As I Was Saying . . .

Jeremy Clarkson began his writing career on the *Rotherham Advertiser*. Since then he has written for the *Sun*, the *Sunday Times*, the *Rochdale Observer*, the *Wolverhampton Express & Star*, all of the Associated Kent Newspapers and *Lincolnshire Life*. Today he is the tallest person working in British television.

As I Was Saying . . .

The World According to Clarkson
Volume Six

JEREMY CLARKSON

MICHAEL JOSEPH
an imprint of
PENGUIN BOOKS

MICHAEL JOSEPH

UK | USA | Canada | Ireland | Australia
India | New Zealand | South Africa

Michael Joseph is part of the Penguin Random House group of companies
whose addresses can be found at global.penguinrandomhouse.com.

First published 2015
001

Copyright © Jeremy Clarkson, 2015

The moral right of the author has been asserted

Set in 14.25/16.75 pt Garamond MT Std
Typeset by Jouve (UK), Milton Keynes
Printed in Great Britain by Clays Ltd, St Ives plc

A CIP catalogue record for this book is available from the British Library

HARDBACK ISBN: 978–0–718–18315–8
OM PAPERBACK ISBN: 978–0–718–18316–5

www.greenpenguin.co.uk

MIX
Paper from
responsible sources
FSC® C018179

Penguin Random House is committed to a
sustainable future for our business, our readers
and our planet. This book is made from Forest
Stewardship Council® certified paper.

Contents

Introduction

After the BBC decided not to renew my contract, I didn't really know what to do next. So I went to the pub and that was very enjoyable. But after a week or so, I realized that I couldn't spend the rest of my life there, so I decided to get a job.

Most people, as far as I know, get one of those from something called the 'job centre', but I didn't think they'd have anything to suit me. A friend of mine once signed on in Kensington, saying he was a shepherd. And then had to look disappointed every week when they said they had no work for him and he'd have to make do instead with some free cash.

I fear it would have been even more difficult finding a job for me. 'Yes, my earning expectations are very high I'm afraid. And qualifications? Well, I can drive a bit too quickly round corners while shouting . . .'

You know that bit in the movie *Taken* when Liam Neeson says he has acquired a special set of skills over the years? Well, I'm the same. But the skills I've acquired are almost completely useless. I make this very clear to my children when they travel. 'If you're kidnapped, all I can do is power slide while gurning and this will in no way help secure your safe return.'

Anyway, to cut a long story short, the Kensington job centre said they had no vacancies for someone who wanted millions of pounds to drive a Lamborghini sideways in a cloud of its own tyre smoke, so I decided after a week or so that I would make a farming programme.

I called up my old friend and former *Top Gear* producer Andy Wilman and said, 'I've decided to make a farming programme.' He came round to my flat to hear my ideas and after three and a half minutes, he looked exactly the same as children do when they are forced to listen to a very boring sermon.

But it was OK, because pretty soon after that someone drove a tank – an effing tank – up to the front door of the BBC's London headquarters demanding my return, and the newspapers went berserk. I was on the front page every day for three weeks. Not just here but all around the world.

And as a result, the phone started ringing. First out of the blocks was a representative from Russia's military television station. 'You come here, make show. Everyone happy.'

Next came some gentlemen from the Middle East. 'Come to Paris,' they said. 'We want to talk to you about making a show. We have table reserved at the hotel. 8 p.m.' So I went to Paris and I made it to the hotel bang on time, and they explained what they had in mind. It sounded very exciting and I said I'd definitely think about it . . .

As I reached for the menu to start making my food choice, they reached for their mobile phones. And after five minutes of general texting and email stuff, one looked up and said 'Thank you for coming'. I made it back to the Gare du Nord after this three-minute conversation exactly one minute after the last train had left.

Feeling a little despondent about my future, I came back to London the next day and my phone rang. It was George Lucas. Imagine my surprise. Mr *Star Wars* himself. He reminded me, not that it was necessary, that we'd met once at the Monaco Grand Prix and then he said he'd like to meet to discuss an idea he'd had. George Bleeding Lucas wanted to meet me. I was very excited.

So, on the day that Chelsea won the Premiership, I left Stamford Bridge, telling my son and our friends that I would not be able to join them for celebratory drinks as I had to meet George Lucas. 'No biggie,' I said, as casual as you like.

At the club where we'd arranged to meet, I was looking around for Mr Lucas when I was approached by another chap, whom I'd also met at the Monaco Grand Prix and who had set a table aside for our meeting. I vowed there and then to get a hearing test as soon as possible.

Not George Lucas was very interesting. He told me that all of the money in the world was Norwegian, and that I could have most of it if I could secure a major TV deal. 'With a Russian military channel?' I asked. 'No,' he replied. 'You need to talk to the Americans . . .'

Well, I was terrified. I've seen grown men pull their own heads off rather than talk to the Americans. Because everyone knows that in the world of US television, there are only two possible outcomes to any deal. Either you're fired after seven minutes if the AB1 twenty-five to forty-year-old male ratio isn't at 62 points. Or, if it is, you're forced to live in Los Angeles for the next five thousand years, where you either join a gym and run about and have your teeth whitened, or you eat so much cheese that you explode.

I was busy pondering all of this when it became clear that Richard Hammond and James May wanted to stick with me. And Richard was very excited about the prospect of working in America. So we decided to get ourselves a big American agent.

We spoke to several on the phone. Some even came over to talk to us. And we learned quite quickly that they are all exactly the same. Anything that isn't a big number is a complete waste of time. Food. Breathing. And other people having an opinion: they have no space in their heads for any of that. 'It's going to be huge,' they all said.

And if you said anything back they said, 'Yeah, yeah, sure, absolutely, yeah, yeah, let's get this done, yeah yeah.' And they kept on saying this for ten or fifteen seconds after you'd finished talking.

James May couldn't really cope with any of it and adopted a strategy of either not going to meetings at all, or turning up and playing constantly with the teapot. Richard Hammond, meanwhile, had become so giddy that on one occasion he turned up after drinking everything in Britain. And me? Well, I was lost. I can drive too quickly round a corner while shouting but I cannot understand what is meant by 'over the top' or 'back end' or almost anything that was being said.

Eventually though, we chose an agent and he was so brilliant that very quickly the job offers started pouring in. I've never known anything like it. I can put in a shift, but God, I was working so hard I had to stop drinking.

Way into the night, the calls were flooding in from California: new offers, new strategies, new ways of putting a show in front of the viewers. I was having to learn about the future, and you can't do that after a couple of bottles of Leoube.

To try and get our heads around what was being offered, Richard and I went with Andy to his house in southern Italy. Which was a brilliant plan, expect there's no mobile phone service down there and his Wi-Fi was a bit patchy.

So, when we wanted to speak to California, we had to drive to the nearest town and then spread out so that on the conference call, we couldn't hear one another live. Or else you'd hear Hammond speak in real life and then, a second or so later, hear him again on your phone.

This meant we were doing vital business to the background accompaniment of light jazz, as the only place Richard could find that a) had service and b) was out of earshot of Andy and I, was outside a café with a live band.

Amazingly, however, we managed to pull it off. And as you'll probably know, we are now at Amazon Prime.

No commercials. No editorial interference. And a budget which is big enough to let us do all the things we want to do.

Which from my point of view is simple: get back behind the wheel of something stupid and drive it round a corner far too quickly, while shouting.

The contents of this book first appeared in Jeremy Clarkson's *Sunday Times* column. Read more about the world according to Clarkson every week in *The Sunday Times*.

Scram, polar bears – we need the North Pole for world peace

We shouldn't be all that surprised that local authorities make a lot of silly decisions because they are usually staffed by well-meaning dimwits or single-issue lunatics with too much armpit hair. This is Gola League politics run by Corner Shop Cup politicians, so naturally your local hospital is going to be full of starving old ladies and all your roundabouts will be back to front.

What's less easy to fathom is why we see similar ineptitude on the global stage. When there is a G8 meeting or some important United Nations seminar, Britain doesn't rummage around in the third division looking for a suitable representative.

We don't send the deputy planning chairman from Macclesfield borough council. This is World Cup politics, so we send the brightest and the best. We send someone who has risen to the top of his game and so do all the other interested parties. And yet still nothing sensible is achieved.

Why? Tony Blair, for all his numerous faults, is not an idiot. Yet somehow he came back from a conference with all sorts of similarly bright politicians and said, 'Yup. We're going to start a war, even though we have absolutely no idea how it will ever end.'

How does this happen? How come normal, ordinary people who got a C in their history O-level can see what should be done whereas a politician who got a degree from Oxford cannot? Well, I've given the question some thought and the answer is obvious. When the world leaders get together, all bar one of them will be suffering from that most debilitating of things: jet lag.

I travel a lot. Really a lot. Last week I was in Siberia. Next week I'll be in New Zealand. And after that it's Spitsbergen in Norway, South Africa, Moscow and Holland. This morning I'm in Australia. I'm hosting a show that features um . . . I can't remember because all I want to do is go to bed. Not that there's any point, because if I were to climb between the sheets I'd just lie there, not sleeping.

After seasickness and trying on trousers, jet lag is the worst thing in the world. There are those who claim they don't suffer from it, but this is nonsense. Everyone does, especially after they've been irradiated and starved of nicotine for twenty hours on an aeroplane.

People say there are cures and ways round the problem, but there aren't. I've tried drinking water on the plane and I've tried drinking sixteen hundred bottles of wine. I've tried sleeping and I've tried not sleeping. Nothing works. Jet lag, after a long flight, is an inescapable hell.

You can't think straight, which is why, whenever I'm in Australia, I say or do something that ends up sparking fury in the *Daily Mail*. I look at breakfast menus thinking, 'All I want is a glass of port,' and then, before bed, I get a craving for a full English. I go for long walks at three in the morning and, at 11 a.m., when I'm supposed to be working, my eyes feel like they are full of grit and my neck muscles collapse.

The only cure is time. It takes one day to move your body clock one hour. So if there's a nine-hour time difference, you will not be fully in tune for nine days.

Of course, this isn't really the end of the world for me because, with the best will in the world, my day job is hardly a matter of life or death.

And it isn't really a problem for holidaymakers either because all they're going to do is lie on a beach, reading about Jack Reacher.

For a politician, though, things are rather different. He doesn't have nine days to adjust. He gets off the plane and immediately he is glad-handing someone in a robe who wants some fighter-bombers. And he can't remember why, because various mealy-mouthed idiots back in Britain insisted he flew all the way there sitting bolt upright, in economy, next to a mewling, puking baby.

This is one of the main reasons why America always seems to get its way at international get-togethers. Because its representatives arrive on Air Force One, feeling fresh, and everyone else arrives on easyJet, having taken some kind of pill to numb the misery.

Sleeping pills are never the answer, though. Take one of those when you are minister for international development and pretty soon you'll be having a fistfight with Monsieur Hollande, having signed an agreement in which Britain takes on the global debt all by itself.

Not that things are going to be any better if you haven't taken a sleeping pill. Because you won't be able to concentrate on what the man in a robe is saying, you'll still want a fistfight with Monsieur Hollande and all you can hear from your similarly affected translator is the sound of snoring.

Why else do you think representatives at the Kyoto climate conference decided the world's electricity needs could be met by burning sunflower seeds? Because it's hard enough to translate John Prescott at the best of times, and nigh-on impossible when your head's full of porridge.

Then we have William Hague. He is super-bright and, I think, an excellent foreign secretary. But at a recent conference on Syria he decided that the opposition forces must be given some blankets in their struggle against President Asda (which is what my jet-lagged spellchecker thinks he's called).

Really? Is that a good idea? Because they are either hardline Islamist nutters, in which case they get nothing, or they are not, in which case they should have some guns. Blankets is the correct answer only if your head thinks it's three in the afternoon and actually it's five in the morning.

Happily, however, I think I have a solution to all of this. A solution that eliminates jet lag. We simply host all future conferences where it's whatever time you want it to be: the North Pole.

Oh, and to level the playing field with America, can we buy the people who are going in to bat on our behalf the sort of jet on which they can arrive having had a bit of bloody sleep?

10 March 2013

It's a simple choice, caller: your money or your daughter

If you were God and you were all-powerful, you wouldn't select Bethlehem as a suitable birthplace for your only child, because it's a horrible place. And you certainly wouldn't let him grow up anywhere in the Holy Land. What you'd actually do is choose New Zealand.

New Zealand causes anyone to question the wisdom of God. Because if He really were all-knowing, children at Christmas time today would be singing 'O little town of Wellington' and people would not cease from mental fight until Jerusalem had been built in Auckland's green and pleasant land. Jesus would have been from Palmerston North.

I'm in New Zealand right now and it really is absolutely stunning – bite-the-back-of-your-hand-to-stop-yourself-crying-out lovely. But sadly, because of modern technology, I can't enjoy any of the things it has to offer. Not its wine or its sunshine or even the scrutiny of its fastidiously attentive paparazzi. Because on the way here I lost my credit card.

Obviously I had to cancel it. Which meant ringing a cheerful computer that asked me to say my sixteen-digit number. I read it out. But it didn't understand. So I used my best Richard Burton voice and tried again. It still didn't understand. And then I lost the signal. And had to start again.

Eventually, after tapping two billion numbers into the handset, I was transferred to a man in India, who asked a few security questions and then said he'd cancel the card immediately . . . along with all the others in my name.

'Whoa,' I said. 'No.' Because that would include cancelling the emergency card I'd given to my eighteen-year-old daughter, who's now travelling through Namibia. The Indian man was most apologetic but said that if I cancelled my card, then she would be at the mercy of every rapist and vagabond in southern Africa.

So because of a computer program, Barclaycard was faced with a simple choice. Either it keeps my stolen card operational, knowing that someone could use it to buy a private jet. Or it allows my daughter to be left, cold and alone, in the home of a former Nazi dentist who wants to know if it's safe.

The Indian man said he'd find his supervisor and transferred me to a piece of music that went on for so long that the battery in my new iPhone went flat.

Speaking of which. Recently in Australia I sat on my last phone and the screen broke. So I bought a new one, assuming that because I'd backed up all the information it would be transferred seamlessly. How naive I am.

What it did was transfer some of the information. So, of the 1,600 emails I know to be sitting in my inbox, it selected just one: a party invitation sent in February last year.

Then there's the phone itself. It's an iPhone 5 and unlike on the previous model the space bar doesn't work unless you hit it hard and repeatedly. Which then causes it to write a full stop. Also, it can't be charged by any of the 2,000 chargers you currently own.

Apple must have known before it put the phone on the market that this was a problem. It must have. But it went ahead anyway. Barclaycard must have known that when someone loses a card, it would be stupid to cancel all the cards in that person's name. But that didn't stop it.

And it's the same story with HSBC, whose Master-Card I have just tried to activate. The Welsh woman I rang said she'd send a Pin code to my home address within six working days.

How can HSBC think this is good enough? Does it now spend so long in meetings, working on yet more annoying airport advertising, that it hasn't realized people on the other side of the world may need access to their money immediately? Not in six working days, 12,000 miles from where they actually are.

But we see stuff like this everywhere. Yesterday I tried to speak with my colleague James May on a satellite phone. These devices are commercially available and are billed as vital life-support systems if you are travelling to very remote, dangerous parts of the world where you may need rescuing and there is no mobile phone signal.

Can I let you into a secret? They don't work. They didn't work when I went to the North Pole, they didn't work when I was in the Atacama desert, and when I tried to speak to James yesterday it sounded as if I was connected to a group of seagulls that had gathered around a drowning eunuch.

To try to see if he was indeed dying, I turned on a satellite tracking device that would pinpoint his precise position. This type of system is available to fleet managers so they can monitor the speed, direction and location of all the vehicles in their charge. Guess what. It didn't work. I'd have been better off trying to work out where James was by using nothing but a forked stick.

I know exactly what's wrong, of course. Such is the pace of change these days, and so heavy is the competition, that companies put products onto the market long before they work in the real world. We're expected to buy an iPhone 5 because it's new. And we sign up to an HSBC MasterCard even though it will cause us to end up under some newspaper on a park bench if we stray from our semi-detached house in Dorking.

What fascinates me, though, is that modern technology works perfectly well when it's designed to make our lives miserable. Get caught by a speed camera in Australia and you can be absolutely certain it will record all the information accurately, that it will instantly glean your name and address from the company that hired you your car and that the lines connecting it to the database at the Driver and Vehicle Licensing Agency in Swansea will be functioning perfectly.

Likewise, if you arrive in New Zealand with some lamb in your rucksack, scanners will find it and you will go to prison. But go online to book a ticket to the theatre next Tuesday, and the best you can hope for is a message from British Airways saying, 'Thank you for your booking to Auckland, Barbara.'

17 March 2013

Pah to apostrophes! And dont do me dinner, I can eat my sons

When a local council in Devon announced that it would no longer be using apostrophes in its street signs, middle England painted its face blue and erupted in a rousing, teeth-gnashing chorus of, 'They can take our savings. They can take our land. They can take our children. But they cannot take our apostrophes.'

Such was the ferocity of the attack that last week Peter Hare-Scott, the leader of Mid Devon district council, said he would be recommending the decision is reversed.

Middle England was still furious, though. 'Is reversed?' it bellowed angrily, while waving spears and axes and jumping up and down. 'Why does he not use the bloody subjunctive? Is the man an imbecile?'

Now I would dearly love at this point to say that this slavish adherence to correct grammar is foolish and small-minded. But I'm afraid I can't. Because when I see a sign advertising CD's and DVD's I become so angry that my teeth start to fall out. If I receive a letter that is full of spelling mistakes and apostrophe misuse, I don't bother replying. When a British Airways steward says, 'Any bread items at all for yourself, sir?', I am filled with an urgent need to punch him to the ground, because in my mind reflexive pronoun abuse is worse than trying on trousers or being stabbed. It's the worst thing in the world.

I know this is idiotic. And I also know there is nothing wrong with splitting an infinitive. If *Star Trek* had been in Latin the *Enterprise* couldn't have been on a mission 'to boldly go where no man has gone before'. Because 'to go' was one word. But in English it isn't. And since there's a gap, why should we mind if Captain Kirk fills it?

The whole point of language is communication, so, really, it doesn't matter whether you go boldly or boldly go. Because we get the gist.

A number of years ago we were all consumed by a book called *Eats, Shoots & Leaves*. The idea was that the removal of a single comma changed the sense of the words completely. Not in context, it didn't. If you're talking about a panda, it's one thing. If you're talking about an inattentive boyfriend, it's another.

It's the same story with apostrophes. If you said you were going to Joburg, I'd understand what you meant. And if you wrote a note to your wife saying, 'There's no need to cook me a special supper. I'll eat our sons,' she wouldn't suddenly decide you had taken up cannibalism.

It's frankly amazing how far from correct grammar and spelling you can stray and still make yourself understood.

A A Gill suffers from what used to be known as slovenliness but is now called dyslexia, and as a result his texts can take a moment or two to decipher.

When, for instance, he suggests meeting for lunch in 'worsy', common sense dictates he doesn't want to meet you in the small town of Worsy, 90 miles east of Warsaw. Even though four letters are missing and one is wrong, it's obvious he means the Wolseley restaurant on Piccadilly.

And when your children send you a text saying it would be 'gr8 2 C U 2 at 8 txt bk' you don't assume that a cat has walked across their telephone keypad. You may despair a little bit but you know perfectly well what they're saying.

Then we have Shakespeare, who is known to have written his name down only six times. And on each occasion it was spelt differently. Does that mean we dismiss him as an illiterate fool? And what of Chaucer? A man who thought it perfectly acceptable to spell 'nostrils' as 'nosethirles'. That doesn't stop his work appearing on the school syllabus.

We even see this with the spoken word. When a person from Barnsley is overheard saying, 'Washewiersen?', it is obvious they mean, 'Was she by herself?' And when a Scottish person says, 'Do ye ken Peebles?', you don't walk away imagining that he is a madman.

French people, meanwhile, speak in a language that makes absolutely no sense at all. It's just a collection of grunts and shoulder shrugs, and somehow saucepans are female. But even here we can communicate.

I once went into a chandler's in Cannes and, using skills gleaned in many Christmas-time games of charades, held myself on an imaginary lead and jumped up and down while barking. Had the sales assistant been a middle Englander and a stickler for correct grammar, punctuation and speech, he would have called the police and said there was a lunatic in his shop. But instead he reached below the counter and produced precisely what I'd wanted: a set of jump leads.

Language evolves. We gave up on Latin when we realized that you couldn't decline a table. And in modern times only the Archbishop of Canterbury and Diana Ross use the word 'thee'. Today, thanks to text and Twitter, we are undergoing a complete revolution, and it's no good hanging onto rules that were laid down hundreds of years ago.

I mean, seriously, if you're looking for a street called Baker's View, and the sign reads 'Bakers View', you're not going to keep on searching, are you?

Grammar is like the speed limit. Sure, a few people stick to it, but when the vast majority don't, it really is time to change the rules. And I have an idea.

Plainly, what people want from the written word these days is speed, and we should accommodate that. Why use the word 'congratulations' when 'congrats' does the job just as well? And why sign off with 'I have the honour, sir, to remain your obedient servant' when instead you can use 'Best'?

In fact we could go further. When I take notes in shorthand, words are abbreviated, letters are truncated and punctuation is not used at all. This means I can never read any of it back. But some people can. Shorthand is an affront to language but it works.

Write normally, and correctly, and you'll manage maybe fifty words a minute. With shorthand you can rattle along at more than twice that rate. It's time, then, to do away not just with grammar but with the alphabet as well.

24 March 2013

Warm the gunboats: it's −58C in the world's next tinderbox

By and large, the world seems to have sorted out most of its boundary disputes. Yes, there's still a bit of argy-bargy in the south Atlantic and the Palestinians would argue that their allotment is a bit meagre. But even in the former Yugoslavia new nations can play football against one another without having to dig a mass grave afterwards.

However, way up in the Arctic, in a place called Svalbard, I sense the mother of all boundary disputes is brewing.

Svalbard is a collection of islands that appear to have been sprinkled like icing sugar on the top of the world. They were formed several hundred million years ago and then absolutely nothing happened until a Dutchman arrived in 1596. He decided there was nothing of any interest there, so he went away again. And nothing continued to happen until 1920.

At this point the world decided it couldn't really have a land mass larger than Denmark that nobody actually owned. A treaty was therefore signed that meant Svalbard became a part of Norway.

Today, though, cigarettes in Svalbard cost £1.40 a pack, which tells me one thing: this is most definitely not a part of Norway. And that's the problem.

Svalbard is really far away. Several years ago I drove

to the magnetic North Pole. It was a gruelling eight-day journey over a frozen ocean, through some of the most inhospitable weather you could possibly imagine. And I genuinely believed when I arrived that I was the most northern person in the world. Apart from Michael Parkinson.

But Svalbard is even further north than that. So it's horrendously cold. Idiotically, savagely cold. When I was there last week the midday temperature was −58C.

Incredibly, though, the Nors are trying to develop this place as a tourist destination. And they seem to be pulling it off. Mainly, I suspect, because this is the only place on earth that has polar bears and a scheduled air service back to civilization. So you fly out there. You see a bear. You take out your camera to snap a picture. It isn't working because it's too cold. And then you die, in agony, of hypothermia.

Alongside the bear-huggers, you also have the thrill-seekers. The sort of people who have surfed the biggest wave and climbed the highest mountain and who now want to hike around the world's northernmost inhabited settlement. Top tip: if this floats your boat, don't bother buying a return ticket, because after you leave the airport you will get about a quarter of a mile before you are eaten by a bear. And you will be grateful because inside its stomach you will at least be out of the wind.

Me? Well, I was up there filming sequences for a new documentary about the Arctic convoys. This meant I spent five days sailing around the island of Spitsbergen trying to get an idea of what it was like for those poor souls in the merchant navy.

I couldn't see much because the porthole in my cabin was frozen over on the inside but I did learn something. It turns out that you can get bored with crashing into icebergs. The first time it happens, you are scared and you rush about waving your arms in the air. The second time, you whimper and make your peace with God. But after the hundredth graunching impact you just turn over and go back to sleep.

We made it all the way to South Cape before we hit ice so thick we couldn't go any further. At this point I climbed down a ladder and went for a walk on an iceberg. That was pretty cool. So pretty cool, in fact, that soon I climbed back up the ladder and made some soup.

Back on dry land, I went to the town. It's called Longyearbyen and there are many restaurants where you can buy whale, and reindeer heart. There are bars, too, and shops that will sell you slippers made from bits of a seal.

Beyond this small settlement, however, there is nothing but mile after mile of enormous scenery. It is utterly bewitching. I'd like to call it jaw-dropping but in temperatures such as this your jaw doesn't do much of anything at all. And after about half a second your eyes freeze over so they don't work, either. And then you die.

As a tourist destination, then, it doesn't really work. Iceland is better. It may be diet-Arctic but it offers everything you can get in Svalbard, apart from the polar bears, and that's no great loss; disgusting, ugly, man-eating bastards, the lot of them.

But if things are bad for the visitor, imagine what it's like to live and work in this remote place. Not many do. In fact, when my Airbus A320 landed, the population of Svalbard increased by 10 per cent. Many are Thai. This is because one of the hotels employed a cleaner from Bangkok, who set up a laundrette. She employed two Thais to help her and pretty soon it was Australian rabbit syndrome.

The government has provided them, and everyone else, with a school and a concert hall and it gives them tax breaks. It plainly wants people to live there. And so do the Russians. They continue to run a coalmine in the hinterland, even though, by all accounts, it produces only enough coal to keep the miners warm.

Why? Ah, well, that's the tricky bit. You see, the treaty that gave Norway sovereignty over Svalbard also said that the forty or so nations that signed it had the right to exploit whatever minerals and resources lay under the permafrost. And guess what they've recently found in the waters off Svalbard. Yup. Oil.

So now you have Norway putting in the infrastructure and the Russians killing time. The Chinese are there as well, along with the Americans and the British. The Canadians are beefing up their navy. The Norwegians are claiming that the treaty applies only to Svalbard and not the waters that surround it. Denmark disagrees. So does Belgium. It's all very ugly.

To sort it out, I'd normally suggest Britain send a gunboat. But the problem is that the Arctic is a terrible place to have a fight. The men who sailed on those Arctic convoys will testify to that.

31 March 2013

Don't forget the body armour for that relaxing beach holiday

At the extreme sports games in Colorado earlier this year, a young chap called Caleb Moore attempted to do a backflip on his snowmobile.

It went wrong, and although he walked away from the crash, he suffered a bleeding heart and died later from other complications.

You would argue that this is entirely predictable – that if you're going to backflip a snowmobile or cycle down a ravine or bungee jump into a shark, you must accept that one day it'll all end in tears. It's far safer – you'd think – to go for a nice walk.

Actually, though, it isn't. Because most of the appeal of an extreme sport is 'the kit'. People don't paraglide off an active volcano unless they are togged up in a purple jumpsuit and equipped with a vast range of lime-green carbon fibre and titanium skid plates. Whereas when you go for a walk, you think you're ready for anything if you are wearing wellies.

You're not. When the cloud comes down, you will wander around in circles until you fall over a cliff. Or you will get stuck and have to saw your own arm off. Or you will die of hypothermia. The main reason why America is home to such a high percentage of fat people is because all the slimline walking enthusiasts are dead.

By far and away the most dangerous pastimes are

those that appear to be safe. Take skiing. It looks about as hazardous as a yoghurt commercial: gentle slopes, joyful rosy-cheeked children and maybe a family snow-ball fight.

But have you ever been to a doctor's surgery in an Alpine town? I have, and it's like a scene from *The Texas Chainsaw Massacre*. There is blood on the walls, and in every chair there is a gaunt-looking accountant type with his legs pointing in completely the wrong direc-tion. Once, I sat in the waiting room next to a chap who had a ski pole sticking out of his eye.

Skating is just as bad. You may imagine that your local ice rink is a lot of jolly Torvill and Dean whole-someness, and that as a result the 'first aid room' is full of nothing but a jolly nurse with a tin of sticking plas-ters. But it's like Damascus in there. There are four-year-olds with their spines sticking out of the top of their heads, and every flat surface is littered with sev-ered hands.

Which brings me on to the perils of a beach holiday. It's a beautiful day and you need to cool off, so you decide to go snorkelling. What could possibly go wrong with that? You won't be more than 30 yards from the beach and you've seen bigger waves in the bath.

So you wiggle your face mask in the water and spit on the glass. No one knows why you do this. But you do. Then you pop it over your head and take the plunge. Then you go back to the snorkel shop to see if it has got another mask that isn't actually modelled on a colander. And then you're off and it's all just too beau-tiful. There are fish that look like an Airbus A380 and little blue ones that whizz about at top speed, and the coral looks like the cover of a Yes album from 1974. You are very happy.

You should, however, be absolutely terrified, because in my experience, for every five people who go into the sea, one comes out either in tears, or in half.

God's not daft. He made dry land for nice stuff such as giraffes and koalas and supermodels. And for all the failed experiments – anything dangerous or ugly – he created an environment where the nice stuff couldn't breathe. The sea. The snorkel, then, is a tool that messes with Genesis. It's an affront to God Himself.

You may not realize this as you bob about. But then you accidentally swim into a completely invisible bloom of jellyfish larvae. You know when you've done this because you are suddenly overcome with a sense that you've somehow caught fire, and the certain knowledge that if you do make it back to the beach alive, some know-all in Speedos is going to make everyone stand back while he urinates on you because it is supposed to calm down the sting.

However, if you manage to miss the swarms of so-called sea lice, and the fire coral and the rays that want to stab you in the heart, you will eventually need to readjust your mask. So you find a nice bit of sand to stand on and - whoa – what's this? Oh no. You've trodden on a completely invisible stonefish that has filled your foot with a venom that will be fatal unless you get to a hospital in a big hurry. And that isn't going to happen because someone on the beach is going to say, 'Don't call an ambulance – I have a cure for that . . .'

Frankly you'd be better off being bitten in half by a shark. Because everyone knows urine does not help. And you'll probably get to go in a helicopter.

Certainly you'd better hope you don't encounter a stargazer. This is an aquatic honey badger. It's a seemingly harmless creature with a benign name and a gormless face but don't be fooled because in fact it's armed like a Navy Seal. Lots of reef fish can sting you. And lots can Taser you with an electric shock. But some stargazers do both. Their eyes can produce up to 50 volts, which stun you, and then they sting you with enough venom to cause paralysis.

This means you will soon be run over by a speedboat that is being driven by a man who has spent the morning smoking what the *Daily Mail* likes to call a 'suspicious-looking cigarette'.

And how have you prepared yourself for this vivid and silent world of teeth, venom and electric shock treatment? Are you wearing a suit of armour? A neoprene and Kevlar helmet? Titanium shin pads? Nope. You're in a pair of Boden trunks.

The message, then, is clear. All sports are extreme. So you should prepare for a swim in the same way that you would prepare for a spacewalk. And if that sounds too much of a palaver, forget beach holidays. Check into the Ritz instead and spend a few weeks lying in bed, watching TV. Then you'll be as safe as houses.

14 April 2013

Life in an awful prison is a better, tougher punishment than death

Last May, a fifty-five-year-old British grandmother called Lindsay Sandiford arrived in Bali with 10 lb of cocaine in her suitcase. She was arrested, tried, and in January – much to the surprise of even the prosecutors who wanted only a fifteen-year jail term – sentenced to death.

Now as we know, the death penalty was very popular when the sun was viewed as a god and the woods were reckoned to be full of witches. But nowadays, a state has to be exceptionally muddleheaded and backward to think that it has the right to take someone into a room, lay them down and kill them. In front of an audience.

The Indonesian government has a particularly grue-some fate in store for Sandiford. Even though it has the wherewithal to inject her with some kind of painless drug that sends her on her way, it has decided that she will be taken to a small clearing on a remote island, chained to a post and shot by a firing squad.

And to make things even worse, it hasn't actually said when this will happen. Or whether the whole event might at some point be cancelled by an appeal court.

Understandably, Sandiford has apparently told other inmates that she can't really face years of hopeful law-yers and endless court cases and that she'd rather they just shoot her in the head now and get it over with.

If I were in her shoes, I'd want the same thing. Because as a species, we are able to cope with despair and regret and shame. But we are useless at dealing with hope. Hope eats away at our souls. Hope can drive a person insane. And what is she hoping for anyway? Because if she loses, she dies. And if she wins, she gets to spend perhaps the rest of her life in an Indonesian prison.

Compared with the jails found in other countries in this part of the world, they're not bad, apparently. Only some mouthfuls of food contain insects, and many of the latrines are occasionally emptied. In addition, the straw in your mattress is changed from time to time, and the hospital is said to have a complete set of pliers.

Small wonder, then, that Sandiford would like to be shot now. Because whatever horrors hell has in store for a convicted cocaine smuggler, they cannot be worse than the horrors she faces by being kept alive. And that raises a question. Should Amnesty International be campaigning for the introduction of more Bangkok Hilton prisons?

Amnesty, like all right-thinking, level-headed people, is vehemently opposed to the death penalty. But how do you convince the Indonesians, and Johnny Turk and Uncle Sam, that it's immoral and barbaric and wrong? And what do you say to two hysterical parents whose little girl has been murdered? They want the killer dragged through a salt mine. They want him boiled and eaten by dogs. And they want the *X Factor* crowd on hand to boo and hiss as he screams and gurgles his way into the next life. And it's pretty tricky to say, 'Wouldn't it be better, don't you think, if we put him in a nice warm room and gave him a table tennis bat?'

You often hear people in Britain calling for the death penalty to be reintroduced and I know where they're coming from. It's always the same argument: why should this paedophile/murderer get to spend the rest of his days watching *Cash in the Attic* reruns, and playing table tennis and tucking into lashings of hot shepherd's pie, while we have to pay our taxes and work in estate agents to keep him there?

There's a sense that prisons are too cushy, and that the cost of keeping a prisoner locked up is too great. There's only one way of winning the debate: to convince the braying hordes, the bereaved parents and the Indonesian authorities that if prison were really terrible, then life inside would be worse than death.

Of course, the wishy-washy liberals usually jump up at this point and say prison should be a place of rehabilitation, not punishment. And that's fine. Because in my new regime, not all the prisons would have slime on the walls and guards who have studied the art of chakra torture.

If you get done for something trivial you can still have *Cash in the Attic* and table tennis, and a nice biscuit if you promise to behave in future. These would be places of rehabilitation, full of soft music and inspiring posters featuring whales.

But if you've done something abhorrent, and you've been given life, what's the point of rehabilitation? You're not coming out. Ever.

Better then, surely, to silence the pro-death-penalty lobby by making sure the crim is locked in a cell and told he can eat only what he can catch.

No one could complain about this because you'd be able to keep someone locked up for 10p a day; less if the guards could be persuaded to turn up as a hobby. And with awful prisons, there'd be no more silly nonsense about bringing back hanging.

Because then, you'd be able to say to those in favour, 'Right. And who wins, exactly, if we hang them?'

Sandiford has already told us – and she is not alone – that she would rather die than lurch through life in a hellhole. So by imposing the firing squad as a punishment, the courts are simply extending a kindness. And I'm sure that's not what they had in mind. Nor what the braying hordes want.

21 April 2013

This is no coat hanger; this is my £25,000 gullible fool grabber

So you're online, chatting with a pretty girl from Lithuania. She seems keen on getting together but says she can't fly over unless you send some money for the ticket. So you do. And then, much to your surprise, you never hear from her again. Nobody knows how often this happens because very few people will ever own up. 'Hello, officer, I'm a fifty-seven-year-old health and safety officer for a West Midlands council. My teeth are yellow, my tank top is stripy and I've been ripped off by a willowy twenty-four-year-old from eastern Europe who said she found me attractive.' Nobody's going to say that because they know it would make them seem foolish.

The trouble is that we live in a world where we feel protected from scam artists. When British Airways gives you some mixed nuts, it says on the packet, 'May contain nuts'. We are given best-before dates and notices advising us that we may fall over. We feel safe all the time. Protected. So we assume that when a 'traveller' offers to tarmac our drive, nothing can possibly go wrong. The state will not allow it.

Which is why we've become a nation of suckers. Buying insurance we don't need and signing up to warranties that don't exist and imagining that Lithuania really is full of girls who like comb-overs and bad dentures.

We often see the victims on regional news programmes, all teary-eyed and resentful, and we're
supposed to feel sorry for them. But I don't because
they are idiots. When you pick up the phone in the middle of the afternoon and it's a man claiming he can clear
all your debts and help you lose weight at the same time,
you have to have the IQ of a vole to think, 'Hmmm.
This sounds interesting.'

And when something appears on your laptop suggesting that you can have sex with a hundred women in
your area that very night, you have to be much dafter
than a brush to reach for your credit card. But people
do. All the time.

It happens everywhere. Stone-clad houses. Hideous
double glazing. Disease-infested cruise liners. And the
Iberian peninsula, which is a graveyard for the broken
dreams of a million suckers. 'You can have a villa by
the sea for just £1.99.' No. You. Can't.

Many years ago Anne Robinson and I decided we'd
like to host a television show that highlighted these
scams. But instead of castigating those responsible,
we'd celebrate their ingenuity and laugh openly at the
stupid gormless fools who'd fallen for the spiel. Which,
of course, brings me on to the absolute king of
scammers: James McCormick.

He's the king because he realized that gullibility isn't
just the preserve of the elderly, the fat and the lonely.
Gullibility is everywhere – even at the UN and at the
very top of the world's governments.

So what he did was buy a £13 Christmas stocking
filler that, said the packaging, could locate lost golf

balls. Of course, it almost certainly could do no such thing. It was just a gimmick, an amusing but quickly-forgotten-about toy. He then took it to various governments and agencies, passing it off as a machine that could be used to sense the presence of nearby explosives. It definitely couldn't do that. You just had to look at it, with its cheap plastic and its Ford Cortina aerial, to know it couldn't find much of anything at all.

But here's the genius. If he'd gone for a 100 per cent mark-up and quoted a price per unit of £26, no one would have taken him seriously. So he didn't. He went for a price of up to £27,000. And they snapped his hand off. This sort of thing works well. I know a man who tried to sell the oil industry a tool that cost him about a fiver. He failed, until he started to charge £100,000. Now he's so wealthy he doesn't even appear in *The Sunday Times* Rich List.

But back to McCormick's golf toy. The UN bought five. Other customers were the Egyptian army, the Kenyan police, Hong Kong's prison service, Thailand's border control and the Saudi Arabian government.

Even with a bit of discounting for bulk orders, the cash he generated was substantial. He was able to buy a yacht, along with homes in Bath and Cyprus. Investigators say that over several years he raked in an eye-watering £50m. And I doff my cap to the man.

Of course, there are those who say he was playing with the lives of people in Middle Eastern compounds. People who felt they were safe but, in fact, weren't because cars and people were being given the once-over by a machine designed to locate golf balls in long grass. Not nitroglycerine in the back of a Toyota Land Cruiser.

Actually, though, it's not strictly true that he was responsible. Because if I convinced Nasa to buy a new type of rocket fuel that was really just cheese, it's the space agency's daftness that would cause the rocket to just sit there when the countdown was done. And so it goes with Johnny UN.

What were they thinking of? Did no one say to McCormick, 'Right. We've hidden a bit of dynamite in this car park. Let's see if your machine can find it'? Did no one do any tests at all? Is that the way, perhaps, when people are spending government money?

Apparently some people did wonder how this small handheld device could work without batteries. They were told that if the operator shuffled his feet, enough static electricity would be generated to keep the thing going. The UN obviously bought that. And these are the people who run refugee camps and make noises about North Korea. It beggars belief.

Naturally they won't go to prison. But it's possible McCormick will. And what's the betting that while he's in there, he spends his time selling discarded room keys to the inmates, saying they will open any known door. And headache pills that he claims will make you unattractive to other men in the showers. He'll probably be released richer than when he went in. Because plainly he understands a simple truth. Nobody ever went bust by underestimating the general public's intelligence.

28 April 2013

Enough cringing, Auntie; stand up and face the rottweilers

After a BBC journalist had a suspected heart attack at his desk, worried colleagues immediately called 999. But when the ambulance men arrived, it's claimed they were prevented from attending to the patient because the news was on air and the newsroom in which the stricken man worked was in the back of shot.

This, of course, is yet another example of the BBC making a complete hash of absolutely every single thing it does. As we speak, it is spending a considerable amount of its time and your money investigating the antics of Jimmy Savile, who, last time I looked, was still dead.

And now there will be a second inquiry into whether, as has been suggested by one person, Stuart Hall was able to go about his vile business while on BBC premises.

Then we have so many accusations of bullying and ageism and drug abuse that we get the impression the corridors are full of charlied-up gangs of media types, smashing up wheelchairs and making fun of the fatties.

The message is clear. The BBC is run by a bunch of champagne-swilling lefties who spend all day gorging on peach and peacock at swanky London restaurants before popping back to the office for a spot of light paedophilia. That's why they fill the news with Labour party propaganda and the rest of the schedules with reruns of *Dad's Army*. Because they're too sozzled and aroused to think straight.

And how does the BBC respond to these accusations of profligate waste, political bias and child abuse? Very tamely, usually. But I've had enough. Because the BBC that's portrayed in the news is nothing like the BBC that I've known and loved for nigh on a quarter of a century.

The first thing you need to know is that there is no such thing as 'the BBC'. In your mind, it's run by a small group of sage old souls such as Lord Carrington and Baroness Williams who sit in an oak-panelled board-room making considered decisions on what we watch and how. But the truth is: it's actually run by a morbid and constant fear of distressing *Daily Mail* headlines.

No, really. It's a collection of 23,000 employees who operate like Richard Harris in that scene from *Juggernaut*. If they cut the red wire, all is well. But if they select blue, they upset the tabloids and are passed over for promotion. As a result they mostly sit there sweating and not cutting any wires at all.

I read often about how I've had my wrists slapped by BBC 'bosses' and you imagine me being hit on the knuckles with a blackboard rubber by some kind of whizz-kid who's fiercely loyal to the concept of public service broadcasting. Not so, I'm afraid. With the exception of Alan Yentob they'd pretty well all jump ship to commercial television tomorrow if the price were right.

I've given up trying to get to know any of them. Because if you go for a coffee, which you pay for yourself to avoid embarrassing headlines, you know that none of your ideas will be accepted in case they fail, causing more embarrassing headlines. And then the next thing you know, they're at ITV. Which means you have to buy yet more coffee as you chat to their replacement who just wants to keep her nose clean until she too can get the hell out of there.

Look at all the recent major developments. The move to Salford. Designed to avoid tabloid accusations of metropolitanism. The refusal to continue following the lead of every other organization and give staff big lump-sum payoffs. Designed to avoid tabloid accusations of financial impropriety. The Savile inquiry. The Hall inquiry. The bullying inquiry. All designed to keep the red-top dog at bay.

I'm not suggesting for a moment there should be such arrogance that nothing is investigated. That would be stupid. But surely it is time for the much-talked-about BBC chiefs to man up. And, where necessary, tell the moaning minnies to get stuffed.

Almost everyone I've met at the BBC wants most of all to make great shows. Many are extremely talented. But every single one is so terrified of blotting their copybook, they spend all day under their desk saying in a panicked squeak, 'Can we just show that episode of *Dad's Army* where Mainwaring breaks Godfrey's pearl-handled butter knife?'

This has to stop. The BBC has to Faccept that newspaper proprietors are duty-bound to attack the very notion of public service broadcasting and that, actually, it makes no real difference.

I'm constantly being hauled over the coals in the *Daily Mail* and the *Daily Star* and the *Mirror* for all sorts of things. Calling Gordon Brown a one-eyed Scottish idiot. Saying public sector workers should be executed. Sparking fury with fox enthusiasts. I'm portrayed as an evil, racist, homophobic misogynist who goes through life stabbing baby badgers for fun.

And I've worked out that it makes no difference. Taxi drivers still pick me up. People still watch my television shows. My books aren't remaindered for weeks; sometimes months. That's because the endless criticism is just a background hum.

The BBC should accept this. It should make decisions on what it thinks to be right, not on how that decision will be reviewed in the next day's papers. It should remember that despite Savile and Hall and the jubilee debacle, most people still like and trust Auntie.

I do. When I'm abroad, I am filled with pride when I tell someone I work for the BBC. I still get a shiver of excitement every time I walk through its doors. I think the concept of commercial-free broadcasting is a good one and – whisper it here – I think it's good value too.

I can say that, of course. Because I'm old and rich enough to not really care if I'm sacked for offending the tabloids. Sadly most of my 23,000 colleagues are not. So they must continue to whimper and acquiesce and apologize with yet another half-hearted, shoulder-shrugging admission of guilt, shame and embarrassment.

12 May 2013

When the grim reaper calls, stub out your fag on a lettuce and grin

When I heard that Angelina Jolie's breasts had been removed, my first thought was, 'Ooh, can I have them?' But then it transpired that Angelina elected to have her bosoms removed because she carried the BRCA1 gene, which meant she had an 87 per cent chance of developing cancer at some point in, perhaps, the not too distant future. Her mother had died from the disease aged just fifty-six.

I don't fully understand the relationship between a woman and her chest. Women spend millions a year on surgery to make their breasts bigger or more pointy or whatever. Millions more are spent on dresses that show them off. And yet every single woman has heartily congratulated Angelina. Which gives me the impression that they aren't important at all.

It's confusing, so to make it more relevant for me, I asked myself a question. If I were to be told I had an 87 per cent chance of catching testicular cancer, would I whizz round to the doctor and ask him to snip off my bits? And if I did, how would I feel on the day when I died of something else?

I face a similar dilemma every day with smoking. I realize that lung cancer is a very real possibility and that I should pack it in. But what if I go through the cold sweats and the bad temper and the weight gain and then get run over by a bus? I should imagine my last words would be something along the lines of, 'Oh, for f***'s sake.'

There are all sorts of things you can do to keep the grim reaper at bay. Run to work, drink water, eat lettuce, take the stairs and chew everything 72 times before swallowing.

Or you can get radical. You can remove all the things that may cause trouble later on: your breasts, your colon, a lung, a kidney, your eyes. And, for sure, what's left would stand a good chance of getting a telegram – or is it an email these days? – from Mrs Queen. But here's the thing. One day, you are going to die of something.

The world sometimes seems to forget this inescapable truth. After every car crash, policemen have to measure the skid marks and assess what they call the 'vehicle' to see if such an accident could be prevented from happening again. It's the same with plane and train crashes as well.

After every death in a hospital, meetings must be held to see if it could have been avoided in some way. And every school yard is full of people with clipboards and safety goggles, making sure that none of the children can ever fall over.

We spend a fortune – trillions every year – making sure we don't die. And yet despite this, we all do.

The NHS was set up essentially as a distribution network for aspirin. Now there's a cure for pretty well everything and patients want it all free. Just so they can go home and die from something else.

Of course, what we are all trying to do is postpone

death for as long as possible. We read about people in southern France and in Japan living to be 112 or more and we all think, 'I fancy a bit of that.' But do we? Really?

The problem is simple. The human being is designed to be like one of those toads that emerges from the mud, has sex and then dies. We are supposed to be in the ground shortly after our children are old enough to kill a deer. But thanks to modern medicine, that no longer happens.

And what's more, thanks to good dentistry and a plentiful supply of food, people in their forties and fifties are not just alive but active too. They can climb stairs and think straight. So they imagine that if they cut off their breasts or testicles and live a deprived life of wheat germ this and sugar-free that, they will continue to be active long after their smoking and drinking friends are dead.

Not so. They are cashing in all the fun that life has to offer simply so they can be the fittest oldie in the care home.

Do I want to live to be a ripe old age? Yes. But only if in that ripe old age I can still do all the things I do now. And that isn't going to happen. I could saw off my scrotum and pack in the fags and banish the booze; I could deprive myself of all the things that make my life fun – but life later on will not be the same as it is now. There will be arthritis and leakage and pain and disability and one day I will walk into a bank and not know why I'm there, or what a bank is for.

Every single day I wake up to find that a bit of my

body, which worked perfectly well the day before, has broken. This will continue to be the case no matter what I do. Which is why I choose to do nothing at all. And there's another reason as well . . .

The world is a fantastic place full of people you want to meet and things you would like to put in your mouth. There are places to go and things to do and stuff you would like to try. But your time here is extremely short so you must rush and never say no to anything. Except butter beans.

If you do, you are depriving yourself of a memory. You are wasting an opportunity. You are making a life that could be bright and vivid beige and dreary.

19 May 2013

Bums on saddles, folks – let's rout the pushbike Bolsheviks

If you selected a random group of British people and asked them to name everything that's wrong or odd about Germany, the answers would be many and varied. But when I once gathered together a group of Germans and asked them to name everything they didn't like about Britain, they were stumped. Only when pushed did one put his hand up and say, 'Your taps.'

The others nodded enthusiastically. 'Yes,' they all said. 'Your taps. We don't like the way you have one for hot and one for cold. Why do you not have one that mixes hot and cold to make warm?' Are you smarting? No. Thought not. So let me hit you with something that will sting a bit more. When I asked an Italian professor to name the thing he thought most strange about Britain, he said, 'I once went to a pub which had a sign in the window that said, "Children welcome". I found that very odd.'

It implies, of course, that there are establishments where children might not be welcome, and that to an Italian is just plain bonkers. Actually it's just plain bonkers, no matter where you're from. Last week, however, I saw a sign on a restaurant door that was even more mystifying: 'Cyclists welcome', it said.

I have nothing against those who ride bicycles. This

week half my family and many of my friends will be cycling from Paris to London to raise money for wounded soldiers. I have a bicycle that I use for short distances of up to 100 metres in London. But I cannot see why because of this I should be more welcome at a restaurant than those who choose to go about their business on the bus.

What about people who play chess? The implication is that they are not particularly welcome. Nor are travelling salesmen, racing drivers and those who take part in dressage competitions. Why would there not be a sign saying, 'Teachers welcome'?

I'll tell you why. Because teachers are a specific group of people who teach stuff. 'Cyclists', on the other hand, does not refer to people who simply ride bicycles. These days the word means so much more than that.

You have those who ride a bike to work, and then you have cyclists who are very angry about everything and do not eat meat. By putting up a sign saying, 'Cyclists welcome', what the owner is actually saying is, 'I have many vegetarian options on the menu and I pursue a fanatical anti-smoking policy. Also, I vote Labour.'

Cycling used to be how you got about when you were poor. Then it became a pastime for children. Now, though, it has evolved into something more. It's gone beyond a way of life and become a political statement. A movement.

Its leaders even have a uniform. They wear skintight black leggings over which they put a pair of shorts. Yes, they actually wear their underpants on the outside of their trousers. There is no practical reason at all for doing this; it looks stupid. But that's the point. It tells everyone that they are not interested in capitalism's drive to make us all spend a fortune on fashion and looking good. It says, 'I'm proud to look daft.'

This also explains the cycling helmet. If you actually wanted to protect your head, you would wear the sort of thing that motorcyclists use, and if you wanted all-round visibility you would go to the people who supply the British Army. But instead cyclists choose to wear five hardened bananas on their bonce. It's the twenty-first-century equivalent of a British Leyland donkey jacket.

And often it is fitted with a GoPro video camera so that the shortcomings of van-driving painters and decorators can be uploaded to YouTube. It's all part of the workers' struggle against imperialism's self-employed foot soldiers. Humiliate Gary the plumber on the internet and pretty soon you'll bring down the stock exchange.

Twenty-five years ago we had cyclists, but back then they were called peace campaigners and they were chained to the fences at Greenham Common. Thirty years ago they were throwing rocks at policemen in Orgreave. And 180 years ago they were demanding the release of their brothers from Tolpuddle.

The Ramblers Association was born as an offshoot of the Young Communist League. It was designed to demonstrate that property is theft, and that the working man has a right to walk wherever and over whatever he sees fit. Well, today's cyclists are simply bringing that tradition to the nation's towns and cities.

As far as they are concerned the roads are theirs by right. And the pavements. They do not ride through red lights to make their journey quicker; they do it to show the Tories that they will not be enslaved by convention. It's political.

And now they are demanding that their ecological, high-visibility, fair-trade, non-nuclear, meat-free lifestyle be accommodated into the mainstream, with junctions designed to put the bicycle first. They want the car and the van banished. Today the Embankment. Tomorrow the Bank of England.

There's only one way they can be defeated. And that's for normal people to start riding bicycles. We need to swell their ranks with moderates, people who ride a bike because they've had a drink and because taxis are too expensive. Ordinary people who ride in jeans and T-shirts and with no stupid helmet.

People who will walk into a restaurant with a sign on the door saying, 'Cyclists welcome', and ask for meat, with extra meat.

I've started the ball rolling by buying a bike. And when I ride it I have a sign on the back of my jacket that says, 'Motorists. Thank you for letting me use your roads.'

Manners. That's what the Germans say they like best about Britain and the British. So let's use them to defeat extremism's latest attempt to upset the applecart.

26 May 2013

Weapons down, Mr Hague – you can't interfere in a divorce

The EU is often criticized for its stance on the shape of bananas and the correct size for a cod. But I'm a fan of Europe in general because once in a while it's needed to provide a reasoned, thoughtful and civilized viewpoint in a world that would otherwise be dominated by trigger-happy lunatics, despots and Americans.

Last week it did just that when it raised a questioning eyebrow at calls from both Britain and France to arm Syria's rebel fighters. Syria depresses me because I spent some time there a few years ago and thought it was all too wonderful for words.

I met a man in a Damascus market who sold quite the most fabulous light fittings and he said, yes, it would be no problem to ship some over to London. He had a website and everything.

Up in Palmyra a colleague banged his head and was taken to a hospital, where the doctors and nurses were first class. Friendly, worldly and with all the supplies they needed to make people better.

It all seemed so normal. You could buy near enough everything you can buy here. And a lot more besides. Girls wore jeans and pretty tops. The people I met talked about Jack Bauer and the weather. But then one night, while I was dining with some architects and

lawyers, the conversation turned to Israel, and all of a
sudden it didn't feel normal at all.

For about a million reasons they felt it should be back
in Palestinian hands and that all of the Jews should
either leave or be killed. What's more, if these seemingly reasonable, well-read people were given the
chance, they would leave their jobs, strap a huge gun to
the back of a pick-up truck and charge down an Israeli
tank division without a moment's hesitation.

This is the problem. We here in the West, with our
exotic cat food and our sing-along hymns, simply cannot begin to comprehend the deep-seated hatred that
seeps from the pores of even the most benign-looking
souls in the Middle East.

And it's not just Jews. My Syrian friends also hated
Bashar al-Assad and many weren't that fond of America either. Then you have the bigger picture in which
the Sunnis hate the Shi'ites, and the Shi'ites hate the
Sunnis, because of some seemingly incomprehen-
sible 1,400-year-old row about who should succeed
the prophet Muhammad.

I've tried to get to grips with this. I really have. I've
read books and talked to people, and just when I think
I'm seeing it more clearly, the Lebanese Hezbollah
arrive in Syria to fight alongside Assad's government
and I'm all at sea again.

I wonder if William Hague, the foreign secretary,
has a greater understanding of the issues. He's a bright
fellow and he has access to all sorts of intelligence.
But does he feel the struggle in his bones? I seriously
doubt it.

He says that Britain should supply arms to the rebels, but only after they've been carefully vetted. I see. So they will only be given to, say, architects and vets and those who have lighting shops in the market. People who seem reasonable but who, I know, want to murder every Jew in Israel.

We heard recently that one rebel fighter had eaten the heart, or maybe the liver, of a dead government soldier. It now turns out this wasn't the case. Experts, having examined the video footage, say that it's fairly clear that actually he ate the poor chap's lung. Is Mr Hague proposing that Syria's answer to Luis Suarez should be sent into battle with British weapons? Or maybe a Sheffield-made knife and fork?

And how does he propose to train these rebels in the art of using our guns and our missiles? By letter? Through a fence? Or will he send 'advisers' over the border in much the same way as America did in Vietnam all those years ago? I hope not, because I suspect they might be a little out of their depth.

When protesters are angry about the government in Britain, they throw plastic furniture through the window of the nearest McDonald's. Or they put a bit of turf on the statue of Winston Churchill. They do not kill a policeman and eat his internal organs.

You've got to be really angry to do that. And I'm sorry but I don't believe that any western person has even the vaguest inkling of what causes that anger, or what might happen to it should it be fed with – or hit by – a stream of British bullets.

We're told that since the Royal Navy intervened in

Libya, all is well in the region. Oh good, so Tripoli is now twinned with Bourton-on-the-Water, is it? No. Because it's now run by a group of chaps who didn't just arrest their former leader. They chased him into a drain and killed him in the back of a pick-up truck.

Is that what we want to see in Syria? People armed with British weapons, storming into the presidential palace and eating Assad's kidneys? I'm not sure we do, which is why I'm so grateful to the EU for counselling restraint.

It's understandable, given the level of awfulness in Syria, to want to do something. And, of course, it's natural for the British to send a gunboat. That's ingrained in our souls. Wherever there's trouble, we go over there, bop the baddies on the head and teach them how to play cricket. But today I wonder if there isn't a better way . . .

When a couple split up, it's often hard for friends to understand why. We rarely know what went on behind closed doors or what caused the love to turn into simmering hatred. Which is why everyone with a shred of wisdom does not take sides. Yes, it's painful to sit by while the children sit in their rooms at night sobbing, but we still don't scrub one party out of the address book and shower the other with treats and affection.

It's because we know that when we don't understand the issues, we don't get involved.

2 June 2013

You can't salute a hero in here, sir – this is gormless Britain

In the not too distant past when a mill owner was allowed to clip the earhole of a slovenly worker, everyone knew their station in life and, as a result, society was extremely unfair.

People who knew how to hold a knife and fork properly were allowed to do pretty much as they pleased while those with flat hats and warty noses were expected to grovel and fawn and tug their forelocks. It was all too ridiculous for words, but happily, we were rescued from the nonsense by Mr Blair, who insisted we call him Tony and strive to create a society in which everyone was equal. Even the pigs. Especially the pigs.

For some, Tony Blair is the man who took us to war in Afghanistan and Iraq. For others, he will be treasured as the chap whose government banned fox-hunting. But for me, he will be remembered as the man who made it OK to ridicule the bright and the successful.

He created bus lane Britain, where the poor and the daft can whizz about at top speed, leaving the clever and the rich to sit in traffic jams. He told us to show kindness to the fat and the weak while plunging daggers into the backs of those who fly around on private jets and have thin wives. He made the little man a king.

In the days before Blair, when you went to collect your parcels from the post office and the gormless slob

at the counter couldn't be bothered to go and find
them, you could call him names and get him sacked.
Not any more. Now, if you argue even a tiny bit, he
points at a sign saying that abuse of staff will not be
tolerated and that you face prosecution.

Unfortunately, while this is all very noble, I'm afraid
it doesn't work. Because if you empower the stupid, the
1,300 cyclists who arrived in London's Horse Guards
Parade last weekend after a gruelling charity ride will
be prevented from celebrating their achievement with a
refreshing glass of beer.

A number of my friends and family members had
been on the Help for Heroes ride, which, by all accounts,
had been something of an ordeal. They'd left Paris
seven days earlier expecting a leisurely Enid Blyton-style,
summertime jaunt through northern France. They'd
imagined stopping at agreeable little cafés for a glass of
cognac and then relaxing in the evening over a plate of
mussels. It was not to be.

On the first day, they left Paris in the pouring rain,
cycled non-stop for more than 70 miles and then arrived
at a hotel that had a number of features, most of which
were walls and none of which was a bath. And it continued in this vein for the next week.

Despite the hardship and the hills, none dared pull
out because among the riders were a number of amputees. Men such as Josh Boggi, who was riding with no
legs, and no right arm. If he could keep going, then the
able-bodied had to keep going as well.

I understand that my friend and former boss Rebekah
Brooks once threw her bike in a hedge, and my

daughter had several tearful moments, having only learnt to ride a bicycle six weeks before the event began. Both had trained by going to the pub and smoking but both kept going into a world beyond the pain barrier.

The *Sun*'s deputy editor, Geoff Webster, and my PA, Lucinda, motivated themselves by swearing, constantly, because they knew that when they arrived at the hotel that night there would be no lovely supper, no bath and that the bar would be shut. Amputees talked of having to take their arms off because they were sweating so badly.

The text messages and emails I received as the week dragged by suggested that they were in some kind of hell, that the organizers had miscalculated the number of miles and that it was only the wounded guys who were keeping them going. And what was keeping the wounded guys going? God alone knows that. Probably an extremely noble quest to show soldiers who'll be hurt in the future that life can go on.

On the day the ride was due to end, I met other supporters and decided that we should have some treats to hand as our friends crossed the finish line in Horse Guards Parade. It was a hot day and we reckoned that champagne, wine and beer would be best. That's what I'd want after a ride from Paris. A drink. Especially if I didn't have any legs.

Sadly, though, there was a problem. The entrance to the finish line was being guarded by two security men who, between them, had the IQ of a wasp. 'You can't take drink in there,' they said. We implored. We pleaded. And we threatened. But it was no good. It was like talking to two farmyard animals. So we asked to see their boss. 'She's busy,' they said.

And that was that. All of those people had ridden their bicycles to London to raise millions for a genuinely worthwhile cause. They were all hot, broken, exhausted . . . and thirsty. And they were going to be denied a drink because power today resides in the hands of people who do not have the intellectual capacity for reason, compassion or logic.

We see this everywhere. We spend our lives being bossed around by people who've taken their orders from someone – who probably learnt their management skills by watching *The Apprentice* – and they are simply too stupid to realize those orders are idiotic and wrong.

Happily, I have a suggestion. Employers should come up with new wording for those notices that tell customers what penalties they will face if they abuse staff. Something along the lines of: 'We employ morons. They are incapable of thought. So there is simply no point arguing with them.'

It won't get you anywhere either. But at least it's honest and you'd feel better as you heave the drink over a fence and take it into the event anyway.

9 June 2013

I didn't get a PhD and CBE playing by the rules, Mr Gove

So, GCSE examinations are to be made more difficult, and the government is studying proposals that would see them replaced, in England at least, by a new, more internationally respected, test. Many people seem to think all of this is a good idea. But I cannot see why, because as far as I can tell, the changes encourage liars and favour people who have nice breasts.

Schoolchildren are always told that they must work hard in lessons and pass their exams or they will end up as a health and safety officer. But this is emphatically not the case.

I did not work hard at school and, in the middle of my final summer term, was invited by the headmaster to pack my bags and revise for my A-levels at home. My parents were a bit cross about this and immediately suspended my £15-a-year allowance, thereby forcing me to think about getting a job of some sort.

I applied to a local newspaper, and in the interview it transpired that my grandfather, a local GP, had visited the editor's poorly mother in the middle of a wartime air raid. To repay this kindness, he offered me a position in the newsroom. But it was made plain that it was only a provisional job, and that if I failed my A-levels, I'd have to go.

Unfortunately on the evening before the first exam I

got a bit drunk and overslept so heroically that I never made it to the school at all. I was an hour late for the second, and in the third I scored a U. My job on the newspaper seemed doomed until I had a bit of a brainwave . . .

The day after the results were announced, the editor summoned me into the oak-panelled boardroom, sat me down and asked how I'd got on. 'Rather well,' I said, crossing my legs and flicking some imaginary fluff from my trousers. 'I got two As and a B.' And as a result of that barefaced lie, here I am now writing for *The Sunday Times.*

So they can change the name of the exams, switch the grades from letters to numbers and fiddle about with the curriculum, but for cheats like me it'll make not a jot of difference. We will still be sitting there, in interviews, knowing full well that claims are never checked, saying: 'Yes. I got top marks in everything. And a first from Oxford. And a Nobel prize for cracking cold fusion.'

For foolish people who tell the truth in interviews the situation is bleak, because employers have enough on their plates without keeping abreast of all the changes to school exams. Spool forwards ten years and imagine you are interviewing three people for a job. One has six GCSEs that were passed in 2014. One has six that were passed in 2016. And one has six of the new tests that were passed in 2017. Finding out which sat the hardest exams would be time-consuming so you'll simply give the job to whichever candidate has the nicest rack.

However, the biggest problem for me is the new curriculum, which starts in September 2015 and is modelled on the system used in that most carefree and easy-going of places, Singapore. Pupils will study entire Shakespeare plays, rather than extracts. There will be more advanced algebra, a greater emphasis on grammar in French and a requirement for longer essays in history, and pupils will be expected to grapple with complex mechanical problems in physics. All of this will cause an epidemic of stupidity to sweep the land.

I had to study *The Merchant of Venice* for my English O-level and I emerged from the experience with a profound and never-ending hatred of Shakespeare. If I could go back in history and make one alteration to the way the world has turned out, I would not throttle the infant Adolf Hitler, or uninvent the GoPro camera. I'd stab the bloody Bard before he'd had a chance to fill his inkwell.

It's the same story with religion. I was forced to spend my Sunday mornings in chapel, and as a result I now have no time at all for vicars. And because I was made to do cosines and fractions in my maths lessons I fly into a rage even today when I need to do a sum. School therefore turned me into an idiot.

And harder tests will make the situation even worse. If you give a fourteen-year-old boy a Jack Reacher book, he will enjoy it and develop a taste for reading. He may, as an adult, pick up a copy of *The Tempest* and enjoy that too. But if you start him off with Shakespeare you're going to put him off reading for life.

And now the government is going to exacerbate the

situation by forcing this generation to learn in even greater depth about yet more things in which they are simply not interested.

The government says the tougher exams will be much respected abroad and are needed because in recent years British pupils have been slipping down the international league tables.

Aaaaaaaargh. League tables ruin children's lives. They are already expected to spend all day in the classroom, learning about stuff that isn't useful, and then four hours in the evening doing homework, simply so their school does better than the school down the road. And now they are going to have to work even harder so Britain can beat Belgium. I hate league tables even more than I hate Shakespeare.

Which brings me on to my three-point plan for the future. No. 1: abolish league tables. No. 2: because employers need consistency, pick an examination system and enshrine it in such a way that it can never be altered. And No. 3: make school fun. Blow stuff up in science. Read fun books in English. Have loads of free time when kids can play and learn how not to be gormless and fat.

Oh, and forget maths. It's not important.

16 June 2013

Hoist the Jolly Wet Roger, my flag for a Lesser Britain

These days the British flag is everywhere. It's on posters on the back of every American kid's bedroom door. Pretty girls have it on their belt buckles in South Africa. Poles are to be seen walking the streets with it emblazoned on their T-shirts.

And, of course, wise people have many reasons for this. It's a legacy from the Olympics. It's because of Britain's never-ending quest for world peace. It's because of Adele. But actually it's none of those things. The real reason the Union Jack has become a fashion statement around the world is: it's a really nice flag.

What sets it apart from other national flags is the complexity of its design. Anyone could draw a German or an Irish flag, but if you gave someone a red and a blue pen and told them to draw ours, from memory, they'd be stumped. I know I would.

There's more, though. See a Union Jack on the tail-fin of an airliner and you know it won't crash. See it fluttering from the stern of a warship and, these days at least, you know you aren't going to be attacked for no good reason. It represents decency and fair play and David Attenborough. And the colours are good too.

Which is why I worry a little bit about what would happen if Scotland decided to go the whole hog and separate itself not just from England's government but from the crown as well. Because if it did that, the Union Jack – a symbol of English and Scottish unity – would be rendered pointless. And we'd have to get ourselves a new one.

This is by no means unprecedented. In 1959 America unveiled its new flag with 13 stripes to represent the 13 colonies that stupidly decided to leave Britain, and 49 stars to represent the 49 states. Which was fine until, a year later, Hawaii became a part of the union.

Afghanistan, meanwhile, changes its flag pretty much constantly. There have been twenty versions since it became an independent state in 1709. Then you have all the countries that didn't really exist when I was at school. They're always coming up with new designs.

The French, of course, change their flag to suit the situation at hand. When things are going well it's blue, white and red, but at the first sign of trouble it's plain white.

In fact it's pretty hard to find a country that doesn't change its flag a lot. Denmark's dates back to about 1370 and apart from a fiddle with the dimensions in 1893 it's the same today.

The Dutch came up with theirs in 1572 but kept altering the colours. Ours is the oldest unchanged flag in the world. But we must face up to the fact that soon we may need to have a rethink.

Obviously we can't simply use the cross of St George because it would annoy the Welsh and the Northern Irish. So we are going to have to come up with something that keeps all the nation happy. This is tricky.

Albania has my favourite flag. It's plain red with a

black double-headed eagle on it. Mozambique went for something even scarier in the 1970s when it added an AK-47 to its flag, along with a hoe and a book. Not sure why. That said, I like a symbol on a flag. Chosen wisely, it hints at history and ambition and power. Unfortunately the only symbol that would suit what's left of Britain is a teapot. And I'm not sure that's quite right somehow.

Canada made this mistake. It went for a symbol of its favourite breakfast-time treat. El Salvador was silly too and chose bushels of what appear to be cannabis plants, and Barbados opted for a Maserati car badge.

Cyprus, meanwhile, has a drawing of itself, Fiji's looks like the runner-up in a primary school painting competition and Bosnia-Herzegovina has gone for something modern and unusual, which means it resembles an IT company's letterhead.

You need to be careful, then, with the symbol you select. And you need to be careful with colour too.

Green would seem the perfect way of appeasing the Welsh and people who think of England as green and pleasant. But the first rule of commerce is: don't do business with any country that has green in its flag. Sweden, Norway, Canada, Japan, America. Yes. Libya, Italy, Bolivia, Mali. Just sort of no.

Besides, we should try to think of a colour no one else is using. Pink? Hmmm. Not sure. Not even Gay Pride went down that route. Brown? No country uses that at all. And I think for a good reason. It's a bit, how can I put this, faecal. Which leaves us with the only other colour not used by anyone else: grey.

Now we need the symbol. I'm sure you have many ideas of your own. Two crossed Minis. A dragon. Noel Gallagher's hair. But I must urge caution. People in smaller, developing nations are always obsessed with how many world heritage sites they have and they travel miles to see the country's longest factory. Their flags always hint at the only thing that puts them on the map, so we need to be careful to avoid anything such as York Minster or the JCB plant in Uttoxeter. It's supposed to be a flag, not a tourism brochure.

And, besides, this is Great Britain we're talking about. We need to show confidence. And there is simply no better way of doing that than with self-deprecating humour. Only the truly strong can laugh at themselves. It's why there are no Cambodian comedy clubs.

So how's this for an idea? A battleship-grey flag with small diagonal black slashes on it. That's not only a nice bit of design but also an internationally recognizable meteorological symbol for incoming drizzle.

The Union Jack was perfect when we had an empire and the world trembled at the sound of our cannon. But when we've shown we can't even hang on to Scotland, it's time to say to the world, with a smile, 'Yes. And our weather's a bit rubbish as well.'

23 June 2013

Sex, blood, mumbling . . . it's Guessing Game of Thrones

Not that long ago I'd have scoffed and tutted at the beautiful and very excellent Imogen Stubbs, who said recently that younger actors have started to imitate American film stars by mumbling their lines.

Of course she would say this. Ms Stubbs learnt her craft in the theatre, where even the most tender love scene must be delivered in such a way that you can be heard at the back. 'YOUR EYES ARE LIKE POOLS OF MOONLIGHT AND YOUR SWEET BREATH CARESSES ME LIKE A GENTLE SUMMER BREEZE.'

Theatre is make-believe. You have to wear make-up that's 6 inches thick, you have to prance about in preposterous clothes and you have to enunciate at a volume that is heard in real life only when someone has a very bad mobile phone connection. 'I'm on the train!'

American film stars can be more true to life. They can whisper, safe in the knowledge that sophisticated microphones and Dolby surround sound will make their near-silent utterances audible in the cinema. In the theatre, actors need lungs like Spinal Tap's amplifiers because they are talking to a thousand people. In a film they're talking to you. It's about small movements and small sound. That's what makes it real.

However, that said, on a long flight to Johannesburg

recently I tried to watch a film called *Zero Dark Thirty*. Early on, there's a meeting of spies and it's obvious that what is being said is vital to the plot. But even though I was using expensive, noise-cancelling headphones, I could not make out a single word that anyone said. It was as though they were speaking in a language that had no consonants. So I gave up.

I am partial to *Game of Thrones*. But I have to watch with the subtitles turned on or I simply don't understand who the man with the beard is, or why he is having sex or being stabbed. Much of the time the actors don't even move their lips. It's as though they were trained to be ventriloquists, to take diction out of the dictionary.

And it's not just while I'm watching TV either. Often when I am interviewing someone on *Top Gear*, the audience bursts into peals of laughter and I have no idea why, because I simply haven't heard what the person has just said. My elder daughter, being a teenager, speaks at 5,000 words a minute, and while I know some of those words are 'like' and 'I'm not even joking', the rest, I'm afraid, are just noises. It's like listening to a goose, most of the time.

At parties, when someone is telling me an anecdote, I have learnt to wait for their mouth to stop moving and say, 'Really?' Because a well-delivered 'Really?' works, no matter what they've just said. 'My children are teenagers now.' 'I have just won £700m on the lottery.' 'My husband has just exploded.' 'Really?' works for all of them. It's the No. 1 catch-all response for the hard-of-hearing.

Of course, you might think it'd be better if I simply owned up to my problem and asked them to speak more like Patrick Stewart when he's on stage at the National Theatre, or the bridge of the USS *Enterprise*. But I'm afraid that this is not possible.

In our cruel world, deafness is like insomnia. People have no sympathy for it. My family will ride bicycles across mountain ranges and swim the largest oceans to raise money for those who have cancer and soldiers who have lost their limbs in Afghanistan. Their capacity for giving is boundless. But when I ask any of them to repeat what they've just said, they laugh in my face.

And I can't complain because for years my elderly mother has struggled to keep up with fast-moving kitchen table chitchat, and I've found it extremely exasperating. She also says that my car phone doesn't work properly, that the sound on her television is broken and that all Americans are inaudible, and I've rolled my eyes in despair.

Deafness is annoying for the sufferer, but, truth be told, it's worse for everyone else. That's why I've spent the past year or so nodding and saying, 'Really?' and smiling politely and pretending I understand what's going on in *Game of Thrones*.

But recently I'd had enough and decided to research the issue. So I turned to the *Daily Mail*, which, of course, knows exactly what's causing it. Surprisingly, it's not Romanian immigrants or the BBC. It's because I eat too much. Yup. It published a story recently saying that overeating can damage the hair cells in the inner ear, causing hearing loss. Fat hair? Who knew?

Mind you, the *Mail*'s medical experts say that drinking one glass of wine a day is good for you and that drinking two glasses of wine a day can cause brain damage. And no doubt make you an immigrant too. So I'm not sure we can take its medical advice seriously.

It's more likely I'm going a bit mutton because I've seen the *Who* thirteen times. And because I've been to a rocket test in the Deep South. And because I spend half my working days being assaulted by the sound of internal combustion. And, if we're honest, because I'm fifty-three and thus many years past my sell-by date.

But can something be done? To find out, I went to see a doctor, who put me in headphones and asked me to push a button each time I heard a small beep. Some sounded like baby bats giggling in the next room, and some like faraway oil tankers in the fog. It was therapeutic and rather nice.

But not as nice, it turned out, as the results. There is absolutely nothing wrong with my hearing. Pete Townshend's G-string has had no effect. Nor has the immense wall of noise created when solid fuel is turned into a huge amount of thrust. I'm fine. My ear hair is not even slightly fat.

Which must mean that Imogen Stubbs does have a point. The reason I can't hear what actors are saying is that they've all seen Marlon Brando at the end of *Apocalypse Now* and think that's how it should be done.

30 June 2013

The AK-47's fine, sir, but please switch off your mobile phone

These days, as I'm sure you know, nobody is allowed to die of anything other than extreme old age. And if someone does dream up a new and unusual way of dying, such as eating themselves, or getting stuck in a suitcase, no expense is spared in the headlong rush to make sure that it can never happen again. When the floor of a shopping centre is wet, we must have a sign telling people that the floor is wet. When it's foggy, we must have a sign telling us there is fog. And with its severe weather warnings, the Met Office now treats an incoming low pressure system like the imminent arrival of an ebola bomb.

At work I am shadowed constantly by a health and safety officer who's on hand to provide helpful tips on how I can perform the next task without tripping over my shoelaces, or falling out of a tree, or exploding. And if I choose to ignore his advice, he has the power to call a halt to the shoot and send everyone home.

That's why every BBC reporter now delivers the news in a hard hat and a high-visibility jacket. And it's why we are no longer warned not to 'try this at home'. Because anything that can't be done at home can't be done on the television either.

All of this means that we can do pretty much anything we want, safe in the knowledge that billions of man hours have been spent making sure that we will come to no harm. Anything even remotely dangerous was banned long ago.

But wait. What's this? British Airways has just announced that passengers will be allowed to use their mobile telephones while the plane is taxiing. Surely this is madness. We know because we've been told a million times that the signal from your mobile phone will cause a petrol pump to explode.

We also know it will give us cancer. And we definitely know that if we switch on our BlackBerrys while we're on a plane, even when it is trundling along the ground at 4 mph, it will immediately veer onto the M4 and rush into London, where it will crash into Harrods.

There are many scare stories. Back in 1998 a Qantas Jumbo went out of control over London. It lurched upwards, fell onto its side and was careering towards the city centre before the pilot managed to regain control. A subsequent investigation found that the autopilot had gone bonkers and that this might have been caused by signals from a passenger's mobile phone.

In fact, there have been fifty incidents in recent years that investigators say could well have been caused by mobiles. And yet British Airways has decided that it's OK to use them when on the ground. Most airlines say it's OK above 10,000 ft. And an Emirates Airbus I used the other day even had wi-fi to encourage their use. How on earth we managed to land in Dubai, I will never know. So many people were making calls, I fully expected to touch down in Leicester.

Except, of course, I didn't, because I simply do not believe that mobile phones interfere with the safe passage of an airliner. Never have. And neither does any pilot I've met, or else they wouldn't sit up there in the cockpit ringing their wives and their bookmakers pretty much constantly.

Think about it. To make sure the plane does not crash or explode, passengers are told to place their cricket bats and bows and arrows and toothpaste in the hold. And before they are even allowed into the departure hall, they must pass through a machine that allows security personnel to have a look at their genitals and their breasts.

Before take-off a lady with a Manchester accent will come on the public address system to lay down a few rules and why they are necessary. You must remain seated with your seatbelt fastened in case of turbulence. For health and safety reasons you are not allowed to smoke in the lavatories, and detectors are fitted to make sure you comply. Drinks will not be served to anyone who's had one too many already. Everything electronic must be turned off completely. And then you are told how to put a mask on. The announcement usually goes on until you are over the Azores.

And then it's time for the announcement about preparations for landing. On Virgin, in particular, this takes about sixteen hours. They tell you that things may have moved in the overhead bins and how to position your seat and what sort of headphones to use, and that smoking is still not allowed anywhere at all, ever. And then they come through the cabin to make sure that absolutely nothing at all is on the floor in front of your seat. Or on your knee. Even a sheet of newspaper or a sock is deemed to be hazardous and must be stowed.

You know, as the lady from Manchester drones on and on, that the airline and the aviation authority have addressed every conceivable issue. That every possible danger has been eradicated.

Which raises the question: if you are not trusted to travel with a tube of toothpaste, do you really think for a moment that they are going to let you board with a device that can cause the plane to lurch about and crash? You think they would trust you to turn it off? Not a chance.

If phones were even the slightest bit dangerous, I can absolutely guarantee that you would be told to put yours in the hold with your deodorant and your rounders bat and your cigarette lighter.

And it's not just me saying this either. Airbus has subjected its planes to such a fearsome radar bombardment, the skin of the plane was hot enough to toast bread. And none of its equipment was affected. Boeing has done much the same thing with similar results.

So I reckon using your phone on a plane is no more dangerous than driving a van into 3 ft of water. But two weeks ago I wasn't allowed to do that either.

7 July 2013

A 2:1 in post office robbery and the world's your oyster

In these times of economic misery the future must seem pretty bleak for the nation's young people. They work hard for their A-levels, study furiously at university and emerge with a decent 2:1, only to be told that if they are lucky they might be able to get a job steam-cleaning fat from London's sewers or working as an estate agent in Fulham.

As the father of three teenage children, I spend many hours chewing the end of a Biro, wondering what might be done about this. And I think I have a suggestion: rather than settling for a dreary job flogging crappy flats, school-leavers should be encouraged to take up a life of crime.

In the olden days this would not have worked at all because you'd soon be caught by Mr Dixon or beaten up by Jack Regan. And then you'd appear in front of a red-faced beak, who'd give you a damn good talking-to before sending you to prison. Now, though, things are a bit different . . .

Today, because the police devote approximately 90 per cent of their resources to phone hacking and disc jockeys who are already dead, they have had to get fairly radical when it comes to investigating burglary and acts of extreme violence.

Mostly this involves not investigating them at all.

And as a result of that, three out of every four crimes committed in this country remain unsolved.

So instead of applying for a job with Foxtons, why not hold up a post office? Provided you don't leave your name and address on the counter, or stare into the CCTV camera for too long, or light a cigarette while you're waiting for the postmistress to put the cash in a bag, there is a 75 per cent chance you will get away with it.

And even if you don't, there's no need to worry. Because the police now spend so much time working out who listened to Sienna Miller's voicemails, they really don't have the resources to process your pesky robbery. So they have devised a cunning way of letting you go.

Today crims are regularly dealt with using what's called a 'community resolution', which is as weak and as lentilly as it sounds. The offender is simply made to say sorry to his victim and in return he will not get a criminal record. In the past twelve months more than 30,000 people have been dealt with in this way. They've kicked someone's head in. And after saying 'sorry', they've gone home to bed.

Of course, if you shoot the postmistress in the head with a sawn-off shotgun, they will put a couple of bobbies on the case, and if they find you, they won't be able to make you say sorry to the victim. Because she'll be spattered all over the Benson & Hedges and the lottery ticket dispenser.

This means you will go to court and you may be given a life sentence. But again, there's no need to worry unduly.

I'd estimate that today 75 per cent of the population would say a life sentence is the right punishment for shooting a postmistress in the head, while 24.9 per cent would say you should be hanged. And that leaves 0.1 per cent who'd say you should be sent to live in a cottage at the seaside. And luckily for you the 0.1 per cent are judges who sit in the Grand Chamber, the highest echelon of the European Court of Human Rights.

Last week they decided that it is inhumane to lock up Jeremy Bamber – a man who killed his entire family – for life and that he must be allowed to seek parole. They agreed with his claim that the time he'd served already had left him depressed and in despair.

Of course, this doesn't mean that he and the other forty-eight people currently serving whole-life sentences in England and Wales – Rose West is one of them, and Peter Sutcliffe is another – will actually get parole; only that they can apply for it. And this may put you off the idea of a life of crime. But don't be disheartened, because if you try to escape, there's really not much anyone can do to stop you.

Last week we heard about a chap called Jimmy Mubenga. After he had served two years in Britain for actual bodily harm, the authorities decided it'd be best if he spent the rest of his life in Angola and issued a deportation order. But, sadly, when the plane landed in Africa, he was all dead.

Guards from the private security firm G4S said that Mubenga had tried to attack one of them on the trip and that they'd had to restrain him. But last week an inquest jury in Isleworth, west London, decided he'd been unlawfully killed. So the guards will probably face charges, which means G4S will doubtless return to its original policy of simply letting prisoners wander off, willy-nilly.

Add all this together and it's easy to see why crime is a sensible option for today's school-leavers.

Except for one thing. The reason why people choose to earn a living by chiselling fat from a rat-infested, foul-smelling sewer rather than shooting postmistresses in the head is that they have a moral compass. They know that even if they ended up, scot-free, in a villa in Spain, they would never be happy again.

And that's what the system seems to have forgotten: that West and Bamber and all the others who are currently serving life aren't wired up like ordinary people. They're odd. Weird. Dangerous. We may like to think that with help they can reboot their inner workings, but it's most likely they can't. Which is why, for them, life has to mean life.

Let me put it to you this way. I know people who have not touched a drop of alcohol for thirty years. It is easy to assume that after all that time and all that hardship, they must be able to drink socially and occasionally like normal people. But they daren't even have a mouthful of sherry trifle, because they know that once you've become an alcoholic, you are an alcoholic for life. And you have to pay the price.

14 July 2013

You really want full disclosure, Mr Assange? OK, here goes . . .

I spent most of last week watching a film called *We Steal Secrets*. It's about Julian Assange and the WikiLeaks affair and it is very long.

If, like me, you didn't really pay much attention to the whole sorry saga, it's worth seeing because it raises some interesting questions.

You probably know that Assange is currently holed up in the Ecuadorean embassy, attempting to avoid deportation to Sweden, where he faces all sorts of unpleasant accusations about sexual matters. But that's just flimflam.

So let me recap, briefly, the important points. Assange is a weirdo with daft hair who seems to have spent his formative years attempting to leave rude words on Nasa's computers. Then one day this self-styled campaigner for freedom and truth and justice stumbled upon a man – who thought he might be a woman – in the US army. The he/she in question bundled up a load of secret information, and Assange put it on the internet.

Now, supporters of Assange – and I count many of them as friends – say that this was a reasonable thing to do. They say that we should all be aware, for instance, of what American politicians said in private about the leaders of other nations. But I'm not so sure about that.

Over the years the huge oak beam that plunges into the wall above my bed has shrunk. This means there's now a big gap between it and the plasterwork, which allows me to hear exactly what house guests are saying in the spare room. Often it's not good.

Many talk about how a man of my means can possibly think it's acceptable to have a spare room that cold. Some talk, in a not entirely flattering way, about other guests who have been for dinner. A very few have sex. And you know what? While it's jolly interesting to hear this stuff, and amusing in the short term, ultimately it makes life a lot more complicated.

Imagine how hard life would become if your best friend were told by a third party exactly what you thought of them. They wouldn't be your best friend any more. Imagine how long a marriage would last if everything a wife said to her friends over lunch were reported back to her husband. Imagine if your kids knew what you said about them after they'd gone to bed.

I suppose all of us have dreamt about how enjoyable it would be to read other people's minds. It would certainly make life easier for teenage boys at a party. Does this girl fancy me? Or am I about to make a gigantic fool of myself? But the truth is: knowing what people think about us would be a living hell.

When I appeared on *This Is Your Life* about two thousand years ago the final guest through the doors was Alan Whicker. I'd written in a school exercise book at the age of ten that I wanted to be him when I grew up, and there he was, in the flesh, singing my praises in front of millions. I was desperately proud.

But then a few years later I was told by the man who'd chauffeured him back from the television studio that he'd said, 'That Clarkson chap really is the most jumped-up little shit.'

I wish I'd never known that. I really do. I'd hero-worshipped Alan Whicker and would feel much better now if I thought the feeling had been mutual.

That's what morons such as Assange simply don't get. Except, of course, he does. Because he is now doing everything in his power to make sure we don't learn the truth about his sexual antics in Sweden.

If you are a freedom of information enthusiast, try this for size. You're on an airliner midway over the Atlantic and in the cockpit the pilot has just noticed a worrying warning light. Do you want him to wake you up immediately and say, 'Well, ladies and gentlemen, I'm afraid there's a fault with all four engines and soon we will all be dead'? Or would you like him to work through the issues and discover it was all a false alarm first?

Most of the time we have to be able to speak freely in the absolute certainty that what we are saying will go no further. And that is certainly the truth if the US ambassador in London is talking to President Obama about Ed Miliband.

Imagine. If he thought for a moment that Little Ed would one day get to hear his opinions, he wouldn't be able to say, 'He's an adenoidal little twerp with the power of a pencil sharpener and the vision of a goat.' He'd have to say instead, 'He's an impressive man with a deep, booming voice and great vision.' And that would end up skewing US–British relations quite badly.

All of which brings me back to the concept of WikiLeaks and a hypothetical situation . . .

There's a man sitting in a bunker somewhere and he knows that there was an accident on board one of Britain's nuclear submarines. He also knows that the Ministry of Defence is trying to keep it all quiet because it doesn't want the public to know how close they came to being fried. And he decides this is wrong. So, acting all on his own, he decides to send the files to some jumped-up computer hacker, who promptly puts it all on the internet.

As a result there's an outcry, the government is forced to abandon the nuclear deterrent and Britain ends up like Belgium. Do we really want that? Individuals deciding what should be a national secret and what should not? I know I don't.

That's why I think we need newsgathering organizations that are accountable and responsible. Organizations in which there are lawyers and experienced newsmen and links to the highest echelons of government. Organizations that know what's a genuinely good story and what's sensitive material.

The great thing is: we have such organizations. They're called newspapers. And when it comes to obtaining my information, I'd rather get it from them than some idiot with mental health issues and a laptop.

21 July 2013

The tears of a clown engulf Detroit, factory of dreams

Shortly after writing last week's column, I began to hear news that Detroit had filed for bankruptcy. This made me sad because, while I'm no great fan of most American cities, Detroit is different. Detroit is special. Detroit is tremendous.

It all began, of course, when Henry Ford started making cars in the city, using mass-production techniques he'd learnt from the gun maker Smith & Wesson.

Pretty soon Mr Chevrolet, Mr Chrysler, the Dodge brothers and, er, Mr Motors were doing the same thing, and the promise of steady, well-paid jobs was causing vast numbers of black workers to abandon the plantations in the Deep South and head north.

This led to the birth of a vibrant music scene in Detroit, and that, of course, led to the birth of the Motor City's greatest gift: Motown. This was run in pretty much the same way as the car industry. The writers poured ideas in at one end and, after the producers and artists had worked their magic, short, snappy pop songs poured out of the other. Songs that, incidentally, were designed specifically to sound good and right on tinny car radios.

Motown gave us Stevie Wonder and Diana Ross and Martha Reeves and the Temptations and countless more besides. But Detroit's contribution to modern music runs even deeper than that. Because other people with strong links to the city include Bob Seger, Ted Nugent, Madonna, some of the Eagles, Alice Cooper, Iggy Pop, Suzi Quatro, the White Stripes, Eminem and, of course, Sixto Rodriguez. There is simply no city anywhere in the world that has contributed more to the happiness and wellbeing of humankind. None.

However, in 1967 everything went wrong. There were race riots. Big ones. Bob Seger recalls coming home from a gig one night to find tanks parked on the streets of what had been until that point one of the richest places in America.

This caused what's been subsequently called 'the white flight'. A massive and sudden emigration of middle-class people from the city to a safer, more Surrey-like area north of 8 Mile Road. The rot had started.

I first started visiting Detroit in the late 1980s, and by then the situation was dire. Whole chunks of the city had been abandoned. Huge houses built by ambitious Motor City executives in the 1930s lay empty and over-grown and burnt. The magnificent Detroit Institute of Arts, which houses Diego Rivera's staggering frescos, sat in a wasteland. I had the Henry Ford museum to myself.

Imagine coming to London fifteen years from now and finding the whole of Knightsbridge had been des-erted by every living thing except weeds. That's how fast and deep Detroit's disintegration was running.

Then the car firms began to move their factories not

just out of the city, or out of the state of Michigan, but out of America – to Mexico, for example, where the workforce was cheap and plentiful. Motown had long since moved to Los Angeles. Detroit had become the murder capital of the world. The whole place was falling apart.

In the mid-1990s I made a television show about its collapse and decided we should visit the ruined eighteen-storey railway station. I wanted to stand on its desolate concourse and do a piece to camera about how 'commuting to work by car' was invented in Detroit.

The police thought this was a very bad idea. They told us that rival gangs fought one another for control of the station's top floor, that it was a war zone in there and that if five Limeys went inside, they would take our camera, our clothes, our watches and our van and kill us. And that no rescue would be possible because it was a no-go zone for the officers of law enforcement.

We ignored them, and after a little while in the ruined marble interior began to wish we hadn't because a guy who was approximately 17 ft tall emerged, brandishing a machine gun that fired 12-bore cartridges. It's known, understandably, as a 'street sweeper'.

The big man wanted to know who we were and what we thought we were doing on his turf. He had yellow eyes and was plainly not thinking straight. Nor was any of the other equally large guys who began to materialize from the shadows. All had guns, and after a couple of minutes' questioning, during which we explained we were from the BBC – something with which they were unfamiliar – and Britain, which flummoxed them too, I really did think for the first time since I'd been in a Russian-made former Angolan air force plane over Cuba that I was about to die.

But then the gang leader whistled, and into the mix arrived a short girl with green hair and many earrings in her nose. She was barely able to stand and she seemed to be very fascinated by me. She stared for a good while before saying, 'Aren't you da guy off *Top Gear*?'

Now this was before *Top Gear* had even crossed the English Channel. There were few satellites and no bit torrents, so she couldn't possibly have seen it in America, even if she had a TV, which, by the look of her, she didn't. I looked suitably perplexed until she explained: 'I used to be a producer on *Newsnight*.'

And so the guns were lowered and, much to the surprise of the cops, who were watching from a distance, we left with our new best friends and went to one of their parties. It was amazing.

Over the years I've had many epic nights out in Detroit. Bob Seger took me on a tour of the city's lap-dancing joints. And then there was the windowless bar where I drank with mates of the film-maker Michael Moore. And dinners in the Ren Cen – the Renaissance Centre. Once I sat with Martha Reeves in a park on Belle Isle drinking Guinness at nine in the morning.

I don't know what bankruptcy means for Detroit. But I hope it means the same as it did for General Motors: the debts were shrugged off and the company began again with a slightly different name. I don't want

Detroit to be abandoned, as some have suggested, to the prairie. I want this factory of dreams to survive. Because, in the words of the Motown star Brenda Holloway, You've Made Me So Very Happy.

28 July 2013

Tit for tapas: they covet the Rock, we conquer Spain

Crikey. It all seems to be kicking off in Gibraltar. In June Spanish police opened fire on a jet skier in Gibraltan waters, and last weekend Spanish border guards decided to inspect every single vehicle leaving the British overseas territory, causing six-hour delays.

Meanwhile, Spanish fishermen, who are normally a model of restraint and common sense, have been going nose to nose with the Royal Navy, and there are reports of Spanish jet fighters streaking low over the Rock. It all sounds very ugly.

Apparently the recent bout of trouble stems from Britain's decision to build an artificial reef in the Bay of Gibraltar.

We claim it's to benefit nature but since Spain, with its long tradition of stabbing bulls and throwing donkeys off tower blocks and hoovering every living thing from every ocean in the world, has no real understanding of environmentalism, it presumably imagines that it must be some kind of underwater nuclear submarine base. This is why the Spanish have got all uppity again.

In some ways I can't blame them. Because if Lizard Point in Cornwall belonged to France as a result of some 300-year-old treaty that was drawn up by a bunch of posh boys in wigs, I dare say we might feel a bit aggrieved today. And we'd feel especially aggrieved if the treaty had been the result of a conflict as daft as the War of the Spanish Succession.

To recap: Charles II of Spain died childless and Philip of France reckoned he was the rightful heir. But an Austrian called Charles disagreed, saying that he quite fancied being king of Spain. This caused a huge split in Europe that, naturally, the British decided to solve by having a big battle in Belgium.

We also decided that we should attack some Mediterranean ports and dispatched the fleet, which sailed around looking for likely targets. Toulon was considered, along with Barcelona, but eventually the top brass settled on Gibraltar. A battle was fought. The Spanish lost. And the residents all scarpered.

Eventually Charles of Austria decided he wasn't bothered about being king of Spain any more and said Philip of France could have the crown. Which caused the British to say, 'Yes. But only if we get Gibraltar. Oh, and you'd better throw in Minorca as well or we'll come and taunt you a second time.' And that was that.

Except it wasn't. The Spanish subsequently invaded Minorca and forced the British garrison to withdraw. But a few years later we decided that though we'd lost the battle, it was still ours. So we went back and had to be kicked out again. Gibraltar, though? Well, despite endless battles and sieges and much diplomatic pressure the 2½-square-mile lump of superheated, monkey-infested rock is still ours today.

But whisper this: we don't need it any more. Yes, it has been strategically important in the past but today it's only real purpose is as a tax haven for William Hill's computer servers. As a result it's guarded by six blokes and a Land Rover. Oh, and there's a jet fighter on the runway but – and I'm not making this up – it has to be parked with its guns pointed out to sea or the Spanish get all cross. I'm not sure why. It's such an old aeroplane that its guns are actually better described as trebuchets.

So we're in a tricky spot. The Spanish want Gibraltar back and behind closed doors we'd probably like to give it to them. But we can't because pretty much 100 per cent of the locals want to stay British. If you go there it's like you've landed in Nigel Farage's head; there are Union Jacks everywhere and all you can eat are eggs, and chips.

So here we are. It's 2013 and we are in a seemingly impossible Falkland Islands-style spot. We're sitting here with the Spanish flying their jets through our airspace and taking potshots at our jet-ski enthusiasts. And all we can do is shrug and say we understand but ultimately there's nothing we can do.

Or is there? Yup. Happily I've hatched a plan. Instead of sitting around biting our fingernails and worrying that one day Gibraltar will be taken by force, we turn the tables and invade Spain.

On paper this sounds like a daunting task. In the air the Spanish have 50 Eurofighter Typhoons and 86 F/A-18 Hornets. At sea there are 11 frigates, 3 submarines and an amphibious assault ship that can be used as an aircraft carrier. And on land there are 327 main battle tanks. And 75,000 troops.

However, while they have a great deal of hardware,

they have absolutely no money at all. And a Eurofighter is no good if you don't have any euros to fill its fuel tanks.

I was there just recently and saw first-hand the sheer number of towns and airports and motorways that were never needed and which are now rotting. And if they can't afford to keep a motorway open, what chance do they have of mounting a full-scale military operation to keep a British invasion at bay?

There's more. We have thousands of battle-hardened troops who when the conflict in Afghanistan is over will need to be kept amused. A gentlemanly scrap in Spain would do the trick nicely.

Plus, finally, I'm not sure the Spaniards would be that ill disposed towards a British takeover. The South American cash cow stopped producing riches centuries ago, and now even the EU money lorry doesn't drop by any more. I think many would therefore quite like it if we were in charge.

It'd be good for us too. Certainly a short war would be a far better capital project than the HS2 rail link, and the benefits would be greater.

I have no doubt, of course, that my plan will never get beyond the drawing board. We will never invade and conquer Spain. But look at it this way; if they thought for a moment we were looking into the possibility, they might stop shooting at our jet skiers and closing the border every time the mood took them. In short, they might get back in their box.

4 August 2013

Doubtless you'll be back up the tip today, dumping Granny

Like many people I was shocked and amazed by those photographs of all the litter left behind by your children at last weekend's music festival in a town called Reading. However, my shock and amazement had nothing to do with the quantity – which was considerable – so much as the quality.

You would expect, of course, the ground to be covered in a veneer of excrement and body hair and all the other flotsam and jetsam that go hand in hand with living like an animal for three days. But having studied the aerial photographs of the aftermath very carefully, it is plainly obvious that hundreds of fans also left behind their tents.

Those of a *Daily Mail* disposition might suggest that the teenagers were so completely out of their heads on exotic smoking materials and vodka that they simply forgot. But I find this hard to believe. Because the checklist when leaving a festival is not that long. We're not talking about Joan Collins packing after a month in the south of France. All they had to remember was a) phone and b) tent.

I suspect the real reason that half of the list was left behind is simple: they couldn't be bothered to pack it away and carry the damn thing home on the train. It's easier to simply buy another one next year when the festival season begins all over again.

And that's odd. We keep being told about how hard it is for young people to get a well-paid job and how they must work until they are ninety-three to pay off their student loans. And yet here is graphic evidence that having spent more than £200 on a ticket, and another £200 on nasal sustenance, they are prepared to simply abandon their £200 tent. Because it's too much of a faff to take it down and carry it home.

This brings me on to Jamie Oliver. Jamie is not backward in venting his spleen, having suggested in recent times that the British don't know how to work and that northerners eat too many badgers. Or something like that. But earlier last week he said the poor waste too much of their supposedly meagre income on junk food. He may well be right.

Recently my colleague James May took to Twitter to say he was at home preparing a mushroom risotto. Don't be alarmed. That's the sort of thing James likes to talk about in real life as well.

And almost immediately he was harangued by a young chap who said that because he's on the minimum wage he couldn't afford a risotto and had to make do with sandwiches from Tesco.

Well, I'm proud to say I have no idea how much a Tesco sandwich costs but I'm willing to bet the difference that it's considerably more than James May spent on his mushroom risotto. Which means our friend on the minimum wage is simply throwing away his cash because he's too bone idle to cook for himself.

Or maybe he's saving up for a new tent. But whatever. It's not just teenagers who are feckless and wasteful. While riding my bicycle – I'll just say that again, while riding my bicycle – through Holland Park last week I was forced to stop. Partly this was because I was extremely weary but mostly it was because the whole sandpit area was full of fair-haired blue-eyed children called Arabella. All of whom were being minded by Filipino women.

So it's come to this. People are now so slap-happy with their cash, and so lazy, that on a sunny bank holiday Monday they will pay someone to go and look after their children in the park. So what was the point of all that sex if you can't take the result to the park, and laugh as it falls off a swing into a big splodgy bit of dog dirt?

I recently spent a morning at what I'd been told was a 'community recycling centre'. You probably know it as a 'tip'. And I simply couldn't believe what people were throwing away. Computers. Bras. Lawnmowers. Bicycles. One man pulled up in a brand new Mercedes-Benz, opened the boot, removed a brand new sink, took it to the sink skip and lobbed it inside. He then drove off.

Then another man arrived with a small plant pot full of earth that he emptied into a skip marked 'garden waste'. This means he was actually throwing his garden away. I was only mildly surprised that there wasn't a skip labelled 'grandparents'.

It's strange, isn't it? The television these days is rammed with programmes on how to make do and mend, how to eat for nothing and how to decorate your home by wombling around in the undergrowth. But plainly no one is watching. Probably because they've thrown their televisions away.

You probably have, actually. When the flatscreen systems arrived on the market I bet you bought one even though your old box worked perfectly well. I also bet your kitchen drawer is full of cameras that you replaced because you lost the charger and your garage is chock-a-block with barbecue sets that you no longer use because they were too difficult to clean.

Today the internet is full of websites that tell you where you can buy the cheapest petrol and which supermarket is currently selling the least expensive lamb chops but nobody seems to be paying any attention. You just fill up when the tank's empty and pay Ocado to deliver your chops when you're feeling peckish. And who these days chooses which pub they like based on the price it charges for a pint?

Today convenience is king. Anything that buys us time to do something else is worth it. Until you sit down and calculate how much you spend every year on stuff you already have. Then it becomes frightening. Then you start to wonder if it really is worth lobbing your still-serviceable 3G phone into the phone skip at the tip and spending £500 on a 4G replacement.

Or whether it's worth spending upwards of £50bn on a new railway line from London to the north when there's absolutely nothing wrong with the railway line you have now.

1 September 2013

Wandering lonely as a vegan amid a host of humdrum lakes

United Nations world heritage sites were created so that important cultural and natural landmarks could be preserved for all humanity for all time. Or until the Taliban blow them up.

It was a good idea, but after all the big stuff had been covered – which didn't take very long – the scheme became nothing more than an ego boost for smaller, less important countries that could rush about saying, 'You lot in the developed world may have your nuclear weapons and your literature and your space programmes, but we have these jolly interesting rock formations.'

Plus, as an added bonus, when a landmark is awarded world heritage status, the UN gives the country's government some money, all of which can be used by the official in charge to buy a shiny new Mercedes.

Naturally, the latest small and unimportant country to leap onto the bandwagon is Britain. There are twenty-eight sites in the UK and its overseas territories; places such as Blenheim Palace and Bath, and the Giant's Causeway in Co. Antrim. But now, people with titles and CBEs are campaigning for more to be added to the list. And it seems the No. 1 contender is the Lake District.

They argue that when the former resident William

Wordsworth claimed that the Lake District was 'a sort of national property in which every man has a right and interest', he created the very essence of conservationism and that for this alone, the area deserves recognition. And some money. Please.

They concede that the cost of staking the claim could be as high as £570,000 but say that if they are successful, the award could increase visitor numbers from the current annual level of about 8m by as much as 1 per cent. This, they say, would bring an extra £20m a year to the region.

Yeah. Right. But only if the extra 1 per cent is made up of Roman Abramovich, Elton John and the Sultan of Brunei. Because a 1 per cent increase would see 80,000 more visitors a year, and for them to dump £20m into the local economy, they'd each need to spend £250 in the sweet shops of Keswick.

It's not the wonky cost benefits, though, that worry me about making the Lake District a world heritage site. Or the slightly tragic notion that we now think such things matter. No. My main concern is that I really don't think the award would be justified.

Because while Buttermere is very pretty, it doesn't cause you to bite the back of your hand in the same way that the Grand Canyon does, or the Pyramids. Or Ha Long Bay in Vietnam. And, I'm sorry, but the centre of Ambleside is in no way a match for the centre of Rome.

Writing last week in the *Guardian*, the mad old eco-fool George Monbiot went even further, saying that the Lake District is a chemical desert, devoid of wildlife and that the tradition of hill farming – the very thing the people with titles and CBEs want to preserve – is responsible. Because the sheep are eating the trees and the mountains and causing floods. Earthquakes, too, I should imagine.

The fact is then that no one who takes a global view could see the Lake District as being a world heritage site. But I wonder: could it be something else?

At present, it is popular among ramblers and tenting enthusiasts; bitter, lonely people with wizened legs who strut about pointing at stuff that doesn't matter and telling everyone that they enjoy the constant rain. These people add absolutely nothing to the local economy, and with their cagoules and bobble hats are actually an eyesore. Nothing ruins a view quite so comprehensively as a tent full of Keith and Candice Marie.

And to make matters worse, the local authorities actively encourage such people to tarry awhile. They create camp sites, and build footpaths and discourage anything that might be boisterous or fun. Which, if it's money they're after, seems to be muddleheaded and stupid.

I recently spent a week on the shores of Lake Como in Italy. This is prettier and more dramatic than any of the British lakes but is not a world heritage site. It's not being preserved by the UN for all humanity for all time. Nature will do that. And in the meantime, all humanity can play with it.

As you may know, there is now a speed limit of 10 knots on all the lakes in the Lake District. This means that water-skiing and jet skis and powerboats are pretty much banned. So that the aquatic ramblers in their idiotic dinghies can have a bit of peace and quiet.

On Lake Como things are rather different. Every day I was woken to the glorious sound of someone parting the morning mist with their wondrous Riva Aquarama speedboat. Then the ferry would go by, its jets turning the tranquil green water into a foaming, vibrant white spume. There are no speed limits on Lake Como and, providing your speedboat has less than 40 brake horse-power, you don't even need a licence.

This attitude attracts people with spending power, and to help them along, the nearby towns are rammed with shops selling expensive trinketry and restaurants full of beautiful people eating the beautiful wildlife. Let me put it this way: when George Clooney was looking for a house in Europe, he chose Como, not Derwent Water.

This then is what the people with titles and CBEs should be doing: getting rid of the coach tour mentality, and replacing the vegans and the ramblers with Hollywood high-rollers and billionaire speed freaks. They should accept that there are plenty of places in Britain where the lonely can go to be by themselves and that the Lake District should be a playground for the young and the interesting.

It's time to forget about what Wordsworth did for the Lake District and concentrate more on the contribution made by Donald Campbell. Because blasting across Coniston Water at 297mph is more appealing to more people than wandering through a field of daffodils. Which you can't do any more, anyway, because the sheep have eaten them.

8 September 2013

Day 893: Tim from accounts is attacked by bats on Mars

In recent years we have become accustomed to TV reality shows in which people with bright orange skin and many tattoos spend some time in a confined space, talking gibberish and being rude about one another.

Well, now a Dutch-led foundation has decided to take the idea one step further. So, instead of contestants being sent to a jungle or a strange house in north London, they will go to Mars, where they will remain until they die.

This is all deadly serious. Mars One, the foundation behind the idea, has a website and everything. And it says that the venture will be up and running by 2023. In other words, it is planning to construct a Mars base, get some spaceships there and populate it three years before the British government can get a railway line from London to Birmingham up and running.

Which is all very well but who, pray, would want to spend the rest of their lives on another planet, eating earwigs for the edification of various gormless youths? Well, such is the desperation to be on television these days that more than 200,000 have volunteered. And I'm one of them. Although I did make a bit of a mistake on the application form and said my name was Piers Morgan.

The next question that raises its ugly head is: who

exactly will foot the bill? Well, the foundation is already selling bumper stickers and T-shirts but I'm not sure this will cover the costs completely. So, to make up the difference, it has been rather clever.

Premier League football and Formula One motor racing are rich because of the television deals. And that's exactly what the Mars One team is trying to emulate. It will film the candidate selection process, which will be shown on global television, and then wc, the viewing public, will have a say in who goes.

That's brilliant. Because you are not voting for some halfwit to win a singing competition or deciding who's been best at eating stick insects; you're voting to send someone to another planet for the rest of their lives. Which means they are going to end up with a spaceship full of Tony Blackburn and George Galloway. People whom we really don't want cluttering up the Earth any more.

What television company wouldn't buy into that as a ratings smash? And then, of course, once the motley crew of misfits and ne'er-do-wells has set off, we'll all be praying they crash-land and explode. So the cost of being allowed to transmit this event will make Mark Byford's BBC pay-off look like the bill for a stamp.

It gets better. Because even if the boffins have done their sums right and Messrs Galloway and Blackburn do arrive safely, we'll all continue to tune in every night to see if a hull breach has caused their faces to turn inside out. Or whether they've been attacked by Martian bats.

Naturally they will be expected to build their own power station and water filtration plant, which sounds a bit dreary. But imagine their little faces when they fire up the atmosphere generator only to find it doesn't work. That would be a piece of comedy gold to rival Basil Fawlty's broken-down Austin Estate.

Oh, and one of them is bound to become ill at some point, which means we will be able to see, oh, I don't know, Esther Rantzen taking out Nicholas Witchell's appendix. With hilarious consequences. God only knows what the bill for an advert in that commercial break would be. And what about the day they all die? Tonight, live: George Galloway breathes his last on Mars.

Of course, it all sounds preposterous; like the brains behind this madness have spent rather too long in one of Amsterdam's coffee shops. And yet . . .

Over the years, Nasa has convinced us all that space travel is very tricky and that colonizing another planet is nigh-on impossible. It needed to maintain this illusion so it could go to Congress and say, 'We need more money or everything will blow up.'

But if you watch the film *Apollo 13* you realize that, actually, it is perfectly possible to drive three men round the moon and land them at a precise point in the ocean even when their spacecraft is leaking and has only enough battery power to run a toaster.

This demonstrated that anyone with a welding torch and some oxygen can go into space. A point that was made again recently when a test version of Sir Branson's forthcoming tourist spaceship reached Mach 1.43 and an altitude of 69,000 ft.

Now if he can do this using nothing but the proceeds from Mike Oldfield's *Tubular Bells*, I'm fairly certain that a television audience of 4bn would enable our Dutch friends to put George Galloway on Mars. I hope they succeed – for another reason as well.

Nasa has managed to make the whole space thing incredibly boring. We were expecting warp drive and rocket suits but all we ever get are men in slacks on the space station, growing watercress. Why can't they do something more interesting? Have a fight, for example. I'd love to watch a zero-gravity scrap. It would be hysterical.

And what's the Mars Rover all about? It plods about, sticking its prongs into the dust every now and again, and I can't be alone in thinking, 'Why don't you make it do a doughnut?'

Then you had the space shuttle. It was a fabulous piece of machinery but why did it have to look like it had come from the design studios of Playmobil? To keep our interest, it should have been more pointy and fitted with guns.

Certainly the Mars One team will need to think about this when the time comes to start designing its spaceship on the back of a Rizla. Job one: make it look like the Starship *Enterprise*.

I wish the team well, I really do. It's tragic, of course, that there are 200,000 or more people on the planet who are so friendless and lonely that they'd rather live out their days in the freezing cold Martian desert. But if the spending power of the world's television networks can put them there, it'd be the most interesting and watchable extraterrestrial event since the cow jumped over the moon.

15 September 2013

As Her Majesty knows, a proper sponsored swim includes sharks

Last Friday a noble charity with laudable aims invited its supporters to raise funds by wearing jeans for the day. Which, of course, was a bit of a problem for me since I can't very well ask friends and colleagues to sponsor me for doing something I was planning on doing anyway.

I therefore checked on the website and discovered that I could turn things around, and get sponsored for not wearing jeans. Really? Is the charity suggesting I ask my friends and colleagues to pay me for wearing a different pair of trousers? Because that's not really much of a sacrifice.

But then again I'm asked on an almost daily basis to sponsor someone who really doesn't seem to be putting themselves out at all. 'Dear Mr Clarkson!!! I am raising money for the NSPCC by exhaling after every single inward breath!!! For a whole day!!!' they say.

Then you have those who say they are going on a 'gruelling' trek across South America and wonder if I'd like to give them some money. Why should I do that? As often as not they are keen ramblers, which means that, actually, they are asking me to fund their holiday of a lifetime.

Paying a walkist to stomp about in the Andes is the same as paying Simon Cowell to sit on a yacht in

St Tropez. And you wouldn't do that, would you? Well, you would. In fact, you do. Every time you vote for one of his acts on *The X Factor*. But you know what I mean.

My eldest daughter recently sought sponsorship for making a cycle ride from Paris to London. And she received my wholehearted support because her usual exercise regime is smoking, and six weeks before the event began she couldn't ride a bike. She was therefore asking people to pay her for something she would not find even remotely enjoyable.

And that's the key, really. Sponsorship should only really be requested if you are about to do something that you find unpleasant, boring or scary. Sitting in a meat locker for a year. Eating nothing but dead flies. Going to work with a brick tied to your privates. I'd support anyone who did any of these things. Certainly I'd give a large sum if Piers Morgan announced that for charity he was going to be eaten by a lion.

Which inevitably brings us round to Her Majesty the Queen. In effect she is sponsored by everyone in the country to do good deeds but does she spend her entire time working with equestrian charities, and opening homes for distressed corgi dogs? No. She does not.

Instead Her Majesty has spent pretty much her whole working life doing stuff that must drive her out of her mind. When it comes to being sponsored to do things she doesn't want to do, she is the, er, king.

I have had the honour on a couple of occasions of watching Mrs Queen doing her sponsored charity work and it's mesmerizing. She is shown into a room full of sweating, stuttering men in silly freemason outfits who genuinely think she is interested in why she's there and what they've done. 'And this, Your M-m-m-majesty, is the new p-p-p-p-processing facility . . .'

For these people it's the highlight of their lives and hopefully another rung on the ladder that leads to becoming a CBE. They will keep photographs of the event on their mantelpiece and treasure the memory until they die.

But for her it's all just a blur of botched curtseys, puce-faced women in nylon overalls, oversized scissors and exciting new health centres that aren't exciting at all.

And it never stops. I've looked at her diary over the past few months and there is not one single thing that I would choose to do. She's said goodbye to the ambassadors from various islands around the world and welcomed puffed-up, chicken-headed dignitaries whose English doesn't extend much beyond 'Where is the postman?' and 'The pen of my aunt'.

And, unlike you or me, the poor old dear can't even slope off after half an hour or get drunk. She has to sit there listening to them droning on and on about how George V once came to their flea-infested country and why they have sixteen wives. And then they steal all the teaspoons. And she knows that the next day she's off to Dorchester to nod a lot while someone explains in great detail why the new community drop-in centre is a vital lifeline for the town's single mothers.

For other members of the royal family it's even worse.

Because at least the head honcho does occasionally get to speak with presidents and kings. The Duchess of Gloucester, meanwhile, has to content herself with a fundraising evening for prostate cancer. And Prince Andrew . . . Actually, let's not go there.

There's even an entry on the palace website for Queen Elizabeth the Queen Mother. But when you ask what she's been up to recently, it says 'no results found'. Maybe that's because she's dead.

Prince Edward is much derided but instead of doing good deeds that he finds interesting and amusing, early last week, in his capacity as master of the Worshipful Company of Gardeners, he tarried a while with a chap who has a keen interest in orchids.

Would you do that? Would you do a sponsored chat with a man who likes orchids? I suspect not. I'm fairly sure I wouldn't. But the Earl of Wessex did, just three days after a visit to the new business showcase centre at Barnsley town hall. I definitely wouldn't do that.

The royal family, then, are a beacon for us all. They define the meaning of sacrifice. Propelled by duty, they engage in charitable pursuits, almost none of which are fun, and I urge you to remember that next time you are planning on raising money for good causes. Don't have a party for all your friends. Don't wear jeans to work. Don't go on a nice walk. Do something that makes us wince and say, 'Rather you than me.'

I'll start you off, if you like. I'm spending the weekend with James May. Who'll give me a tenner?

22 September 2013

You're a hit with the kids, Mr Balls.
We adults are trickier

Did anyone else feel a little bit nauseous last week when they were presented with those pictures of Ed Balls playing with some plastic zoo animals in the playground of a children's centre? Plainly the whole thing was a setup designed to convey a message of some kind. But what message? That Ed likes plastic animals? That he's an infant? Or that he has an interest in small children, perhaps?

Later he made a speech in Brighton in which he made a joke about the smallness of David Cameron's gentleman part, and again I want to know what I'm supposed to think.

Mostly what I think is this: that I don't want a chancellor of the exchequer who spends his free time making sandcastles with other people's four-year-olds. And making silly gags.

There was a time, I'm sure, when it was deemed important for politicians to be seen as human beings. That's why we occasionally caught a glimpse of Mrs Thatcher at the kitchen sink, and Tedward Heath on his sailing boat. Once, we were even treated to an image of Winston Churchill building a wall. But now, the obsession with making them look down-to-earth and normal has exactly the opposite effect. Because who, for goodness' sake, goes into a sandpit to play with a bunch of kids they've never met before?

Then we had Mr Cameron, when he was leader of the opposition, cycling to work . . . while wearing a helmet. This implies that the wearer is such a spanner he may fall off his bicycle. And that he is a coward. And these are not qualities we look for in a prime minister.

Speaking of which. Apparently when Gordon Brown was running the show, someone suggested he should smile more. Why? Because anyone with a functioning face must have been able to see that when Brown smiled, it looked like he had just suffered an embarrassing accident in his trousers.

And now we hear about a time when Brown was to be asked by a journalist whether he preferred James Blunt or the Arctic Monkeys. The correct answer for a British prime minister is: 'I don't listen to either of them because I am a prime minister so I prefer Bach.'

But no. The back-room boys felt that would have made him look elitist, or German. So they had a meeting. And at the meeting they realized that James Blunt's mates were all called Rupert and that he might be a Tory. So we had the ludicrous situation where Brown, the most dour man to walk the earth, admitted that he preferred the Arctic Monkeys. Which meant that every single reader knew instantly, and beyond doubt, that he was a massive liar.

One of the reasons Nigel Farage does so well is that when he appears in public he's doing something the public actually does as well. Such as drinking a pint of beer – not a half – and smoking a cigarette. He even let hacks take pictures of him laughing at a joke about UKIP on the front of *Private Eye*.

Why don't other politicians do this? Let us see them being normal? Washing the car? Staying up late to watch pornography on the internet? Or how's this for an idea – doing some work?

They don't, though. I once met John Selwyn Gummer, and in a small-talk, drinks-party environment he appeared to be normal. He had ears, didn't pick his nose as we spoke and like everyone else couldn't hold his plate and his glass and eat at the same time.

And yet this is a man who once shoved a potentially diseased beefburger into the mouth of his angelic daughter. How do spin doctors get a sentient being to do that? Seriously, how do they get him to say, 'Yes. Me winning the hearts and minds of six people in Putney is more important than the wellbeing of my daughter.'

Which brings me off the seesaw of political balance – Gummer was a Tory – and back to Brighton, where last week we saw Ed Miliband skipping down the seafront with his wife and children.

Does Mr Miliband think we really believe that his family lead the sort of life normally only seen in a commercial for Ski yoghurt, that they all do somersaults out of bed in the morning and then spend the day making paper aeroplanes and playing Swingball? Really? Because if he does, it can only mean one of two things: that he is stupid. Or he thinks we are stupid.

It's bad enough Balls using someone else's children to make him look all warm and gooey. But using your own? How exactly does he think that will play out? Does he think that when they get to school their peers will say: a) 'Gosh. I saw you on the news and you looked great', or b) 'Give me all your milk money, you moron'?

By forcing them onto *News at Ten* and the front page of the newspapers, Mr Miliband will probably win the hearts of those stupid women who waste half their lives flicking through the Mail Online's sidebar of shame. But on the downside, he is guaranteeing that his children will spend most of their time at school with their heads down the lavatory.

The vast majority of children born to famous people will do pretty much anything to stay out of the limelight. Because they know that basking in the glow of a well-known parent is seen as showing off. And at school that's not allowed. Titles. Flash watches. Being the offspring of the leader of the opposition. These are the things kids want to keep hidden. Trust me on this. I know because once, many years ago, I very briefly allowed my children into the limelight. It is one of my greatest regrets.

The whole point, of course, is that politicians want to be seen as normal. They show us their kids as a way of saying, 'I'm just like you. I have a penis and it works.'

But what they're actually saying is, 'I will use my kids, or yours if mine aren't around, to keep my job.' And that is not normal at all. That, frankly, is borderline criminal.

29 September 2013

I'll be days, love; Boris has landed me at Swampland terminal 1

It seems everyone in a suit spent all of last week trying to decide whether the human adenoid's Marxist dad did or didn't hate Britain. And you know what? I don't care either way, in the same way that I don't care if politicians punch one another or have affairs or claim their wife was driving at the time. I do care, however, when they get up in the morning and decide to be stupid. And with this high-speed train business that's exactly what's happening. Because some of them really do believe that London is full of people saying, 'Yes, I would move my family and my business to Liverpool tomorrow if only the journey time was cut by thirty-two minutes.'

We see similar lunacy with this London airport business. Boris Johnson is not a stupid man. He can translate complex manuals into Latin and I bet he even knows the French word for pliers. But somehow he has got it into his head that all of our problems can be solved by building a gigantic new hub on a marsh in the Thames estuary.

Of course, this would be extremely good news for the 3.5m people who live in Kent and Essex. They would be able to get from White Hart Lane to their villas in Marbella much more easily. But on the downside it would be extremely bad news for the people who live in Hampshire, Surrey, Sussex, Dorset, Devon, Cornwall, Wales, the Midlands, the north, Scotland, America, continental Europe, Australia and Asia.

The problem is simple. Getting to and from the Thames estuary is impossible for anyone who has a job, or any sort of commitment in the next seven months. This is because London is very big, very busy and very in the way.

Over the years there have been a number of attempts to discourage the westward creep of London by committee-type people with CBEs and a fondness for using words such as 'community' and 'sustainable'.

They created the Docklands as a sustainable community in which to live and it filled up immediately with extremely unpleasant American psychos. They put the Millennium Dome in Greenwich and initially that didn't fill up with anyone at all. So then they had the Olympics, which was great at the time but – and I can guarantee this – soon the site will be a weed-infested wasteland.

The fact is that you can't force people to live and work in a place where they don't want to live and work. And the last person who wanted to live and work east of London was Boadicea.

Fans of the sustainable estuary airport scheme say it would be close to the M25 and this is true but have they ever tried to go round it? It's possible but only if you don't absolutely have to arrive on time. Which, when you're going for a flight, you do.

They also say that excellent train services could be built, and I'm sure that's true as well. But hang on a minute. What about Heathrow? It already has a train service that gets you to and from Paddington station in fifteen minutes. And from most of Britain you don't have to go through or round London to reach it by car. So if we need more capacity, why not simply build a new runway there? Good idea, surely.

No, says the anti-Heathrow lobby. It may be easy to reach for the passengers but because Britain's winds prevail mostly from the west, aeroplanes wishing to land at the airport must fly over the centre of London, which causes noise pollution.

At least I think that's what it said. It's hard to hear properly in the capital over the traffic, the pile-drivers, the sirens and the excited babble of tourists reliving the exhilaration of that fabulous view as they came into land at Heathrow. It's one of the most exciting and vibrant glide paths you will find anywhere in the world.

Naturally, nearer to Heathrow it is jolly noisy but who cares? Every single person who lives nearby moved into their house knowing full well that they were close to an airport. So they can't complain.

It's a different story out east. No one knows who lives near the proposed site, of course, because it's impossible to get there, so we've never met them. But we can be sure they did not choose to live on an inaccessible swamp so they could listen all day to the roar of a Rolls-Royce Trent engine at full chat.

And what about the wildlife? Today, if you want to build a kitchen extension, you must rehouse all the newts and bats that may be affected, so can you imagine how much work would have to be done if you want to turn a marsh into the busiest airport in the world. You'd need to stage a migration on the sort of scale not seen since Mr Wildebeest decided to go a-wandering. Whereas the number of animals and birds affected by a third runway at Heathrow would be exactly none. They'd all been scared away by 1951.

Oh, and don't think that if Boris gets his way that there will be a choice of which airport you use. Because if the swampland plan goes ahead, Heathrow will be closed down. That's because the powers that be know full well that passengers wouldn't opt to spend the first half of their holiday plodding through Newham on a train and the next bit in an airliner that was in a silent nose-dive because both engines had been taken out by a brace of avocets.

Can you imagine even contemplating shutting Heathrow? Think about all those warehouses along the M4. You couldn't close it. It would be financial suicide. It would be madness.

Look at it this way. If you find that you need a bit more storage space at home, you don't build a castle in the Scottish Highlands. You build a loft extension. Because you'd know that a castle would be ruinously expensive and that commuting every day to your office in Beaconsfield would be impractical.

That's the trouble, though. That's what you'd do. Because you are intelligent. You should be in politics.

6 October 2013

Dai the dustman had better book his Bolivian plague jab

On the face of it, the latest cost-cutting wheeze from Cardiff's cash-strapped council is a good idea. Because, in an attempt to save £125m, it is considering making bin collections of general waste only once a month. Recyclable waste such as food, plastic, glass and paper will be collected every week.

Oh, and don't think you can get round the system by hiding general waste in a recycling bag, because they've thought of that, and if you're caught you'll be fined £100. It all sounds very clever. But it isn't. Because if this scheme is implemented, I can pretty much guarantee that soon the entire population of Cardiff will be suffering from the bubonic plague. Here's why.

My bin at home is divided into three sections. One is for general waste, one is for recycling and one is stuff for the chickens. This is all very *Media Guardian* and cuddly polar bear lovely. But there's a problem, because I don't ever know what goes where.

Is a smashed plate general waste? Will a chicken eat a used tea bag? What about the packaging in which Gillette sells razor blades? Could that ever be recycled, and if so, into what? Apart from as a substitute for a diamond on the end of an industrial drill bit?

If I lived in Cardiff, then, I'd be fined about £17,000 a week for getting it all wrong, and this strikes me as unfair. Because if a council wants to spend its time turning an old pair of shoes into the rear wing of a Vauxhall Astra, then that's fine. But asking me to do the job on its behalf is like asking me to be my own doctor. 'Don't clutter up the hospital with your blocked saliva gland. Go home and mend it yourself.'

There's another problem with the Cardiff idea. It's this: when someone's waste bin is overflowing, I doubt very much they will think, 'Oh, well, we will just have to live with the smell and the rats and the disease until next month, when the dustbinerie come round.' Instead, they will simply pop it into the boot of their car, drive to the countryside and lob it over a hedge.

This already happens with the sort of large items that the men of the dustbinerie do not take away in case they hurt their arms. My farm is littered with old televisions, building materials and mattresses. Some days it looks like a Brazilian favela out there. And if the Cardiff solution catches on, things are going to get worse. There will be so much litter in the streets that rats and plague are sure to follow.

I accept, of course, that savings need to be made and that eventually we will have to wave goodbye to frivolous luxuries such as the NHS, housing benefit, old age pensions, free schools and the Royal Navy.

If we are going to balance the books, this is all necessary and inevitable. But if we are to protect our way of life, it is critical that we draw the line at refuse collection. This must be maintained. This is our line in the sand. Refuse collection is what separates us from the beasts.

I have had the good fortune to do a great deal of travelling over the years, and I've learnt that you can tell much about a country by studying its attitude to waste. In Switzerland there is a good attitude, and as a result you can go out at night wearing an expensive watch. In Brazil there is not, and you can't.

In the worst country in the world, Bolivia, people simply leave their rubbish in the middle of the street. It's like a big, foul-smelling, never-ending crash barrier. And I recall vividly the spectacle late one night of a woman having a tug of war with a wild dog over what appeared to be a pretty much empty crisp packet. That's what happens when a government abdicates its role as refuse collector. That's what's coming to Cardiff.

You may argue that when things become bad, the boyos will take it upon themselves to have a clear-up. But anyone who's been to rural India or Bangladesh or most of Africa will tell you that this simply doesn't happen. It does happen in Rwanda, strangely. On the third Saturday of every month everyone in the country is ordered by the government to clear up whatever mess they've made. On the upside, there is nationwide spotlessness. But on the downside, it's a police state.

So what is to be done? We can't afford to collect every single thing that everyone throws away. And we must not allow it all to build up in the streets. But what if there were less to throw away?

When I spend a night alone at my London flat, I will pop into the supermarket to buy a few provisions. All of which come with enough packaging to fill a skip. You have individually packaged apples these days, and

yesterday I bought a micro-SD card for a GoPro camera, which came in a plastic casing that would have
been big enough to wrap a London bus.

This is where the problem lies. It's not how much we
consume. It's how much we waste. Hotels now serve
sugar lumps that come in their own little plastic jackets.
The newspaper that campaigns to rid the world of
plastic bags sells its weekend supplements in a plastic
bag. Jewellery shops sell rings in boxes big enough
to house fridge freezers. Bread is wrapped. Vegetables
are wrapped. Everything is sold in a box. And it has to
stop.

This, then, is how Cardiff council should move forward. Instead of employing an army of sniffer-people
to root through everyone's rubbish, making sure they've
understood the recycling process properly, give residents less to worry about in the first place. Go out into
the streets and shoot any shopkeeper selling anything
in an unnecessary package. This would save time and
money and stop the city becoming a breeding ground
for rats the size of badgers. It would also save the polar
bear and all that stuff.

13 October 2013

Stroke, then eat. That, veggie fools, is being an animal lover

Four young chaps from Oxford Brookes University were hauled through the newspapers last week for posting 'vile' pictures of themselves on the internet, plucking some partridges they'd shot in 'broad daylight' and then hanging them in full view of passers-by.

So let's just get this straight. Instead of sitting around playing mind-numbing video games all day and then ordering an Indian takeaway, they had been into the countryside, shot some birds and then prepared them for the oven. Presumably they'd chosen to do this in broad daylight because in the dead of night it can be much more tricky.

Plainly the story was written by someone who believes chickens are born with no heads, ready-wrapped in clear plastic. Certainly it was written by someone who has never had much mud on their shoes. First of all we were told there was blood at the scene, which is fairly normal when something has been shot. And then the reporter added: 'A group of four hunters can expect to shoot up to fifty birds.' Which is true, but only if they have their eyes closed.

This story, then, was yet another eye-rolling, shoulder-sagging example of the modern-day assumption that all animals are delightful and wise and everything they do is heartwarming and cute. But it was nothing compared with the reaction of the university's spokes-woman, who said it was important to respect the culture, background and beliefs of other students, and that, clearly, storing and preparing game was 'not appropriate'.

This made me so angry my teeth started to itch. Because she was obviously not talking about Muslims or Jews, who prepare their meat by slicing the animal's throat and sitting about while it bleeds to death. Or Japanese people, who eat stuff before it's dead. Or the French, who put a cork in a goose's bottom to make it tastier. And then eat a horse while they're waiting.

In fact it's hard to think of a single belief or culture that would find the plucking and hanging of a free-range bird offensive in any way. Except one: vegetarianism.

Which brings us to a shuddering halt outside the Leeds branch of Harvey Nichols, where recently a handful of protesters – the pictures show six – turned up with placards to complain about how the store sells clothes trimmed with rabbit fur.

Now I can sort of understand people getting angry if an animal is killed solely because an orange woman in a wealthy Leeds suburb wants a new coat. Certainly I'd be very upset if someone peeled my dog for this reason. But the thing about a rabbit is that you can eat its soft, chewy centre and then use its fur to keep warm on a chilly night. So it doesn't die for a reason. It dies for two.

If I'd been running Harvey Nichols I'd have ignored the protesters, or I'd have gone outside and asked why they weren't jumping up and down outside the butcher's shop as well. But I wasn't running Harvey Nichols. A man called Joseph Wan was. And he arranged a meeting with the animal rights group Peta, shortly after which the shop's fashion director, Paula Reed, tended her resignation.

Once again the *Daily Mail* was on hand to provide us with all that we needed to know about the high street's rabbit-murdering Cruella de Vil. She's married to a wealthy architect and lives in a £4m west London town house. The implication is clear: she murdered Bright Eyes, so she deserved to lose her job. And we mustn't feel sorry for her because she lives in a £4m town house.

But I do feel sorry for her. Because she is yet another victim of the vegetarian plague. Just like those young lads at Oxford Brookes. And the sheep that are killed by foxy-woxy. And me.

Over the years I have upset many people, but it wasn't until I riled the nation's vegetablists that Special Branch arrived on my doorstep. They said that because I'd made a joke about a fox on *Have I Got News for You* I'd gone on an animal rights internet hit list, and that as a result my car's numberplate would have to be removed from the computer at Swansea and closed-circuit television would have to be installed throughout what the *Daily Mail* would undoubtedly call my 'sprawling country estate'.

We're in a chicken-and-egg situation here. I don't know whether lunatics are drawn to vegetarianism or whether not eating meat causes a person to go mad, but, either way, people who live on nuts are nuts. And the hardliners are more dangerous than a mentally ill religious zealot with a wardrobe full of automatic weapons.

A few years ago an academic in East Anglia said BBC wildlife documentaries breached animals' right to privacy, and that they should be allowed to have sex without David Attenborough sticking his nose into the moment.

In America the emergency services are prevented from dropping flame-retardant chemicals into the path of a forest fire by veg-heads who say the practice harms animals. Not as much as the fire, you might think, but there you go.

Then you have those who think badgers must be allowed to vandalize walls, murder hedgehogs and kill cows, and that foxes have a God-given right to eat people's babies. And, of course, we regularly hear about research scientists having to go to their labs under armed guard to prevent them from being blown up by a load of people with angry faces and hair from the 1970s.

There's nothing wrong with having a belief. But there is something dreadfully wrong when you believe that everyone else in the world must share it. 'I don't eat meat and you can't either.' But I can and I will, and then afterwards I shall tend to my pigs and my dogs and my tortoises and my birds and my donkeys.

Because I live on a balanced diet, I have a balanced mind, and as a result I know that animals are like people. Some are for looking at. Some are for loving. Some are for riding. And some need to be shot because they're a bloody nuisance.

20 October 2013

Wish you were here . . . to help rid my shack of a decidedly ill pig

Everyone wants to be seen by their peers as interesting, and there are lots of ways this can be achieved. You can actually be interesting but if that's not possible you can wear snazzy jumpers or have amusing spectacles or buy a Thai bride. Or you can go on holiday to a country that has only just taken its first tentative step into the travel brochures.

There is, however, a problem with doing this. Yes, when you return, your colleagues at work will be most impressed with your stories and your amazing range of new skin diseases. But the holiday you took to achieve these goals will, I'm afraid, have been a total and unmitigated disaster.

I've just spent a couple of weeks in a region of Burma that has been closed to the western world for the past sixty years. And this makes me seem more interesting than if I'd just spent the past couple of weeks in Florida. But if I'd been in Florida I'd have slept in a bed and had many prawn cocktails.

In Burma I spent one night on the floor of a shack, above a vomiting pig. And for supper I had some bees garnished with a dash of grated caterpillar. That's a good post-holiday anecdote. But a lousy thing to have lived through.

The next night I was in a hotel, and to the locals it

must have seemed like a wondrous place full of things about which they had heard only rumours. Electricity, for instance. And chairs. And water that was see-through.

But by global standards it wasn't really any good at all. For instance, the light switch for the bathroom was in the actual shower. And the television could receive only one channel. It was like being in a council house, in Barnsley, in 1958.

I then saw a man with rabies. His arms and legs were contorted by pain into corkscrews, his eyes had rolled back into his head and he was foaming at the mouth. He'd been thrown out of his village to die, and by now that will have happened. It was indeed an eye-opening experience watching the poor fellow stumble about, but on a holiday, I dunno – I'd rather look at the hydrofoils tearing across Lake Como.

Make no mistake, Burma is properly beautiful. And in a couple of years, when Aman Resorts has got there and some blue-blooded third son has started a cool bar in Rangoon, I'd recommend it in a heartbeat. But now? No.

For example: when you get ill – and you surely will – the nearest hospital is likely to be at least three days away. The nearest airport is going to be even further. And on the days when you do not have cholera or typhoid, what exactly are you going to do to kill time?

Go on a guided tour? Ooh, no. I really don't recommend that. Even in countries that have been hosting tourists for many years, guided tours are more dreary than being dead.

But in a country where no one knows what to leave in and what to leave out, they are so bad that pretty soon you will start to taunt the nearest sick-looking dog in the hope that it bites you.

Tour guides in recently opened countries are always obsessed with two things: dates and height. They pull up at a temple and tell you first of all how tall it is. And then when it was built. Then you get back on the bus, and you are told the height and age of every building you pass, until you reach the next temple. Which you are told was built in 1923 and is 417 ft tall.

At this point someone in your group will get all tearful and say it's such a shame the country has opened up because now it'll be ruined. This is what the first wave of tourists never seem to understand. That their definition of 'ruined' means the locals getting headache pills and clean water and an education and a job in a factory making their next pair of training shoes.

Maybe, then, you will decide not to take the tour. So what are you going to do instead? Have lunch? Where, exactly? A country that has been shut for more than half a century is not going to serve you a steak. When I was in Cuba, shortly after it became possible to go there, I was given a spaghetti bolognese that had been in the oven ever since the ousting of Fulgencio Batista.

In Niger, in western Africa, I was presented with a chicken leg that appeared to be juicy and succulent. Right up to the moment when I put my fork into the golden, crispy skin and it just popped. There was no meat in there at all. And I'm not going to tell you what I ate in China in 1984. Only that it used to bark.

So you think you will go to the beach. Bad plan. I first went to Vietnam long before the tourists arrived and we decided to take a day off on the golden sands near the mouth of the Perfume River.

We got there early, laid out our towels and sat back in the sunshine. Lovely. But then ten minutes later we decided we wanted a drink. And there wasn't one to be had for 30 miles. Much better to go to Vietnam now because the splendid isolation has been replaced with whale song spas and private butlers.

I'm sure that the bore in you is already thinking hard about taking his next holiday in Libya. He's heard that things are settling down and reckons that a week in Tripoli will be just the ticket. I'm sure it will too, but only if he ends up on *Who Wants to Be a Millionaire?* and the final question is: 'What is the precise height of the minaret in the Ghut al-Shaal district?'

Certainly we'll all get a huge laugh at his expense when he has to say, 'I don't know. I was vomiting into a bucket when we went past that one.'

So let's have the next contestant: the dreary and unadventurous chap who went on holiday to Spain and learnt all he knows from sitting on the beach, with a chilled cocktail, reading books.

17 November 2013

Grab a plunger, kids, there's only one job left in the world for you

As we know, 30m people are now working in Britain. That's more than at any time in human history and, of course, this is very tremendous news. But I do sometimes wonder: what exactly are they all doing?

Back in the late 1970s, the school-leaver could choose from a thousand types of job. Even someone as poorly qualified as me could be a miner or a typesetter or a cobbler or a librarian or a news vendor. But not any more. All of these jobs have now been vaporized by the relentless binary-numbered march of progress. And China.

I briefly flirted with the idea of getting a job processing people's holiday snaps at my local branch of Boots. I liked the notion of seeing people I knew naked. But that's gone as well now. I'm not even sure you can be a pox doctor's clerk these days.

Soon there will be no journalists either, or car mechanics or, now we have drones, fighter pilots. Furthermore, if you watch a modern film such as *Gravity* you do wonder how much life actors have left in them.

Because if you can create realistic computer-generated space crashes, how hard can it be to create realistic computer-generated people? Not very, is the simple answer.

It won't be that long before there's no such thing as a

supermarket checkout girl or a dairy farmer. There'll be no greengrocers or butchers, and why send a child to school when he or she can stay at home and be taught online? Then there'd be no more dinner ladies.

Of course there are lots of jobs people can do now that they could not have done thirty years ago. But sadly, since they all involve repairing broken laptop computers and unjamming frozen software, no one can do any of them.

I mean it. When was the last time someone came round to your house, identified a problem with your electronic equipment, repaired it and left? Exactly. Never.

When your iPhone jams, you can't take it to a shop full of men in brown shop coats and expect them to be able to fix it. You have to throw it away. And does that give someone a job making a new one for you? Not really, no. Because electronic stuff isn't made by people. It can't be repaired by people. And it does all the interesting jobs that used to be done by people. It's Skynet from *The Terminator*.

The government tells us that we needn't worry and that, thanks to some steady growth, more and more jobs will be coming on line very soon. Which takes us back to the original question. What jobs?

Not everyone can be employed in call centres or checking on the health and safety of those who make wings for Airbuses. And not everyone wants to be an estate agent. Not if they have something other than dried leaves between their ears.

I raise all of this because I had a long chat with my

eldest daughter last weekend about what she'd like to do now she's an adult. She fancies the idea of photography. And certainly that used to be a job. You could earn a living taking wedding snaps, or shots of girls scratching their bottoms on the tennis court. But today, thanks to the camera phone, everyone is a photographer and all it takes to turn Blind Pew into David Bailey is a 79p app.

Eventually we drifted into conversation about the internet and what services she could provide for that. But the sad truth is this: with the exception of a few nerds in America, nobody has yet made one single penny from their online endeavours.

I know countless people who slave away all week at their websites, paying designers to make them fresh and clean, and collating all the information they can about nappy rash or broad beans or whatever it is they've chosen to market, and every month they get a pay packet of exactly nought.

I'd love to know how many people who currently claim to be working are actually doing nothing more than spending their days filling a site that no one ever visits. It's probably about 29m.

So what else is there? Well, I have been racking my brains all week and I've decided that there is only one job left for people who don't have a double first in advanced nuclear physics from Harvard: plumbing.

First of all, the lavatory is not like a newspaper or a book. It cannot be digitized. It cannot be replaced. Likewise there is no app that will make you clean. If you want to smell fresh and scrubbed, you have to have a bath. And if you want central heating or clean clothes or a smooth chin, the water coming out of your taps needs to be hot. You therefore need a boiler. There is no alternative.

This means we will always need plumbing, which, so far as most people are concerned, is witchcraft. Well, it is to me. I listen to it sometimes, burping and groaning, and I have not the first idea what is going on. It's the same story when I flush the lavatory. I do not know how that works or where the waste goes to or how it gets there.

Unlike in the world of laptop computers, though, there are a handful of people who do know. Usually they are called Mr Starnowski. And they have a habit of vanishing shortly after the expensive remedial work they did has caused your kitchen to flood with warm, muddy water.

Can you imagine, then, what would happen if you studied the sorcery and mastered its dark and mysterious ways; if you became a reliable plumber who did good work? And was on hand if it all went wrong? Imagine how much you could charge for a service such as that.

And think of the job satisfaction. You'd be doing the only real job that's left, and think of all those grateful women in their negligees saying how much they admire your ballcock work. Or is that just in the films? Whatever – it's what I shall be suggesting for my children. They shall be plumbers and I shall be proud.

24 November 2013

Oh don't be a chicken, Kiev: tell Putin to put a sock in it

I was caught up in the Kiev protests last week and it was hell. Satellite vans to the left of me, jokers to the right, and all around, hundreds of expensively haired reporters begging directors back at the studio not to go live now because nothing's bloody happening.

'Not now,' they were screaming into their microphones. 'Not now. Not n . . . Yes, Fiona, thanks. You join me in Kiev, where, as you can see behind me, things are quiet.'

I counted six protesters, although I was told that those numbers could well swell to a million.

And for a million people to take to the streets in a country as cold as Ukraine, they really must have their knickers in a twist about something pretty important.

Turns out it's the government, which said it would do some kind of trade deal with Brussels. This annoyed Vladimir Putin, who said that if Ukraine started cosying up to the EU he would send no more railway carriages.

So at the last minute the Ukrainian leadership announced it was going to do some kind of trade deal with Moscow instead. It sounds like two eleven-year-old girls fighting over a best friend, if you ask me, but whatever. Everyone is jolly cross.

The big question, though, is not whether the

Ukrainians want to join us but whether we want them. And obviously, for those of a *Daily Mail* disposition, the answer is an emphatic no.

We've got quite enough eastern Europeans mooching about the place already, eating our dogs and generally making a hash of our plumbing, and we don't want any more.

Then you have the political geeks, who will explain that a country that jails its opposition leader for walking on the cracks in the pavement isn't really welcome at the top table in Brussels. What's more, I doubt very much that Ukraine's fiscal situation meets whatever standards need to be met before membership can be considered.

And that's before we get to Ukrainian business practices, which, well, let me put it this way: I'm not sure that anyone can rise to the top in business over there using nothing but good manners and a winning smile. It's more likely to be elbows and AK-47s.

So that's that, then. Except it isn't, because for me the best way of testing a nation's suitability for EU membership is this: does it feel European?

This is where we went wrong with Greece, because it doesn't. And it's where we went wrong with Romania too. I was lost there once and it was like being stuck in a history picture book.

It was all oxen and grubby-faced children, who thought I might be from space. Anyone who'd been with me on that day, in that village, would have looked at Romania's EU request form and said, 'Let's talk again in a couple of thousand years.'

Things are rather different, though, in Kiev. First of all there's the girls – er, I mean the airport. You don't have to put a coin that you don't yet have into a barely functioning slot to get a trolley, and that's a more important tick in the box of civilization than a country's GDP.

Nor do you have to pay to use the motorways. There's more, too, because as in much of continental Europe, although officially banned, smoking in public buildings is tolerated, provided you ask politely and agree to sit near a window.

Kiev, then, is tremendous. It feels like Berlin or Budapest. Yalta too is magnificent – it's like Juan-les-Pins. Apart from the girls, who really do leave the West behind. But I will concede that the rest of the country does seem to be a bit . . . how can I put this politely? Old-fashioned.

You just have mile after mile of fog. And then it lifts and you rather wish it hadn't because then you have mile after mile of absolutely nothing at all.

It's flatter than a freshly run-over fox. And cold. The sort of cold that eats into your bones and makes your nose fall off. And then you get to a village and it's all a bit Soviet. There's a factory pumping clouds of reddish-brown smoke into the fog, and all the cars are Russian and they're pumping clouds of blue smoke into the fog, and way off in the distance you can see the rusting missile launchers that were left behind after independence. They aren't pumping anything at all into the fog. Thankfully.

It is mind-numbing, and even after two days of solid

driving you are still only about a quarter of an inch on the map from where you started. Ukraine is even more enormous than one of Arsène Wenger's coats.

I stayed the night in one town, the name of which is impossible for this keyboard, and it was shiversome. Potholed roads. Angry, fidgety dogs. Men in black bomber jackets with heads like turnips. Bad skin. And at the hotel a chef who had plainly learnt his craft at the people's tractor factory No. 43. Before it was closed down by a chemical leak. That never happened.

And as I sat there trying to work out whether the food on my plate was an onion ring or calamari, and not daring to go to bed because the mattress was strangely damp, I thought: no, Kiev feels European, and so does Yalta, but out here in the sticks it feels like 1952. Best let them stick with their old mates in the Kremlin.

However, I then realized that rural Ukraine is exactly the same as the north of England. Both have many people who yearn for a return to communism. Both have many towns built to serve industries that have gone. Both have big flat bits. And in neither can you tell the difference between an onion ring and a squid.

And no one is saying that the north of England should be excluded from the EU and all of its many benefits. No one is saying the north of England should be sent cap in hand to Putin. So why should we tell the Ukrainians to get lost?

We should support them in every way possible, and then welcome them with open arms. Especially the girls.

1 December 2013

You'll be glad of a high street nuclear-free poetry centre

As we know, the government makes a hash of pretty much everything.

It decides to be green. Then it decides that's too expensive.

It sells off all our gold at rock-bottom prices.

It declares war on countries for having weapons of mass destruction. Then it finds out that, oops, they didn't have any such thing.

It commissions aircraft carriers even though it has no planes to put on them. It employs nurses who can't nurse and teachers who can't teach and runs an immigration policy that's not a policy at all.

It can't even run a cull. Recently it decided to shoot all the nation's badgers, but then it decided there were too many so it decided not to shoot any at all. Then it decided to shoot some, but we've just heard that all the marksmen it employed learnt everything they knew from Elmer Fudd. So they've spent the past few months shooting at bits of countryside where badgers had been playing only moments earlier.

And this, remember, is central government, which is run by the brightest and the best. These are the guys who went to Oxford and Cambridge and have brains so vast they need to be carted around in wheelbarrows. So can you even begin to imagine what terrible and hopeless things are foisted upon us by politicians at a local level?

They can be considered bright only if you are comparing them with farmyard animals. Some see life in a local authority as a useful way of getting back at the people who bullied them at school for their poor personal hygiene. Others have no other way during the day of staying warm. Many have extremely nasty jumpers.

I have some experience of their world because many years ago, when I was a reporter on a local newspaper, I would often be sent to cover parish council meetings. They were staggering. One group spent forty-five minutes deciding whether to have a glass or a plastic water jug. Another even longer on whether a member's faulty hearing aid meant that, technically, they didn't have a quorum. I used to spend my entire time tight-lipped with fury and wondering what they'd all look like without skin.

They couldn't do anything properly. Nothing. They were there only so they could strut about in what we must now call their communities, with their heads held higher than nature had intended.

And things were not much better at borough level because here, in one meeting, the councillors decided that private companies could not be trusted to run a restaurant and that if the town must have such a thing, they would do it themselves. Well, if you've seen municipal roundabouts or a municipal lavatory, you'll have some idea of what municipal food tasted like. Nutritionally you'd have been better off eating the building.

And so it was with a great deal of horror and dread

that I read a report recently that said local authorities should make 'aggressive' use of compulsory purchase orders to buy up entire town centres. And that planning rules should be relaxed so they would be free to do whatever they liked with them.

This is the stuff of nightmares. Your town centre gets handed over to a bunch of people who would struggle to get a job picking fruit. And they are given carte blanche to do with it whatever takes their fancy. Imagine their muddled, small ideas. Imagine their idea of the greater good. Imagine the number of hanging baskets they'd order. Imagine the forlorn skateboard park. And then start the countdown to the moment when someone says, 'We could open an art gallery for local artists.' Living in a town run this way would be like living in Pam Ayres's head.

And yet I find myself wondering what the alternative might be because the current arrangement really isn't working at all.

We all know the problem. The internet means there's no need to go into a town centre to do your shopping, and that in turn means the big high-street chains are starting to disappear. Woolworths has gone and other big names have shrunk drastically, leaving every parade of shops looking like a tramp's mouth.

In an ideal world the gaps they left behind could be filled by enterprising local people, who could sell flowers and jewellery and knick-knacks. I was in Bruges recently and simply could not believe how many independent shops there were, slap-bang in the city centre. I marvelled too at the rich variety of things they were selling.

Sadly, though, that can't happen here, because of Britain's property prices. A landlord with a town centre shop worth millions is used to charging the big boys thousands a week. Worse, he needs to do that to balance the books. So he's not going to rent it out for £20 a month to some bored housewife who's been bought a mix-your-own potpourri business by her City-boy husband in an effort to stop her sleeping with her fitness instructor.

The net result of all this is simple. The internet will drive the big boys either out of business or online. The landlords won't be able to drop their rents. And the high street will become nothing more than a nocturnal creature that sleeps all day and is then spattered with 2bn gallons of clubbers' vomit at night.

And then what? No, really, I mean it. Then what? A town that's nothing more than two clubs and a selection of burger vans isn't really a town. So those who don't wish to scrape half an inch of partially digested kebab from their car's bonnet every morning will move away. And then you have Detroit. And then you really are in a world of pain.

So I look with cold hands and all the hairs standing up at the back of my neck at the plan to let local councils buy up all the properties and turn them into sculpture parks and ethnic nuclear-free poetry centres. But I simply can't see a more realistic alternative. And if I'm honest, I'd rather live in Pam Ayres's head than the dying moments of a life spent in Gordon Gekko's underpants.

8 December 2013

She's a bit broad in the beam but she shivers me timbers

There are 300,000 cargo ships at sea these days and they transport 90 per cent of the world's trade. Without them the world would stop working. But between them they produce more carbon dioxide every year than Germany. And more, amazingly, than all of America's cars combined.

There are many suggestions for lessening this environmental impact, all of which have been dreamt up by lunatics. In the main the sandal enthusiasts seem to think that reducing the speed at which a ship travels will help most of all, and I don't doubt that's true.

But when you order an iPhone 5C you want it brought to Britain on a class 1 offshore powerboat, not at a speed that's so slow it arrives just after the iPhone 7 has started to roll off the production lines.

The obvious answer is to reduce the number of ships. Which, if you want to keep the capacity, means making them bigger. And that's exactly what seems to be happening.

To us a cross-Channel ferry or a cruise liner is quite large and an American aircraft carrier is vast. But compared with the behemoths that bring the training shoes and the motorcycles to your local Amazon depot they are rowing boats and canoes. Many modern-day cargo ships dwarf the Shard. They beggar belief. And now they're getting even bigger.

Last week Shell's latest vessel took to the water for the first time at a dockyard in South Korea. Called the *Prelude*, it is 1,601 ft long and will weigh more than 600,000 tons when it is completed, and have a 305 ft-high turret. You could put the Sydney Opera House in its hull and not even notice it was there. Nothing bigger has put to sea. But its three engines are not designed for propulsion, so really it's more of a barge.

The biggest actual ship is the Maersk Triple-E carrier. A handful have been made and they are so vast no port in America is big enough to handle them. Each can carry 836m cans of baked beans. Or 36,000 cars. Or so many containers that you would need sixty trains, each a mile long, to handle them all. They're not beautiful, let's be clear about that, but I yearn to see one nevertheless.

Because I love big ships. I love the idea that a crew of thirty can, with a laptop and some charts, control and steer something that enormous, even in the jaws of a hurricane. Really big ships: there's no better example of man's brilliance. They make me proud to be a human.

Strangely, however, the closest I've come to dying was while trying to disembark from the biggest ship of them all: the largest man-made self-propelled object created: a now-scrapped crude-oil tanker called, among several other names, the *Jahre Viking*.

The procedure for landing on board was simple. Pilots on the Huey helicopter would hover over the sea and allow the ship to pass underneath before touching down on the landing pad towards the stern. I was very excited and actually gasped as the prow of the ship slid under the aircraft. But the gasping soon turned to unease because the ship just kept on coming, and coming and coming. I knew there was a six-storey superstructure at the back and felt, when a quarter of a mile of steel had slithered by, we really should be landing. But we didn't. And still the ship came.

You can forget about trivia with something this size. It was so big, it couldn't even sail up the English Channel, and you could get four St Paul's Cathedrals in its holds, but facts like these don't really give you a clear enough picture. Have you seen *Gravity* yet? When Sandra Bullock is all alone in space, with the world behind her? Well, that's what it feels like to hover over the *Jahre Viking*. You feel like an insect.

Happily I did eventually land and all was well until the next morning. After making some tea, I noticed that there were concentric circles forming in the cup, as though a giant dinosaur was approaching.

In fact the tea was registering something I had not. That during the night, we had run into a class-one, grade-A* Cape of Good Hope winter storm. The waves were straight out of a Hollywood disaster movie and the wind was biblical, but on board all was calm, peaceful, serene. Man was laughing at nature. Sneering, even.

I was too until I needed to leave. This would be impossible in a helicopter because the deck was largely underwater. Getting closer to shore, where things were calmer, was out of the question for reasons of cost. As was slowing down. So, as I had plenty of cigarettes, I decided to stay on board until the storm had subsided.

This, it transpired, would be in three days' time. By which time we'd be in the Atlantic, out of chopper range. 'Well,' I said to the camera crew with whom I was working, 'looks like we're going to Texas.'

'No we're not,' said the cameraman. 'I'm getting married on Saturday.'

This meant we had to get a tug from Cape Town, and at three in the morning, a child's rope ladder was lowered over the sheer side of the tanker. Gripping with my fingers to the rope and with only my toes on a rung, I had to wait until the right-sized wave brought the tug to the correct height for me to jump. Too high and I'd be swept off the ladder and washed away. Too low and I'd miss the tug and fall from a great height into the sea. And then be washed away.

To give you an idea of just how scary this was, the sound recordist suffered a heart attack as he jumped. A big one.

And yet as the monster slithered off into the cacophonous, raging darkness without so much as a backward glance at the people it had nonchalantly tried to kill, I felt sad. And I still do when I look at the footage of this giant ship being broken up for scrap on a filthy beach in India.

That's the thing, you see. Big ships have a soul. And they're good for the planet. So let's get rid of the smaller ones – starting with that hideous little smoker the *Rainbow Warrior*.

15 December 2013

Rejoice, all ye hung-over, I've found the God vitamin

When I wake up with a bit of a thick head I often resort to a zesty Berocca. And soon I feel well enough to skip through the park with my dog, tickling its tummy, and generally looking as happy as those girls you see in a commercial for panty liners.

Berocca tells us that each pill contains all the vitamins and minerals we need to lead a full and active life, and when you look at the list, that certainly seems to be the case. There's folic acid and a natural form of caffeine and enough magnesium to build a gearbox housing for a Ford Focus.

But here's the thing; a hangover isn't cancer. It will get better on its own, so how do I know that the zesty drink is responsible for my metamorphosis? How do I know that my head hasn't simply healed itself? There's no way of telling.

'Oh yes there is,' say various friends of mine who travel everywhere with what appears to be an entire branch of Boots in their handbags. I watch them in the morning, as they wait for the juicer to turn a handful of rather nice-looking vegetables into a disgusting brown mush, counting out an endless array of pills that will see them through the day. And eventually into a super-healthy life of dementia and incontinence in an old people's home.

They have brown ones and red ones, and blue ones they got from America on the internet. And all have been recommended by Sally at the book club, who says they contain all you need for a holistic healing lightness of being. 'And Sally's really bright, you know . . .'

Hmm. I've long harboured a suspicion that Sally is in fact extremely stupid and now it seems I am right because last week scientists and academics announced that the entire vitamin business, which is worth about £650m a year in Britain, is pretty much complete bunkum.

They say that supplementing the diet of a well-nourished adult has no clear benefit and might even be harmful. And they may have a point. I recently spent three weeks living on nothing but Diet Coke, rosé wine, grilled grasshoppers and roast bees. And I was fine.

At home I eat well. I have a balanced diet of meat and chocolate and the occasional chicken madras. Occasionally my body telegraphs its need for whatever it is you get in vegetables by sending signals that it would like some greenery. So I make sure at lunchtime that the chef pops a sprig of parsley on top of my eggs Benedict. This then causes me to feel righteous, which means there's no need to do jogging or any of that stuff.

I would know if I had a vitamin deficiency of some kind because my gums would start to bleed and all my teeth would fall out. I would have scurvy or rickets. My legs would bow and snap – and you know what? They haven't.

It's a fair bet that Peter O'Toole did not bother with any vitamin supplements either and he died last week aged eighty-one. Nelson Mandela, meanwhile, spent twenty-seven years in prison, not balancing his diet with extra zinc and vitamin C, and he lasted until the age of ninety-five. And then you have all those 112-year-olds in southern France who have lived all their lives on nothing but red wine and bird fat.

Doubtless the scientists and academics who wrote the report would agree with all this, and that if you want to stay healthy you should forget all those stupid pills and juiced soil. However, their research is flawed because there is one vitamin supplement that the ordinary, happy and healthy soul does need to survive. It's called B12. And it is the single most important thing on God's green earth.

I've seen the morning in the mountains of Alaska, I've seen the sunset in the east and in the west, I've sung the glory that was Rome and passed the Hound Dog singer's home, but nothing has come close to the moment when a South African nurse took down my trousers and injected me with a milk bottle full of what felt like the elixir of life.

In keeping with my thoughts on a healthy diet, it had been a big night out. A monster. And why not? I was due to perform in front of a large audience the next day but this was a Johannesburg summer and the thunderstorms were straight from the really bad bits of the Bible.

There was absolutely no way the show could possibly go ahead so I was free to enjoy all that one of the world's great cities could casually toss in my direction. At one point my mate Mad Dog took me for a late-night spin over Soweto in his helicopter. We fired pistols at midnight to see if the police would come. And I wouldn't have been at all surprised to find a tiger in my bathroom the next morning.

What I did find, however, was worse. There wasn't a cloud in the sky. It was an uninterrupted ocean of blue. The show would be going ahead.

The hangover was catastrophic. This was not something that could be dismissed with a Bloody Mary or a couple of pills. It was, and remains, the worst I've had. And you will get a similar story from my colleague, whose name I shall not reveal here. Save that it begins with J. And ends with ames May.

We could not get out of our rooms, leave alone into a car and across the city to the stadium. And so the nurses took pity on us and gave us the B12. Something used to cure the effects of cyanide poisoning. The results were instantaneous. As soon as the needle was out of my buttock, I felt like I'd just emerged from a deep, nine-hour sleep after an evening drinking only cocoa. And so the show was saved.

I think the message is clear. Vitamin supplements designed to stop you getting ill are like yoga, a complete waste of time. But B12 works the other way round. It lets you get ill and then makes you better. What it is, then, is a knowing wink from God that getting plastered is OK.

22 December 2013

The AK-47 says you don't rule the world, Ronald McDonald

We can argue all we like about which is the world's best-known brand. You could suggest that it's Coca-Cola but there are vast chunks of the world where no one would have the first clue of what you were talking about. The same goes for McDonald's and Starbucks and all of the other things that really only have any traction in the western world. Mercedes-Benz is well known everywhere and so is the US Navy, and *Top Gear* seems to be getting there as well. But while these things are far behind the Catholic Church even the Vatican has to play second fiddle to what I consider to be the best-known product name of them all – the AK-47 assault rifle.

Nobody knows how many have been made over the past sixty-four years since it went into production but if we take the official figure of 100m we can deduce that at some point one in seventy of the world's population has actually used one. And then we get to the number of bullets that have been made to feed this Soviet icon. Some say it's around 30bn. And that's enough to kill everyone on earth more than four times over. Not even the world's nuclear bomb makers could manage that.

People have sung songs about the AK-47. It is featured on Mozambique's flag. It is the standout symbol of revolution. It is often said – wrongly – that

Coca-Cola determined the colours of Santa Claus. The AK-47, meanwhile, has determined the colours of the world map.

It was designed in 1947 by a chap called Mikhail Kalashnikov, who died last week, aged ninety-four. Though he licensed his name to a vodka company in recent years he didn't earn one single penny for his work on the gun. Like a good communist he did it for the benefit of the state and to protect the motherland. Though he did admit not so long ago that he rather wished he'd developed a lawnmower instead.

He was born in Siberia to peasant stock and after a sickly childhood went off to fight the Germans. After his tank was blown up and while he was recovering from a shoulder wound in hospital he overheard two senior officers bemoaning the poor quality of Soviet armaments. He resolved, when better, that he'd put that right.

And so he did. The AK-47 is perhaps the only example of Soviet engineering that was demonstrably better than anything made in the West, chiefly because it had only eight moving parts and would consequently work even after it had been buried for three years in a swamp.

In Vietnam, American infantrymen would often put aside their own rifles and use a discarded AK-47 instead. Because they knew that while it wasn't as accurate or as fast as a standard-issue M16, it wouldn't jam.

Over the years there were attempts to make it more precise and less heavy but each of these improvements simply meant it broke down more often. So they were discarded. I actually own an AK-47 and when you remove the top it's like looking inside a ballpoint pen. There's a spring and that's about it.

You pull the trigger and as a round sets off down the barrel, the gas it leaves behind is used to push back the firing mechanism, the empty cartridge is ejected and another round pops up out of the magazine and into place. It is breathtaking in its simplicity.

And of course this makes it not just reliable but cheap. The cost of a new one is around £500 but in some parts of the world you can buy a good second-hand example for as little as $3. Or a couple of cows. But it is no peashooter. And even though it costs less than a decent water pistol from Hamleys it's no toy either.

I went to a quarry in Switzerland once with a Hell's Angel called Cheesy – I know, an odd day – to test-fire his new AK-47. And it was amazing.

The safety catch is on the left-hand side of the weapon. You push it down once to engage fully automatic and then again to make it a single-shot rifle. This was done on purpose because Kalashnikov felt that you would only ever take the safety off in a panic situation and you might therefore accidentally push the lever all the way down in one go. He didn't want this to engage machine-gun mode because he knew that then you wouldn't hit a thing.

He was quite right. When I fired the AK-47 on fully automatic at a railway sleeper maybe 75 yards away I didn't just miss the target. I missed the quarry. The violence of the thing jiggling around in my hands had to be experienced to be believed. It was like wrestling with a hot, angry metal ape.

And then there was the pain. I'm a left-handed shot so I fire from my left shoulder. Which is fine, except the AK-47 ejects its red-hot spent shells on the right – straight into my right forearm. Result: I was standing there basically shooting myself.

For the second magazine I switched to my right shoulder, which made me so inaccurate I began to wonder: this gun is largely used by untrained soldiers, many of them children. So has an AK-47 at any point in its history actually killed anyone?

To find out, Cheesy suggested I put it back in single-shot mode and aim once again at the railway sleeper. This made a difference. The single 7.62 mm round hit that chunk of wood at more than 1,500 mph with such a punch that it split clean in two. And both parts ended up 6 ft from one another.

You may have seen people in films saying 'ow' after they've been hit by a bullet from an AK-47. Well, I'm afraid that's nonsense. Because if it gets you anywhere above the wrist or the knee you will need binoculars to see the other half of what used to be you.

Which, of course, raises an interesting question about Mikhail Kalashnikov. Was he a villain or a saint? The answer rather depends on which end of his gun you happen to be looking at at the time.

29 December 2013

When stuck in Antarctic ice, be sure to have a patio heater

Like many people, I awoke on Wednesday morning with a strong determination to be kinder and more sympathetic to others in the year ahead. But over breakfast this resolve was sorely tested as I read about the plight of those global warming scientists whose ship, in a delicious bout of irony, became stuck in the Antarctic sea ice.

The new me felt very sorry for them because, after all, here was a bunch of explorers trying to find out if man's activities will one day cause sea levels to rise by 52 metres, or whatever figure they've plucked from the ozone layer this week.

I also felt very sorry for the team's unbiased reporters from the *Guardian* and the BBC, who had to spend the whole festive period waiting for the power of internal combustion to effect a rescue. But it was no good, I'm afraid. 'Ha ha ha,' shrieked the old me. 'They went to Antarctica to show the world how the ice has all melted. And there's so much of it, their ship is stuck. Ha ha ha.'

When will these people realize that it's bloody cold down there? And that even if global temperatures rise by 40 degrees, it'll still be cold enough to snap off a man's nose and vacuum pack an icebreaker?

Of course, the team is trying desperately to extricate itself from the PR disaster by saying the monstrous slab of ice that's pinning the ship in place is somehow the result of your patio heater . . . and presumably the ships that were trying to reach it. 'Er . . .' say the reporters from the BBC and the *Guardian*.

Apparently, the enormous slab was knocked last month from its moorings by global warming and was carried by globally warmed winds and strong, globally warmed currents into the path of the ship.

Well, I have some experience of sea ice. I drove to the magnetic North Pole over miles of the stuff a few years ago, and what they're saying has some traction. But here's the thing. I'm a temperate-based nancy boy and learnt in just eight days how to tell the difference between new ice and old ice.

I also learnt about the effects of the tide and the wind and, as a result, I completed the journey with only a few minor problems. This lot are supposed to be climate scientists and they got stuck. Ha ha ha.

What's more, their trip is supposed to be a rerun of an expedition by the early twentieth-century Australian explorer Douglas Mawson. Which is a bit like Nasa staging a rerun of Apollo 13.

Mawson had toured Earth's soft white underbelly with Ernest Shackleton and was therefore an Antarctic veteran when he arrived on the continent in 1912.

Because he was an actual scientist he made it ashore with no problems, though photographs show that back then, before the invention of the Range Rover and the patio heater, there were no marauding slabs of ice. It was all rocky beaches and open water.

After setting up camp Mawson set off to explore the

interior with a skiing champion called Xavier Mertz and a British Army officer called Belgrave Ninnis who, thirty-five days into their journey, fell down a crevasse with all the best dogs and most of the supplies.

Mawson and Mertz were in trouble. They were 300 miles from base and had supplies for only half a week. So there was no alternative. They would have to eat the remaining dogs and tow the sledges themselves.

Quite soon, Mertz's skin started to fall off. Then he started to feel unwell. He wrote in his diary: 'The dog meat does not seem to agree with me because yesterday I was feeling a little bit queasy.' Anxious not to eat any more of it, he decided to eat himself and that night bit off one of his own fingers. This seemed to agree with him even less because that night he died.

For two weeks, Mawson ploughed on alone and then he too fell down a crevasse. Luckily, however, he was attached by a rope to his sledge, which had not, and so, after a four-hour climb, he was back on the move. It was not easy going, however, because he would have to pause once in a while to glue the soles of his feet back on with lanolin cream.

Amazingly, in a spirit of determination that would be completely lost on the people of Surrey whose turkeys remained uncooked because of power cuts on Christmas Day, he made it back to base. And was just in time to see his ship steaming over the horizon. His mates had given him up for dead. And gone home.

Just in case, though, they had left behind a few men and some supplies in an ice cave on which Mawson lived until he was rescued a year later. That's twelve months. With not much to eat. No warmth. And nothing to do all day but endlessly glue his feet back on.

Mawson was a proper chap. And my admiration for him is boundless. But let's get one thing straight. Most of those Victorian and Edwardian explorers did scientific research in the same way that Hollywood stars plug their movies on *The Graham Norton Show*. Not because they wanted to. But because it was the only way they could get funding.

They went to the deserts of north Africa and the jungles of South America and the frozen wastelands of the poles because they craved the excitement.

I have a sneaking suspicion that this is exactly what drives the scientists who travel to the polar regions today. They are paid by anti-patio-heater organizations to say it's all Land Rover's fault – but come on, admit it. Going to Antarctica on an icebreaker is a lot more exciting than working for a living.

I therefore say this to the scientists who were stuck over Christmas. If you really and truthfully wanted to make a point about man-made global warming, why did you take journalists from the *Guardian* and the BBC? Why did you not take someone who needed to be convinced? In short, why did you not take me?

5 January 2014

Man's silliest invention gets the boot . . . and shoe and clog

We know that at some point in human history a man opened up an oyster and thought, 'Mmm. If I put that globule of slimy mucus in my mouth, I shall be a sure-fire hit with the laydeez.'

Meanwhile, another chap was looking at a cow and thinking, 'You know what? If I peel that and place it above a fire for an hour or so I reckon it would be delicious. Especially its bottom.'

We have to presume that over the years man has tried to digest just about everything. Because how else would you arrive at bread?

You have to grind the seeds from a wheat plant to dust – why would you do that? Then you have to add water and mix in yeast – why not laburnum seeds or chilli peppers or the eyes of a great crested grebe? Then you have to apply heat.

Butter is another astonishing thing. So's cheese. And wine. Who ate a grape and thought, 'I wonder if this would make me happier if I trod on it and then left the juice in a big wooden box for a while'? Did they try it with tomatoes first?

And how many different types of leaf were smoked before someone came across tobacco? It stands to reason that at some point someone must have tried to smoke tea before thinking, 'No. This would be better if

I put it in a cup full of hot water and then added a splash of what comes out from the underside of a lady cow.'

Oh no. I've just thought of something. The first person to make a cup of tea. Did he start out by using what came out from the underside of a gentleman cow? There's a 50/50 chance he did.

But for me the strangest event in man's culinary development occurred in Finland about 5,000 years ago. A chap was wandering about in the woods, eating the trees and smoking the leaves and generally trying to find something more interesting than deer for supper.

And he noticed that when he burnt some bark a strange gooey stuff was produced. Now he could have done many things with this. He could have used it to make some soles for his shoes, or a set of tyres for his cart. He could have used it to rub things out or wrapped it around his private parts. But no. Inevitably, he decided to eat it.

After a while, of course, he would have realized that it had no nutritional value at all and was completely useless. But as he sat there gnawing away, he must have hatched a plan . . .

Back in the village, he gathered everyone around, saying that he had made an important discovery. 'Is it a cure for rickets?' some will have asked excitedly. 'Or is it some kind of pointy thing we can use to shoot wolves?'

'Are you able to bring little Sven back from the dead?' a tearful mother will have blubbed.

After their questions had finished, he will have

unwrapped his stick of tree goo and said, 'No. It's this. You put it in your mouth and you chew it.'

'And then what?' the crowd will have asked.

'Well, after a while you take it out and stick it to the underside of a chair.'

He must have been one hell of a salesman because they lapped up his new invention and soon every idiot in every part of the world was producing the goo from trees and using it to make 'chewing gum'. Mankind's most useless invention. A food you don't eat.

There are other drawbacks too. First of all, people who chew gum look incredibly stupid, unless they are on an aeroplane and the gum is laced with nicotine, in which case they don't.

Second, freshly discarded chewing gum sticks so firmly to the concrete in a paving slab that it cannot be removed by anything . . . except the sole of a man's shoe. And then the shoe will have to be thrown away.

It's a lot of shoes, because every year 3.74 trillion sticks of chewing gum are sold. And even if 95 per cent are disposed of thoughtfully, that still means 187bn pieces are stuck on a pavement right now, awaiting your arrival. And remember, that's 187bn a year.

The cost of trying to clean up this mess is astronomical. The most recent figures suggest that councils in Britain spend about £150m a year.

Discarded gum is so unpleasant that in Singapore sale of the stuff is banned. And at my school we could do pretty much what we liked except pop a stick of Wrigley's into our mouths. Smoking got you a detention. Sex got you a wagged finger. Chewing gum got you expelled. It was even worse than rubbing potassium into the school cormorant.

But despite all the problems and the complete pointlessness of a food you don't eat, the popularity of gum has continued to spiral. Until now.

Figures out last week showed that in Britain there had been an 8 per cent fall in demand in the past twelve months. That's a big chunk, and the industry is worried. It has plainly hijacked the Wikipedia page because it is full of stuff about how chewing gum helps you lose weight and have fresher breath and fewer gum diseases. It smacks of an industry that doesn't quite know what's gone wrong.

Some say it's the cost. But that doesn't quite ring true. I've heard of people selling the family car to save money, or turning the central heating down a notch. But I've never heard of anyone saying, 'Right. That's it. No more chewing gum.'

Others suggest that at long last people have started to realize that discarded chewing gum is a disgusting menace. But again I can't see why this should happen now. We've been hearing the message for decades and it's made no difference.

So why are we now buying 3,000 tons less than we used to? What's happened? Well, I've had a good, long think about it and I believe I know the reason. In May last year Sir Alex Ferguson retired as the masticating manager of Manchester United. That's 3,000 tons of lost sales right there.

19 January 2014

Sun, sand and civil war on the Costa del Myanmar

By the time you read this, the talks in Switzerland aimed at bringing peace to Syria will probably have ended in a blizzard of fury and finger-pointing. Or they may still be dragging on in an atmosphere of sullen recrimination, deep purple faces and hatred.

What won't have happened is that they ended with all the delegates high-fiving Ban Ki-moon, the UN secretary-general, and going out for a jolly fondue and a bit of karaoke on the Lake Geneva shoreline.

Not since Paul McCartney split from his ex-wife have we seen two parties so far apart.

On the one hand you have President Bashar al-Assad's people, who say they will not even talk about a change of leadership. And on the other you have a bunch of people with AK-47s and Toyota pick-up trucks, who say they won't even start to talk unless the leadership is changed.

Then there are delegates from more than thirty countries around the world, including the diplomatic powerhouses of Indonesia and, er, Denmark, who probably want the president to stand down. But don't want the people on the other side of the table to take over. Because if that happened, women in Syria would end up being flogged because they flashed their noses in public. And rapists would walk free if they agreed to marry their victims.

It all sounds completely hopeless, but there is some comfort to be taken from a chap called Colonel Yermakov. Throughout his adult life he was a keen member of the Russian Communist party and at the height of the Cold War he ran a Soviet Army tank division in East Germany. His job was to kill us, pure and simple. And yet on Wednesday I had a lovely lunch of watercress soup and crusty bread with his daughter in Notting Hill . . .

Many years ago I used to spend quite a bit of time at a pub in the Yorkshire Dales. Behind the door to the cellar was a grey box that was connected to the early-warning system at RAF Fylingdales; if it beeped, the landlord knew he had four minutes to tell the local farmers to get the sheep inside because the SS-18 missiles were coming. And yet not that long ago I had a wild night out with the daughter of a man who'd helped to design their rocket motors.

Every time I go to Moscow I have to pinch myself as I walk into Red Square, because for the first twenty-nine years of my life I did not imagine such a thing would ever be possible. I'd watch on the television those endless Victory Day parades with all those tanks and all those soldiers and all those missiles. And all those weird old men in frightening hats. Russians were scary. Alien, almost. And yet now I pay one of them for my season tickets at Stamford Bridge and share drinks with them in the south of France.

So I sometimes find myself wondering: will my children one day be booking a carefree holiday in Kabul? And going on coach excursions to the historical

Helmand province? Will they be enjoying a minibreak in southern Sudan or in the Democratic Republic of Congo? And will they be coming round to my house and saying, 'Dad, did you really used to go to South Africa? And just walk about on your own?'

Which brings me on to Burma. That's been a no-no for donkey's years and one region in particular still is. It's called Shan state and for more than sixty years it's been at the heart of the world's longest-running civil war. I cannot pretend for a minute that I have the first clue what they've been fighting about – heroin, probably – but I can tell you that people with pink faces could not go there. Or rather they could, but they stood a good chance of not coming back again.

Well, I was there last year at a party hosted jointly by all of the warring factions. And it was a very jolly affair. The whiskey flowed. There was dancing. And afterwards we were all invited to enjoy some of the region's local produce: roast bees, toasted grasshoppers and something called yaba, which apparently is a combination of methamphetamine and caffeine.

Normally you can see why some people choose to take a particular type of drug, but yaba appeared to have no upside. It simply made those who partook very sweaty and unbelievably aggressive. But despite this the evening passed with not a single shot fired. And as a result we can be sure that within a year or two it'll be the next must-visit destination for people who like to spend their holidays pointing at temples.

Let's not forget that even before the American tanks pulled out of Iraq, Lufthansa was running a scheduled service to Erbil, and half of Europe was wandering around the local towns, pointing at mosques. The other half, of course, were sunning themselves in Croatia. Or parking their speedboats in Albania. Or playing in the waves in San Sebastian.

You may argue that Syria is different. You may say that it's been a seething nest of violence for 7,000 years and that people there will never stop fighting over who has the best imaginary friend. You may look at the situation today and think that it's worse than ever. On the one hand you have a president who gases children and on the other a bunch of hotheads who like to eat the livers of soldiers they've killed.

I agree, of course, that it would take a special kind of diplomat to reconcile a mother with the 'freedom fighter' who'd eaten her son. But Vietnam today is full of Americans, there are Poles in Berlin and the only real war in Northern Ireland is between the Lannisters and the King in the North.

The truth is that bitterness and rage are invariably softened by time. Today I can be in the same room as Piers Morgan without vomiting. You can warmly greet people in the street who bullied you at school. And one day we shall go to Damascus to point at all the bullet holes and wonder: what was that all about?

26 January 2014

Tumblers, twerkers, cleaning ladies, stoners: find Sochi and win gold

Oh no. The government has issued a warning that terrorist attacks are 'very likely' at the Winter Olympics, which start this week in a remote Russian town that literally nobody could find on a map.

Some say the biggest threat comes from a hitherto unknown organization called Imarat Kavkaz. I've done some reading about it on your behalf but I'm afraid I'm still none the wiser. All I know is that its leader – who may not be the actual leader – thinks that the Olympic stadium has been made from the bones of many dead Muslims and that it must explode as soon as possible.

Then you have a number of women in headscarves who are jolly cross that their husbands have died and feel that the best way of getting back at those responsible is by detonating themselves while standing next to a Swedish curling enthusiast. One is called Ruzanna Ibragimova and by all accounts she will definitely blow up some time very soon.

To try to get round the problem the Russians have drafted in 37,000 troops to the town that no one can find on a map, just in case some of these angry people do, and by all accounts the whole area is now as accessible to the public as a nuclear submarine.

There's another problem too, of course. In the same way as football chiefs decided to hold the World Cup in a country that's so hot even the goalkeepers will die of heat exhaustion, the Olympic bigwigs decided to stage their Winter Games in a city that can't always be relied on for snow.

Maybe they couldn't find it on the map. Perhaps they thought it was in Siberia. But, whatever, the 37,000 troops will be having a gay old time under the palm trees and on the nearby beaches. Except, of course, they won't, because having a gay old time in this neck of the woods is completely not allowed. Which is going to be a problem for some of those heavyweight Bulgarian ski ladies.

In short, then, the phenomenally expensive event is being written off before it's even begun. And that's a shame, because as sporting spectacles go, man has yet to conceive anything that is quite as much fun for the spectator as the Winter Olympics.

You see, when it comes to Wimbledon or the Uefa Champions League or the Ashes, you have the best of the best competing with the best of the best to see who's the best of the best of the best. Which is extremely dreary.

But with the Winter Olympics you have the best of the best competing against a bunch of complete spanners who are going to fall over and crash at very high speed into a piste-bashing machine. And that's not dreary at all.

Have you seen a bobsleigh accident? It's absolutely hysterical, because when you crash a car or a horse, you stop fairly quickly and the viewing pleasure is over. Whereas when you crash a bobsleigh, you keep right on going, often on your head, for miles.

It's even better, though, when people fall off their skis and you watch them in a maelstrom of momentum, flailing about as if they're stuck in an invisible tumble dryer. You could watch cricket for the rest of your life and never see anything as funny as the result of a skier catching an edge at 90 mph.

Some say they like skiing holidays because of the exercise, some claim it's the thrill and others say they enjoy the gin-crisp mountain air. Me, though? I like to sit in a bar at the bottom of a slope and watch people going head over heels. And the Winter Olympics brings that into our living rooms, provided, of course, the cameraman can find the town where they're being held and doesn't get blown up by a widow woman.

There will be a lot of falling over too, because, as I said, many of the participants are actually not particularly good at winter sports. This is because they have come from a country where there is even less snow than at the venue. Jamaica, for instance.

Then you have Thailand, which is represented by two athletes – one of whom is the extremely gorgeous and, er, British classical violinist Vanessa-Mae. And isn't that brilliant? It's like sending Nigel Kennedy out to Brazil this year to play for England, or France or Sumatra or whichever country will have him.

The other great thing about the Winter Games is the way ordinary people can win a gold medal for doing something that is simply not a sport. Curling, for instance. It's just cold crown green bowling with added housework. Being the best at that is like being the best at ingesting sweetcorn through your nose. Or running with your trousers round your ankles. You're the best only because no one else can be bothered to do it.

Then there's snowboarding, the only Olympic sport where you are required to fail a dope test before being allowed to set off. It really is a test to see who can stay upright when off their head on marijuana.

Best of all, though, is ice skating, in which a panel of judges is supposed to decide which girl is best at jumping up and down and spinning round in circles. Obviously this is impossible because they're all exactly the same, which is why each girl twerks as she skates past the panel and the one with the pertest bottom wins.

Some say I have the best job in the world – and I probably do – but being a judge in the ladies' skating championship runs it a pretty close second. Being a judge in the men's skating competition, however, is impossible. Because in Russia sequinned men skating is not allowed.

But perhaps the highlight of the Games will be the biathlon. This is a discipline in which competitors have to ski for a great many miles and then take a rifle off their back and shoot at a target. With tensions running as high as they are, and with 37,000 itchy trigger fingers in the area, I should imagine the sound of gunfire will provoke a bloodbath finale that would impress even Sam Peckinpah.

2 February 2014

Quasimodo. Elephant Man. Sign here – I'm gonna make you rich

SodaStream must have been pleased when the extremely wonderful actress Scarlett Johansson agreed to advertise its fizzy drinks maker in the middle of an American sports event called the Superb Owl.

But then it all went pear-shaped because she had to resign as an ambassador for Oxfam, which noticed that SodaStream had a factory in the Israeli-occupied West Bank.

Naturally this caused the world's peace and love enthusiasts to start bouncing around in a purple-flecked maelstrom of fury, filling their Twitter feeds and their online rant rags with claims that they would instantly take a sledgehammer to all the gently carbonated drinks in their fridges.

Never mind Hugo Boss making uniforms for the Nazis, or Volkswagen owning the company that produced engines for U-boats. This was an all-new Defcon 1 level of horror. Tonic water made from the bones of the Palestinian oppressed.

It was an unmitigated PR disaster and it must have been annoying for SodaStream because while it does indeed have a manufacturing plant in the West Bank, it is staffed by many Palestinians, who receive the same wages as their Israeli co-workers.

But if it was annoying for SodaStream, it must have

been properly thump-your-head-against-a-wall sick-making for Ms Johansson. Because she was being dragged through the mud, and for what? A reported fee of £250,000. Which in the world of Hollywood A-listers is the price of a stamp.

I honestly don't know what she was thinking of. And neither do I understand the motivation for George Clooney advertising, er, I can't quite remember what now. Some kind of coffee. Or Leonardo DiCaprio. Why is he prepared to appear in posters, wearing a watch round his hand? It's stupid.

Because when you sign up to be the face of some giant corporation, you can be absolutely sure that you are agreeing to do far more than turn up on the day, stand in the right place and smile appropriately.

If someone advertises a supermarket, they will be forced by the small print in their contract never to set foot in a rival's shop, even if it's nearby and it's late and it's raining. That's why you never see Gary Lineker eating a packet of KP salted peanuts. Even though from time to time he must get the craving.

It's why you never saw Bruce Willis coming out of a nightclub with his trousers round his ankles when that broadband ad was running – Sky would have wanted its money back. And it was undoubtedly a clause in his Nike contract that stopped Lance Armstrong taking dr . . . actually, scrub that one.

God knows how much I could earn if I chose to sell you a particular brand of vodka, or eat a certain type of corned beef. But, frankly, life is way too short to have some corporate suit ringing me up at ten o'clock every night to make sure I'm tucked up in bed with a good book.

Many years ago I used to do advertisements. But I realized that for every pound you earn you lose two in credibility. And if you are a newspaper columnist you have one hand tied permanently behind your back, unable to speak freely in case you tread on a corporate landmine.

I'd like to say this makes me feel righteous and decent. But in truth it makes me bitter. When I see Paul White-house doing his Aviva commercials and James May on the underside of a taxi seat flogging beer, I can't help thinking, 'That could have been me.' Which is why I've come up with a rather brilliant plan.

Weirdly, Piers Morgan's support for Arsenal was the inspiration. You see, leaving aside my natural dislike of the dreadful little weasel, I think it's fair to say that he is deeply unpopular with absolutely everyone and every-thing that has a nose, and that his much-talked-about affinity with the Boomers, or whatever they're called, must prevent young people from becoming supporters. This made me wonder: how much would Arsenal pay him to support Spurs?

You can spread this out. How much would Manches-ter United pay Mick Hucknall to switch allegiance to City? And how much would Leeds United pay for someone to rewrite the history books on Jimmy Savile? A lot, is the answer.

This could easily be spread into the corporate world. About ten years ago various newspapers suggested that Levi's were becoming uncool and possibly unprofitable because fat old people such as me were wearing them. Which makes me wonder. How much would Levi's pay me to go about my televisual business in a nice pair of corduroy slacks?

This would be a tremendous opportunity for those who represent the sort of 'celebrity' whose private life has lately been the subject of press and even legal interest. I don't recall the name of that young lady whose sex tape ended up on the internet and who was recently charged with cocaine offences. But I bet Apple would pay her a lot to be photographed each week with the latest Samsung.

It could be a whole new world of negative PR. At present people with orange faces who come tripping out of gala dos in London's glamorous West End are given money to wear the latest shoes and get into the latest car. But I'll tell you what. If I made those expensive shoes with the red soles, I'd pay the entire cast of *The Only Way Is Essex* to go out every night in wellies.

All of which brings me back to where we began. With this sorry tale about Ms Johansson and her Superb Owl advertisement for SodaStream.

The truth is that Oxfam was responsible for the whole sorry saga. I'm no fan of Israeli foreign policy either, but before making a stink I would at least check my facts. Which Oxfam obviously didn't.

And what is a charitable organization set up during the Second World War to alleviate a famine in Greece doing sticking its nose into Middle Eastern politics? It needs to be taught a lesson, which is why I'm suggesting that Scarlett shifts her allegiance to a rival organization, and the role of promoting Oxfam is adopted, whether it likes it or not, by someone the world doesn't like very much.

I was going to suggest Kim Jong-un. But there's someone closer to home who'd be much better. Answers to the name of Morgan.

9 February 2014

Coming soon: Top Hi-Vis Gear. No stunts, no tomfoolery, no fun

Last weekend I appeared on television riding a jet ski across Lake Como in northern Italy in a pair of jeans and a rather fetching white linen shirt. I was not wearing a helmet or a life jacket or any sort of high-visibility vest.

As you can imagine, this did not go down well with the BBC's health and safety enthusiasts.

And neither were they very pleased when I simply set off before the safety boat with its squad of trained – and very expensive – divers was on hand to help out if I fell off.

I had tried to explain, using swearwords and much finger-pointing, that it was a lovely calm summer's day and that I wasn't going to fall off. And that even if I did I could swim. But this argument was based on a principle that they simply could not grasp: common sense.

I'm used to this, of course. Before I do anything, a man with a stern face and a lime-green jacket with tubes coming out of it is forced to give me a lecture for several hours on all the things that may go wrong, and I never listen to a word he says. I'm not interested. I genuinely, actively and passionately hate health and safety.

What surprised me after the Lake Como escapade, though, was that my Twitter feed was jammed up by ordinary members of the public who said I should have been wearing safety equipment and was setting a bad example. This made me so angry, my teeth started to itch.

It's not my job to tell people to wear stupid clothes any more than it's my job to tell people to brush their teeth or always wear cufflinks that are smaller than your little fingernail. It is my job, on the other hand, to make jet-skiing across an Italian lake look fun. And I would have failed if I'd been dressed up like a traffic warden.

I am completely fed up with people appearing on television in brightly coloured technical clothing when there is simply no need. Only recently some idiot was filmed at the top of Nelson's Column wearing a hard hat, and I just sat there thinking, 'What do you imagine is going to land on your head up there, you moron?'

Then you have the Somerset correspondents wearing life jackets, while standing up to their ankles in a puddle.

Politicians are the worst. Whenever they appear in a factory of some kind they are always wearing a suit and a tie, which is bad enough, plus wellies, a plastic hat and a high-visibility vest. I want to put my hands round their neck and scream, 'It's a bakery, you idiot. It's not dangerous in any way.'

I simply would not vote for any politician who appeared on television dressed up as though he were about to juggle chainsaws in the outside lane of the M4, while standing in a factory that made chair legs. Because I'd just know he had been told to put on the clobber and he hadn't had the wit to raise an eyebrow and say: why?

There is no answer to this. Only recently an airline stewardess told me to remove my jacket from my knee before coming in to land, and when I asked – very politely – why I should do any such thing, she was stumped. As stumped, in fact, as when you ask why you can't use a mobile phone.

High-visibility safety clothing is the result of an unholy alliance between Britain's insurance industry and the trade unions. The insurers like it because anyone injured while not dressed from head to foot in DayGlo orange is not insured, and the unions like it because their members get a free jacket at the company's expense.

And the whole thing is out of hand. When I was growing up, a policeman looked like a policeman. Now, in his ridiculous yellow jacket, he looks like absolutely everyone else.

'Help. I've been robbed.'

'Sorry, guv, I'm a scaffolder.'

So, what's to be done? We can't abandon the craze for high-visibility hard hats because the insurance industry would simply smile the supercilious smile of the victor, upwardly raise its corporate palms in a 'what can I do?' gesture of impotence and refuse to compensate anyone who'd been injured at work.

But similarly we can't live in a society where a man with a bronze life-saver award is castigated by mealy-mouthed busybodies for riding a jet ski across an inland lake, on a calm day, in a pair of jeans.

We need balance, and for an answer we should turn to nature, where we find that all of the most unpleasant and useless creatures come with high-visibility jackets. The wasp, for example. Its yellow-and-black traffic-officer markings are designed to tell other creatures – us included – that it is pointless, and to be avoided. Surely that's not the signal the police want to send out.

If you wear brightly coloured orange clothes at work you are essentially saying that you are not that far removed from the monarch butterfly, a creature that tastes so awful it can make a starling sick. It's marzipan with wings, and again I'm not sure people want to be sending out this sort of signal.

So what we need is a creature that is capable of becoming highly visible in times of emergency. And the only creature I can think of, off the top of my head, that does this is Bambi.

When Johnny Deer senses danger, it raises its white tail, which acts as a muster point for the weak and the vulnerable. And that's what we need in society. The freedom to go about our business in normal, sober, brown clothes, but the ability to become a beacon instantly when there's been a fire or a crash or a forklift is out of control and heading towards a massive vat of acid.

This, then, is my alternative to the ridiculous health and safety clothes we are now supposed to wear. Instead of a hi-vis jacket, a raisable tail. And instead of a hard hat, some antlers.

Of course this would make everyone look very stupid. To which I say, 'Hope so. Then they might stop doing it.'

16 February 2014

Cuckoo, Switzerland! Sneaky hijackers don't clock off at 5 p.m.

Ethiopian Airlines prides itself, apparently, on being Africa's best carrier. Before last week it had had only sixty-one incidents of note since 1965, and in the past two decades there have been only two big crashes. But it has been a bit prone to hijackings. In fact in 1996 one of its Boeing 767 jets was overrun by three drunken young men, who burst into the cockpit, found an axe and claimed a bottle of alcohol in a bag was a bomb. The drunks had done a lot of research, by studying the in-flight magazine, and had worked out that a 767 could make it without refuelling from Addis Ababa to Australia, so they ordered the pilot to do just that.

He tried to explain that they were only supposed to be going to Nairobi and wouldn't be able to get a quarter of the way there. But they didn't believe him and waved their alcohol about menacingly.

He tried to fly down the coast so that he'd be near land when the fuel ran out, but it was a cloudless day and his ruse was spotted by the hijackers, who ordered him to turn east. Reluctantly he obeyed, but instead of heading for Perth he set a course for a cluster of islands in the Indian Ocean, where, with the fuel at a dangerously low level, he attempted to land.

This started a fight in the cockpit, and that caused

the plane to hit the sea at more than 200 mph. A hundred and twenty-five people lost their lives.

Now you would imagine that after this tragic incident Ethiopian Airlines took every precaution in the book to make sure it was completely hijack-proof. And I'm sure it did. Certainly it will have removed all the spare axes from its cockpits. And yet last week when one of its pilots left his seat to spend a penny, his co-pilot simply locked the door behind him, hijacked the plane and headed for Geneva.

So all those people in the back who'd been searched and stripped naked and poked and prodded to prevent exactly this sort of thing from happening were now faced with a nightmare: that the Swiss air force would be scrambled to shoot them down.

Luckily, however, the Swiss authorities learnt of the hijacking at 4.30 a.m. and – you won't believe this – the country's air force doesn't start work till 8 a.m.

Yup. Hitler once joked that after his armies had conquered Russia he would use the Berlin fire brigade to take Switzerland. But it turns out that, actually, if he'd gone there out of office hours, he could have used the Women's Institute.

The Swiss tell us that all their bridges and tunnels are mined so that they can be destroyed should an invasion take place. They even have stretches of motorway with lampposts that fold flat so that they can be used as runways. And yet despite all this the hijacked Ethiopian plane touched down at Geneva airport, no problem at all.

Doubtless the world's security chiefs are now poring

over the incident in microscopic detail, trying to work out what steps can be taken to make sure it never happens again. And I don't doubt that when they've finished, laws will be passed to ensure that in future pilots are made to pee into bottles as they fly. You think I'm joking, don't you?

Well, I'm not. Before the Winter Olympics began, security officials around the world were warned that terrorists could develop a new type of toothpaste bomb that might be transported to Sochi on an aeroplane. And as a result passengers on every flight into Russia were banned from taking even the smallest amount of liquid, gel or paste into the cabin.

We saw a similar reaction after someone tried to set fire to his shoes on a flight into America. Instantly every passenger was ordered to have their footwear x-rayed before being allowed to board even a plane from, say, Glasgow to London Luton.

This was in addition to all the other security protocols that are in force at any given moment. In Australia, for instance, you may not board an aircraft with more than one cigarette lighter. Quite why this should be I have literally no idea. And neither did the man who made off with my cherished Zippo.

In Barbados, if your trusty travel bag contains a completely harmless brass bullet casing, you will be taken into a small room and stared at until shortly after the flight you were trying to catch has left.

In Nairobi, after you've passed through the usual body scanner and put your shoes back on and your belt, and you've repacked your hand luggage, you walk round a corner and then have to get undressed again for a second body scanner.

And everywhere else people in rubber gloves are legally entitled to touch you anywhere they like. In some places they are even allowed to take photographs of your naked body from behind a screen.

In the next few weeks I shall be travelling to South Africa, Australia, Russia and the Caribbean, and it all sounds terribly important and lovely. But the truth is that I shall spend a damn sight longer standing about barefoot, with my arms in the air, while a man slips his hand into the waistband of my trousers, than I will sipping gently from a glass of chilled Blue Nun.

And I won't be allowed to complain about any of the time-consuming indignities, because we all know that if a plane is hijacked, every government in the civilized world will use its air force to shoot it down before it can be flown at high speed into a tall building.

And yet we learnt last week that despite all the checks and all these threats and all those confiscated Zippos, it is still possible to hijack an airliner and land it safely in a western city.

We also know that, because of this, new rules will be enforced that will make all our lives even more miserable.

But in fact only one is needed. Tell the Swiss to buck their ideas up.

23 February 2014

Cheer up, Piers. You can always get a job as my punchbag

I was going to write about Angela Merkel this morning. I really was, I promise. But then I thought: 'Nah. Come on, Jeremy. Piers Morgan's lost yet another job. He really is down this time. So why not fire up the laptop and kick him a bit?'

As you may know, the ghastly little weasel and I have history.

He ran some unpleasant stories about me on the front page of the *Mirror* several years ago, and whenever we met afterwards he thought it was all a huge laugh. A joke. No harm done.

My wife thought otherwise. And at the British Press Awards gave him one of her hard stares from across the room. 'Why's your f****** wife looking at me like that?' he thundered. So I punched him. And then I punched him again.

And then I thought: 'You know what? I don't think this would ever get boring.' So I punched him again. And, annoyingly, broke my finger.

In another encounter, on the very last flight of Concorde into London, he was seated in the row behind me, droning on about his brilliance, so as we began our descent into London, and an inevitable encounter with the waiting bank of television cameras, I turned round and emptied a glass of water into his crotch.

'Look,' I said to journalists as we walked down the aircraft steps, 'the idiot's wet himself.'

We've tried over the years to shake hands and make amends but he always ends up doing something moronic and the feud starts all over again. Only recently he wrote in his truly amazing *Mail on Sunday* column about how he'd been chatting at a party to Samuel L. Jackson and various other big-name Hollywood stars when I'd walked over.

Apparently I stood on the fringes of their matey chat until the humiliation of being a small fish in a big pond was too much to bear and I sloped off. That simply didn't happen.

It makes you wonder about all the other events that Morgan writes on. All those chance meetings with 'Bobby' De Niro in swish Los Angeles restaurants. All those clever put-downs to his detractors. All that *Hello!* magazine back-patting bonhomie.

How much of it happened only in his imagination? It's more likely he spends his evenings in a hotel suite, on his own, with all the TVs tuned in to his CNN show in a one-man quest to shore up the ratings.

God, they were low. This was a show, remember, that was being aired round the world. Billions had the ability to watch it but few did. In fact Morgan attracted a global audience smaller than the BBC day-time show *Cash in the Attic*. He was even beaten by *Kerry Katona: The Next Chapter*, an ITV2 programme that followed the downward spiral of the dimwitted cocaine enthusiast.

I heard that he was going to be dropped about six

months ago. And have been sitting here for all of that time, loving his stupid Twitter boasts about his huge fame and lavish lifestyle, knowing that he didn't know what I knew.

Things aren't much better for big M, little organ, back home in Britain. Because here his show *Piers Morgan's Life Stories*, in which he makes orange people cry, has obviously run its course.

Gone are the days when he could get the prime minister to come on and sob; now it's Tony Blackburn and Beverley Callard (nope, me neither).

This, then, is a man who was fired from the *Mirror* for publishing obviously faked pictures of British Army bods abusing Iraqi prisoners. A man who was accused of insider dealing. A man who is about to lose his show on CNN and who might very well hesitate over returning to Britain because the police may want to talk to him, again, about phone hacking.

He is a friendless, broken shell. So you might imagine that with his life in tatters, he's sitting in his condo, crying his eyes out over pictures of himself.

But no. Instead he's busy telling everyone that he now has more Google pages than the Pope. Yup. He really does believe that there is only one thing worse than being talked about, and that is not being talked about. And he thinks that so long as he can keep his name in the papers he will get another job. Yeah, right.

Morgan probably thinks he's cast himself as a sort of pantomime baddie, and in time he may indeed end up at the Swindon Wyvern doing just that, throwing sweets into the audience and then trying to duck and weave when they are thrown back – along with all the chairs.

But actually he isn't a pantomime baddie. He really is genuinely awful. It's something we've all known since we first clapped eyes on him with his arm round some teenage pin-up in the showbiz pages of the *Sun*. 'My "pal" Simon Le Bon', the caption would read. Really? So why doesn't Simon have his arm round you?

Later we saw him strutting his stuff on a Simon Cowell talent show and we won't go into detail here about how he got that gig.

And today he's trying to argue his CNN show failed because the Americans didn't take kindly to his misguided attempt to spark a debate on gun control. Nonsense. His show failed because the viewers hated him. Everyone hates him.

And that's a big problem when you are trying to play the fame game. You can upset some of the people some of the time and survive – thrive even. But if you upset all of the people all of the time, you will fail.

And he has. And I couldn't help but notice that as the news broke, it stopped raining and the sun came out.

2 March 2014

Dear Uncle Tim, thank you for this opportunity to mock you for just 62p

What with all the floods and the alarmingly sudden developments in Ukraine, it has been easy to overlook the dramatic news that the price of a first-class stamp is about to rise to 62p. Which, if you employ some rounding-up maths, means it will soon cost a quid to post a letter.

Factor in the cost of some headed stationery and a decent envelope, and the cost of writing to thank someone for a party now exceeds the cost of throwing it.

Of course there are those who will think that more than twelve bob for a stamp is ridiculous and that the boss of Royal Mail should be flogged to death immediately. But I'm sitting here in a state of head-scratching bewilderment wondering how on earth it can possibly be so low.

There is simply no industry that has been hit quite so hard and quite so fast as the Post Office. Only fifteen years ago if you wanted to communicate anything at all to anyone, anywhere, you had to use the post. And the Royal Mail was geared up to deal with that. It had a mind-blowingly enormous infrastructure of trains and ships and vans and sorting offices and postboxes on every street corner. And it meant you could post a letter in Cornwall late in the afternoon, knowing that it would be delivered the following morning. Even if the recipient lived up a mountain in the Scottish Highlands.

But then, in the blink of an eye, electronic communication came along and demand dwindled to virtually nothing. So let's do the maths. If sixteen letters are being posted every day – and it really can't be many more than that – then the revenue with first-class stamps at 62p works out at £69.44 a week. And how do you maintain an army of vans and ships and postboxes for that?

Or, more importantly, why do you maintain an army of vans and ships and postboxes for that? One of the world's last two typewriter makers went west a couple of years ago, so why doesn't Royal Mail throw in the towel as well? Why not admit defeat? Why not let the posties go to seed: let Postman Pat become Postman Fat?

Because, these days, why send a postcard when you have Instagram? Why send a bank statement when most people have one of those calculator communicator jobbies? Why spend money writing when you can email for nothing? Today the postman is nothing more than an irritant who comes round in the morning to annoy your dog and jam up your letterbox with details of a new pizza takeaway service. He's a pest.

Except he isn't. He's vital. Because the simple fact of the matter is this: children cannot thank their grandmother for the present she sent with a text.

I am probably alone on this one but I like writing thank-you letters. Always have. Indeed I remember actually relishing the challenge at the age of ten as I sat down to write a letter of thanks to an uncle who had given me a book called *Christian Art.*

I knew that even the Archbishop of Canterbury would struggle to express any form of sincere gratitude for such a dreadful, ponderous anything-will-do gift, but I was determined not to be beaten. So I turned it into a game: writing a letter that sounded grateful but actually said, 'You utter bastard. I hate you nearly as much as the present you gave me.'

First of all, spell their name ever so slightly wrong. And don't worry if they are called something simple such as Tom. Just call them Tim. This sends out a subtle message that you have written them a letter, and paid 62p for a stamp, but that you aren't even remotely close.

Next, tell them their gift was 'amazing'. This is one of the most cunning words in the English language. It comes dripping with connotations – of Joseph's dreamcoat and many wondrous things – but the truth is that if you really want to congratulate someone, you will use the word 'brilliant' or 'fantastic'.

Amazing is only used to describe your host's soufflé, when it tasted of petrol, or an eight-year-old's bassoon solo, on speech day, when it sounded like a dying wildebeest. Amazing means 'amazingly bad'. You can smile and open your eyes wide and look as though you are showering the recipient with praise, but what you're actually saying is, 'You are a dog egg.'

Next, having said their present was terrible, you need to put it in context. For me as a child this meant listing all of the other things I had received for Christmas. So the letter would go something like this: 'Dear Uncle Tom. Thank you for your book on Christian art. It was amazing. I also got a working crane, a complete Hornby 00-gauge railway set, a 6 ft bear and a speedboat.' None of this was true but he wasn't to know that.

You can apply a similar technique when thanking someone for a dreary party. Simply say it put you in mind of another party you both attended, and pick one that was absolutely fabulous and ended up as an orgy in the swimming pool.

You will then need a sign-off. I used to say, 'It's a shame I'm at boarding school because that means I can never see you,' but that's tricky when you are forty-six and the chief financial officer of a petrochemicals company. But don't despair. Simply say how work keeps you in Nigeria a great deal these days and there's so little time to catch up with old mates.

Once you get into the swing of this, writing a thank-you letter can be as much fun as playing Call of Duty or sitting in front of the television watching Manchester United lose.

And the cost of delivering this letter, if you pen it on a bit of photocopier paper, in your worst handwriting – which you should – is less than a pound.

In terms of value, that's up there with a McMeal, the BBC licence fee and indeed this gigantic newspaper.

And there's a whole army out there waiting to help you humiliate someone you no longer want as a friend. Don't waste it. Get writing.

9 March 2014

My plan for bringing Putin to heel: mutually assured derision

In a moment of boredom last week I solved all the world's problems. A bold claim, I know, but if my plan were implemented, there would be no more war, no more hijackings and no more jealousy, bitterness or rage. And it's so simple: there just has to be a lot more teasing.

At present teasing is seen as a dangerous midpoint stepping stone on the way to the dark shores of full-blown bullying.

It is frowned upon and in some cases completely illegal. You can actually go to prison for teasing someone about their religion or their skin colour. And at school expulsion awaits those who refer to a ginger as a 'mutant' or a short person as a 'Richard'.

But having spent last weekend in Australia, I know that, actually, teasing is a healing balm of righteousness. You see, deep down, the Aussies hate us Poms on a cellular level. They hate our culture and our brilliance as deeply as we hate their ridiculous passion for cooking in the garden. But our differences never come to anything because we tease one another relentlessly.

Walk into a Sydney pub and it begins immediately. 'Backs to the wall, everyone. There's a Pom in the bar.' 'Ha. Nobody ever moved to Australia because of the success they made of life somewhere else.' 'Hide your wallet under the soap – he won't find it there.' 'Jonny

Wilkinson.' 'The Ashes.' 'Peter Andre.' 'He's one of yours.' 'He bloody well is not.'

Sometimes it can be two hours before you actually get round to ordering a beer. And then it starts all over again. 'It'll be cold. I know you fellas like it warm.' 'Better that way.' 'Only because it never stops raining where you come from.'

We see a similar sort of thing in the upper echelons of the Premier League. At Chelsea we tease Manchester United fans for living round the corner, Liverpool fans for the cannibalistic nature of their striker and Arsenal fans for never quite winning anything. And they tease us for the magnificence of our football and the handsomeness of our manager. And as a result there's rarely any fighting these days.

Which brings me on to Syria. Because one man is not allowed to make up football-style chants about another man's interpretation of Muslim history, they are all rushing about in the streets, eating one another.

Good-natured banter obviously wasn't allowed in Ukraine either, and consequently we now have half of Russia's Black Sea fleet at anchor off the Crimean peninsula and Ed Miliband making adenoidal noises about taking very firb action.

Who knows? When Neville Chamberlain and Adolf Hitler met, what if they'd spent the time teasing each other about their moustaches? Maybe if they had, there really would have been peace in our time.

Of course, at this point people with sandals and a fridge full of weeds will be jumping up and down saying that teasing only really works when the two parties perceive themselves to be equal. That we can tease Australians because we're sort of the same and Chelsea fans can tease Manchester United fans because both support big clubs. But it would be wrong for a 22-stone man mountain to tease a small boy.

Well, I'm sorry but this is exactly what's wrong with the world. We feel we can tease only those who have never been persecuted in the past. So it's fine to tease the Germans or the French but it's absolutely not all right to tease Jewish or Irish people. That it's acceptable for the poor to mock the rich but not for the rich to mock the poor.

This makes life almost totally impossible for Americans. Because they are king of the hill, the richest country on earth and the world's only proper superpower, they do not feel they have the right to tease anyone. And with their African-American, Native American, affirmative-action attitude, they don't even tease themselves. Which means the whole concept of ribbing has been pretty much erased from their culture. The result is that if you call someone from the States fat, his natural response is to fire up the gunship.

Right now they are feeling impotent in the face of Russian aggression in Ukraine. They know they can't have a fight and they know they can't not. So they feel stuck. As if they can't do anything. But they can. Obama Barrack can go on television and say, with a bit of a smile, he won't be pushed around by a country that thinks beetroot is a delicacy.

Hopefully this would cause Vladimir Putin to respond by saying Budweiser tastes like mouse pee, and pretty soon they'd be engaged in an Aussie/Pom-style banter war that would lead to nothing more harmful than a couple of back-slapping pints and an agreement that the scallywags can have Crimea if they leave the rest of the country alone.

If Mr Barrack wants some practice I think we'd all be happy for him to start on us. We really won't mind. Make fun of our teeth and our pasty complexions. Then tell us the Rolls-Royce Merlin engine only really worked when it was put in a P-51 Mustang and 'soccer' is for girls.

And when we come back to say that baseball is basic-ally rounders and that the tune to your national anthem was written by a Brit, don't get mad; get on the phone to *The West Wing*'s Aaron Sorkin and ask him to come up with a witty response. Maybe something about how Fleetwood Mac were rubbish till Stevie Nicks and Lindsey Buckingham came along.

When you get a taste for it, have a go at the French and work your way down until eventually you'll be laughing at the Afghans' headdresses instead of drop-ping bombs on them.

I really do believe this: if every country, religious group and social class modelled its relationship with every other country, religious group and social class on the one enjoyed between Australia and Britain, the world would be a much better place.

It's not hard. You just turn centuries of resentment into a good-natured argument about sport and beer.

16 March 2014

Welcome aboard the *Nasty Rash*, cruiser loser. Let's go spoil Venice

Every time I visit a Pizza Express restaurant, I am torn between the Sloppy Giuseppe and the American Hot, but when the waitress turns up, I always order a Veneziana because, as the whole world must surely know by now, a percentage of the bill will then be spent on keeping the world's most amazing city out of the sea.

Pizza Express's backing of the Venice in Peril fund is almost certainly the longest continuous support of a single charity by a business. It's been running since 1975 and to date £2m has been raised. Most of it by me.

But now, it seems, all of that is going to be wasted because the regional authorities have decided to overturn a ban on giant cruise liners entering the city's famous lagoon.

This is the same as allowing coaches to enter the inner circle at Stonehenge. Or quad bikes into Westminster Abbey. It's bonkers.

Environmentalists, of course, are howling more loudly than anyone else, saying that these huge ships damage the local ecosystem. But they're missing the point. There is no ecosystem within 50 miles of Venice. It's just one big turd soup. Nor is there a problem with wash, since the ships are nudged through the lagoon by tugs.

No. The big problem here is aesthetics. Because some

of these ships are a thousand feet long, they are actually bigger than St Mark's Square, so they totally dominate the view. Putting the MV *Chlamydia* in the middle of Venice is like putting a severed horse's head in a bowl of pasta. The chef can waffle on as much as he likes about the delicate seasoning and momma's recipe and the light drizzle of truffle oil, but all you'll be thinking is, 'Yes, but there's a horse's head in it.'

I've just realized that my simile doesn't work. Because while a severed horse's head is fairly grotesque, it is nothing compared with the eye-watering ugliness of a modern-day, slab-sided, top-heavy cruise liner. In fact, I'm struggling to think of anything that man has ever created that looks worse. The city of Archangel in northern Russia is a bit of an eyesore. And Paul McCartney's hair is fairly dreadful. But these are trivial baubles next to the full-bore horror of the MV *Legover*.

Cruise liners are revolting and they have no place in Venice. In fact, they have no place in any of the world's cities. I was in Sydney recently and my view of the opera house was completely obliterated by a ten-storey monster called the MV *Diarrhoea*. Much the same effect was achieved in St Tropez last year by the MV *Hip Replacement*.

And things are only going to get worse because last year the number of people who took a holiday on a cruise liner jumped by 10 per cent to more than 20m. About 1.7m of these were British. And that staggers me because think of the holiday opportunities these people turned down. They could have gone on a coach tour of north Wales, or visited the mining museum near

Barnsley. They could have gone to one of those enema and wheatgrass health farms in Norfolk, or spent a week being stung by wasps. All of these things would have been cheaper, and better, than going on a liner. Surely.

I know that the people on board imagine they're living the life of Billy Zane in *Titanic*, in a wing collar, saying 'Bzzz absurd' when the teaspoon is the wrong shape, but the truth is that a modern-day cruise liner is more like a big floating Pontins.

Genuinely, I cannot think of anything I'd like to do less. A long, vomitous week in a giant shopping centre, trying desperately to avoid the attention of a lascivious sixtysomething divorcée, knowing that soon either you will get food poisoning or you will crash into Sardinia or you will be cornered by a party of four people from Rhyl who want to talk about all the other cruises they've been on.

And what's the upside? Not the view, that's for sure, because every time the sea does something interesting, you will be in the bathroom, talking to God on the great white telephone, and hoping with all of your heart that you do crash into Sardinia as soon as possible.

This is entirely likely, because as far as I can tell, most of the crew on a cruise liner spend most of their time giving all of the passengers thrush.

You may imagine that the captain is a smart Edward Smith-type figure, up there on the bridge, scanning the horizon for obstacles. But he isn't. He's called Giovanni, he's thirty-five and he's in his cabin with an orange *X Factor* runner-up called Michelle.

Doubtless the brochure will speak of many exotic stopping-off points. Venice may be one of them. But the truth is that in most places you'll park in a container port and then you'll be told to be back on board by six. Which doesn't give you time to do anything even remotely interesting.

In Barbados, for example, there is much to see and do, if you go by plane and stay a while. But the best thing you can do is pop into the rather nondescript capital and spend a couple of hours laughing your arse off at the cruise liner people mooching about saying, 'Well, we've seen the Caribbean's oldest synagogue. And now it's time to leave.'

I suppose in some ways cruise liners do the rest of us a service. Because they attract the sort of dullards and desperate divorcées who you really don't want to find propping up the bar where you've chosen to go on holiday.

Maybe that's why Venice's regional authorities have decided to allow liners into the lagoon. Because if the passengers can see the city from on board, they will feel less inclined to get off and clutter up the streets with their nasty clothes and their idiotic opinions.

I'm sorry, though. No. At present, I am happy to pay 25p per pizza to help preserve Venice, because it's not a world heritage site. It's the world heritage site. But if its skyline and waterways become dominated by the 60,000-ton MV *Shagfest*, then it's no longer worth preserving. And I'll simply have an American Hot instead.

23 March 2014

With a banana and a smile I'll see off Putin, killer dust and ebola

As I write, London is bathed in the soft pastel mist of a beautiful spring morning. Children are playing in the parks, the magnolia trees are in full bloom and all the indicators suggest that everyone's house is now worth a billion pounds.

Sadly, though, the magic of the moment has been rather lost because we are told that a giant cloud of killer dust is on its way and that soon the streets will be full of dead pensioners, their lives snuffed out by a deadly cocktail of sand and dust from the Sahara and toxic particles from all of those poorly maintained lorries in France.

Experts have even drawn up a chart, which shows that in East Anglia the level of pollution will be a terrifying 10.

Everyone has been warned to stay indoors, do no exercise and eat seven portions of fruit and vegetables every hour. Jogging, apparently, would be 'sheer stupidity'.

On top of all this, there's a suggestion that a recent outbreak of ebola in rural west Africa has now reached the cities and could be arriving at terminal 5 within hours. And that there is nothing our Border Force can do to stop it because it has been instructed by the prime minister to spend every waking hour finding out what the sinister-sounding Muslim Brotherhood stands for and what it's doing in Britain. And, of course, on the BBC rolling news channel there are many stories about climate change, slavery, Aids, inequality and how the bungled sale of the Royal Mail will bring poverty and disease to all corners of Britain by nightfall.

It's strange. I thought that at lunchtime I might go for a walk in Holland Park to look at the squirrels. But instead I shall be under the bed in a hazmat suit, chomping furiously on my stockpile of bananas and wondering which of the many threats will get me first. The dust, the ebola or a Muslim extremist? Or maybe in the best traditions of multiple choice, it'll be d) none of the above. Because we keep being told that there's a very real threat that the problems in Ukraine could spark an all-out thermonuclear war between Europe and Russia.

In other words, life has never seemed so gloomy and pointless. It's just layer upon layer of fear. Except it isn't, because behind the headlines there is absolutely nothing to worry about at all.

This sandstorm, for instance. 'Experts' tell us it will send pollution levels soaring to 10, but 10 is a made-up figure, designed to make the whole thing seem more serious than it really is. Yes, if you are a chronic asthmatic with one cancerous lung and you go for a long uphill bicycle ride, you will experience a shortness of breath. But for everyone else the worst that can happen is that some dust will land gently on your car.

Then there's the business in eastern Europe, which represents about as much of a threat to our health and

wellbeing as a wet vest. Ukraine was overrun by a mob.
The elected president fled. And those who supported
him, especially in Crimea, were left thinking, 'Well,
that's spiffing.' So, in what historians will see as a political masterstroke, Vladimir Putin simply brought them
under his wing with barely a shot fired. It was a brilliant
solution, and the only real problem is for producers of
the world's atlases.

So what about ebola? We are informed, solemnly,
that if this hideous little virus were ever to board a
plane, the world's population would be dead in two
weeks. And not dead in a nice way either. Because in
the late stages it liquefies your internal organs, which
then leak out. That's not a good way to go, sitting there
with your liver coming out of your eyes, knowing that
soon you will explode, showering all your family with
blood so infected that within hours they'll be leaking
and exploding as well.

But here's the thing. Contrary to what we have been
taught by Dustin Hoffman, it's actually quite hard to
catch ebola. You either have to eat a bat or snog someone who has the disease. So, realistically, it will be
contained in western Africa and will not be popping
round to your house any time soon. Remember Sars?
Remember bird flu? They were going to kill us all, and
they just sort of didn't, because ultimately a virus is stupid and we are not.

Unless, of course, we are talking about this Muslim
Brotherhood business. Because last week David Cameron suddenly loomed out of the smog to tell us that
he wanted to know everything about it. That sounded

very ominous. Especially as we have now handed Afghanistan back to the Taliban. Er, sorry. I meant democratically elected government there.

Well, as I see it, the Brotherhood is a collection of wildly disparate individuals who all share the goal of wanting people to live life according to the Good Book. So in that respect it's a bit like the Church of England. At present it's attempting to change the government, the way of life and the minds of many millions of people in Libya, Egypt, Tunisia, Algeria, Somalia, Jordan, Syria, Iran, Iraq, Saudi Arabia, the UAE, Lebanon, Indonesia, Sudan and so on. I suspect, therefore, that shooting Eric Pickles is a long way down the 'To do' list. Big though the target might be.

Maybe this optimism is foolish. Maybe I should pay more attention to my fruit'n'fibre intake and the quality of the air and climate change and political instability on the other side of the world. Maybe we are all going to be killed by an atomic bomb or a giant meteorite and maybe Ed Miliband really is on course for victory in the next election. There are many, many dreadful things that might happen. And you could spend all of the day and all of the night worrying about them.

Or, how about this for a plan? At present many people say in their will that they would like Monty Python's 'Always Look on the Bright Side of Life' to be sung at their funeral. Wouldn't it be better, though, if you didn't wait till you were dead? Try singing it now.

6 April 2014

I've heeded my snob gene long enough, Rembrandt – just point me to the exit

Recently announced figures show that last year nearly 7m people visited the British Museum. Of course some of these visitors will have been schoolchildren who had no choice in the matter. But a great number will have been tourists and I find that astonishing because what in God's name possesses Johnny Foreigner to say, 'Right. Here I am in London. And what I want most of all is to see an Anglo-Saxon arrow head'?

Things are even worse in Paris, where 9.2m people woke up last year and set off to the Louvre simply so they could look at what is in essence a cracked old stamp with a lopsided woman on it.

I think we have a snob gene. It's the same bit of DNA that causes us to sit on a beach, reading a book we don't want to read about stuff in which we are not interested, because we think that if we sit there reading something with a speedboat and an explosion on the cover we will look idiotic in front of our peers.

And I fear I am a sufferer because I awoke a couple of weeks ago in the glorious city of St Petersburg. It was a beautiful, warm spring morning and I had a few hours to kill. That's my idea of heaven: a city I haven't been to before and nothing to do all morning but snout about in its back passages, stopping occasionally to people-watch in various pavement cafés. But no. I was gripped by the snob gene and knew that I must visit the city's truly gigantic State Hermitage Museum. Must visit. Must visit. Must visit . . .

Upon arrival I was offered the services of a guide but I am wise in these matters and declined because guides never quite know how to throttle back on their enthusiasm, which means you must stand in front of every single exhibit for an hour while she explains in a language that is only on nodding terms with English why this tiny piece of broken pottery is in fact the single most interesting thing in the entire world.

And you stand there with an aching back, thinking, 'If you were any good at languages you'd be working at the EU, earning a million pounds a minute, not working for tips in a room full of old coins.'

I've had trips to the Kremlin, the Smithsonian in Washington and all of the 17,000 houses in which Ernest Hemingway once lived ruined by guides who simply don't realize I'm only there to say I've been. Not to actually learn anything.

I mean, take the Rijksmuseum in Amsterdam. People only visit that because if they didn't all their friends would imagine they'd spent their entire time in the city smoking weed and catching chlamydia. But do the guides get that? Nope. So you're hauled round by a bossy fat woman who really and genuinely believes that we care about the microscopic differences between Rembrandt's paintings, all of which, so far as I can tell, were of businessmen in darkened rooms having meetings.

And don't think the audiovisual alternatives in museums are any better, because all it takes is one moment of inattentiveness – one left when you should have gone right – and you spend the rest of the day being told that the Viking boat in front of which you're standing is a seventeenth-century vase. And the only way you can correct your mistake is to go back to the entrance and start again.

'I don't need a guide dog,' I said as I breezed through the Hermitage's non-wheelchair-friendly entrance and into a room that was decked out like Liberace's bathroom and about twenty-five times bigger than any ocean liner.

It was absolutely vast and it was stuffed from floor to ceiling with various bowls. Some were for the storage of potpourri; others were tureens for soup. None was interesting.

As the minutes ticked by I must confess that I started to skip some of the cabinets. Because I didn't have all the time in the world and I could see through the haze – a few miles away – there was a door into another room, which turned out to be even more enormous and even more vulgar.

And guess what. Yup. It too was filled from floor to ceiling with more bowls. And about six billion teapots.

Now I know that around the world there are many museums dedicated to slightly odd things. In Britain there is a museum for lawnmowers and in San Francisco there's one for sex toys. The French have one for instruments of torture and the Icelanders – as I'm sure you know – have a room in which penises from all of the island's species are displayed. But teapots? I mean, come on.

Eventually, while trying desperately to find the exit so I could have a nice sit-down at a pavement café, I stumbled across a room full of paintings. Mostly they depicted businessmen in darkened rooms having meetings, so I knew them to be Rembrandts. But one caught my eye. It showed a naked woman lying on a bed welcoming the Greek god Zeus, who – get this – impregnates her with a 'shower of gold'.

This is the trouble with museums. Each usually has one thing that makes a visit worthwhile. London's Natural History Museum has the huge dinosaur. The Louvre has the lopsided lady. The Smithsonian has the Bell X-1 supersonic aircraft. The penis museum has the sperm whale's member and the Hermitage has a woman who's been immortalized for all time because she told her husband she'd got pregnant after a god peed on her.

It makes me wonder. Instead of having a museum with one good thing and then filling the rest of the space with arrow heads and teapots, why not have a world museum full of all the one good things? It could be the world museum of excellence and we should put it somewhere such as Dortmund, which has no other attractions worth speaking of.

That way we could be free to enjoy our time in Amsterdam or London or St Petersburg without the constant nagging need to visit a museum simply so we don't look as stupid as we'd rather be.

20 April 2014

Today's explorers only boldly go where everyone's gone before

Nine days ago an enormous avalanche on Everest killed sixteen Sherpa guides and now their colleagues have staged a walkout, saying that the government compensation of around £240 per victim isn't really enough. They may have a point.

An all-out strike would leave around 330 fee-paying western climbers stranded at base camp, as most have neither the skill nor the know-how to reach the summit without assistance from the Sherpas. And I'm sure at this point you're thinking the same as me – 330!

Yup. It seems the world's highest mountain has become something of a conveyor belt in recent years. On one single day in 2012, 234 people reached the peak, and last year an altercation between two parties climbing the mountain led to a mass brawl. To date 4,000 or more people have climbed it. Many even got back down again.

The mountain has become big business for the Nepalese government, which charges each climber £5,900 in permit fees. And that's on top of the cost of the expedition. It also insists that each climber takes home 8 kg of rubbish to try to reduce the mounds of litter that are to be found at the camp sites.

And all of this raises a question: if you want some

fresh air and a bit of a thrill, what's wrong with Alton Towers?

Hmmm. From the late eighteenth through to the early twentieth century hardcore expeditioning made sense because much of the world was unknown. We had Roald Amundsen, the Norwegian who went to the South Pole because, well, because it was there and no one else had been. And all of those sailors looking for the Northwest Passage. And John Hanning Speke stomping about in Africa, having a wonderful time and occasionally hunting for the source of the Nile.

Back then we had chaps such as George Mallory, who stayed on at Cambridge for an extra year so he could write an essay. Yup. Twelve months to write an essay. Then he decided to climb Everest to see if there were any fossils up there. Important work.

This all sounds terribly romantic and interesting but most believe it's no longer possible to do exploring these days. Africa is full of tourists pointing at hippos. Everest is a rubbish tip. And if you want to go up an Alp you can simply take a chair lift.

Being an explorer, then, is like being a town crier or a typewriter manufacturer or one of those men who went around at dawn extinguishing streetlamps. It doesn't matter how much the idea appeals, it's pointless and nobody is going to fund your expedition.

You'd expect people to move on and get jobs designing iPhones. But no. They simply think of new ways of going where absolutely everyone has been before. This is why we are forever being treated to stories in the newspapers about some steely-eyed Oxbridge chap who's just become the first man to hop to the North Pole, just weeks after he became the first man to climb Mont Blanc wearing nothing but a jockstrap.

Expeditions are getting more and more bonkers. The Atlantic is chock-full of servicemen who had their legs blown off in Afghanistan and are now rowing to Barbados. And the Andes is awash with people licking rocks to get a bit of moisture. Soon even space will jam up with Richard Branson and various loony Austrians jumping out of their helium balloons.

I'm just as bad. When I arrived by car at the magnetic north pole I climbed out and thought, 'Nobody's done this before.' It made me happy. Similarly in Chile several years ago I kept on driving up a volcano, even though I felt like death, because I wanted to drive a car at a higher altitude than had been achieved. Only when we reached 17,200 ft and the film crew started to faint did I see sense and come back down again.

For most people the modern world is a wondrous place full of medicine and food and fizzy drinks in vending machines. But for explorer types it's a miserable place. Because almost everything that can be done has been done already. And our thirst for firsts is not going to be quenched by sitting at a desk designing apps.

All of which brings me on to the missing Malaysia Airlines flight, which – best guess – is sitting 17,000 ft beneath the surface of the Indian Ocean. That's only about three miles or so down. But realistically we can't get there. A modern nuclear submarine, for instance, can dive to around 2,400 ft before its hull collapses. And that's not even half a mile.

In the early 1960s a manned submersible did reach the bottom of the Mariana Trench, which is almost seven miles down in the Pacific, but no one attempted to repeat the feat until 2012, when the film director James Cameron successfully piloted a torpedo to what is the deepest part of the ocean. It's more than a mile deeper than Everest is high. The pressure down there, using the internationally recognized unit of measurement, is like lying on your back with fifty jumbo jets sitting on your chest.

Of all the living space on the planet 99 per cent is under water. And we've only explored 5 per cent of it. Today we know of 212,906 marine species, but scientists reckon there could easily be 25m down there in the murky depths. That's almost 24.8m species here on our planet that no one has ever seen.

Don't you find that remarkable? We're building rockets so we can travel at least 35m miles to Mars while all we've come up with to explore the sea is a snorkel. We're going to explore strange new worlds and seek out new civilizations before we've even had a look over the garden fence.

Even more strangely, the world is full of people who will climb the highest mountain and hop across the Sahara. But ask these people to check out what's under the waves and all you get is, 'Ooh no, I might get my hair wet.'

Why? Because if you truly want to be alone and to go where no one has gone before, it's the only place left. There's no litter. No queues. No noise. It is, as the writer Jules Verne said, 'the living infinite'.

27 April 2014

Look at the mess you've made, Mr Executioner – try doing them this way

I think most people now realize that I really didn't say the n-word. But as a result of the lurid headlines I realize I must turn over a new leaf.

I've been told by BBC chiefs that I'm drinking at the last-chance saloon so from now on I shall arrive at work on a bicycle with a copy of the *Guardian* under my arm, and at lunchtime, instead of moaning about how everything on the menu is vegetarian, I shall cheerily ask for extra lentils in my nuclear-free peace soup. Also I must remember when I'm in a lift to not goose Mary Beard.

I've even been informed that I must maintain these standards when I'm not at work. So no more sneezing into my hand just before I press the flesh with Ed Miliband. No more drunken shooting parties. And I shall immediately change the name of my scotty dog from Didier Dogba to Tony Blair.

Here, of course, in my little corner of *The Sunday Times* there can be no more columns about how badgers have killed all the nation's hedgehogs and must be exterminated immediately. To keep my job I must become like the love child of Polly Toynbee and Brian May.

So. Here goes. Did you see that dreadful story from Oklahoma about the botched execution? Orderlies spent nearly an hour trying to find a vein in the condemned man's arms and legs before finally deciding to stick the needle into his groin.

Then, after the cocktail of drugs had been administered, a doctor noticed that the intravenous line had missed his vein and that instead of flowing into his bloodstream the drugs had been absorbed into his muscles.

So now he had half a pint of potassium chloride in him, and writhed about in unspeakable agony for a number of minutes until mercifully he was killed by a gigantic heart attack. Naturally the whole sorry affair has caused the nation to think more carefully about using lethal injections to kill people.

Obviously, like all left-thinking people, I am dead against the death penalty. It is completely muddle headed to think that the state has the right to kill people. Unless they've driven into a yellow box, of course.

But in the land of the free, more than half the population – and the US president himself – supports it. And now in all the thirty-two states in which it is legal everyone is trying to decide what method to employ when the supply of lethal drugs dries up.

Some are suggesting a return to the electric chair. Really? Do these people really think that in the twenty-first century it is acceptable to shave off a human being's hair, put a colander on his head and then feed up to 2,000 volts of electricity into his body until he is dead? This is not quick. Or pleasant.

In a 1985 court case in America the presiding justice – an opponent of the electric chair – described the gruesome process: 'The prisoner's eyeballs pop out and rest on his cheeks. He defecates, urinates, and vomits blood and drool. The body turns bright red. Sometimes the prisoner catches fire.'

As a result some states are thinking of using a gas chamber instead, while others reckon a firing squad is the solution. I dunno. Perhaps they could adopt the old French way of tying the guilty man to his wife and throwing them into a river.

Other methods that have been used around the world over the years include being crushed by an elephant and being torn in two by horses.

It's strange. It's very easy to kill a person quickly and cleanly, and yet when the job is given to a state it invents all sorts of cruel and unusual methods that verge on the ridiculous.

I mean, what was stoning all about? And what deranged halfwit thought it was a good idea to sentence someone to death by pendulum? You shall be tied down and an axe will swing back and forth over your body, getting lower and lower until eventually it cuts you in half.

Things were even worse for miscreants in various navies. Because although the captain had access to a gun, so he could shoot the guilty man, and lots of rope, so he could be hanged, many decided that the best method was to lob a chap over the side and drag him under the vessel where the barnacles would act like a cheese grater and peel his skin off.

On land, meanwhile, the king, with his manners and his airs and graces, decided that if somebody had misbehaved, he should be hanged until he was not quite dead and then placed on an operating table so that all his internal organs could be brought into the fresh air, where the poor man could watch them stop working.

Usually there was an audience for this. And in Vietnam there still is. I visited a school there once that was right next to a jail. Which meant that every so often the pupils in form VIb could look out of the classroom window and see a blindfolded man in the courtyard below being tied to a post and shot in the middle of his heart.

Countries that have the death penalty really need to address this sort of thing. They need to stop fannying about and come up with a system that's quick and as decent as a state execution can be.

How's this for a plan? After the man is found guilty, he is sent to the county of Midsomer. Because one of the many murderers there could do the job on the court's behalf. Or Sweden, where it's much the same story.

4 May 2014

You can't sex up cricket – it would wake the dead at the Pavilion End

Well, there we are. After a rollercoaster ride in which four different teams looked set at various points to win the title, the Premier League is drawing to a close and now sports fans must aimlessly wander the streets like the undead until the World Cup kicks off in Brazil.

But hang on, I hear you say: the cricket season is now under way. And surely this will provide ample entertainment for the enthusiast of balls and men and back-slapping communal showers.

Hmmm. I'm not sure about that. As with all sports, nobody really knows how or when cricket began but we do know from records of the late sixteenth century that it was played in Britain.

And that makes sense. There were no computer games then, or trips to the garden centre, and cricket was a good way of passing the time until you caught diphtheria or your house burnt down.

It really got going in the late nineteenth century, when a great many extremely stupid former public-school boys were sent to run hill forts in various far-flung corners of the empire. They would wake every morning and think, 'Right. I need to fill my day somehow. So either I shall spend it face down in a bucket of gin sling, or I shall do a game of some sort.'

Cricket was ideal because, unlike backgammon, or

playing hide the sausage with the maid, it went on for about six weeks.

What's more, it was a game that could be played against Johnny Local. Until, of course, everyone realized that they were in fact much better at it than us. And that was that. People, in Britain at least, lost interest.

Today figures show that the average attendance figure at a county cricket match in England is around 3,500. Which means that in terms of popularity it's on a par with Cypriot first division football. And far behind women's football – or soccer – in America, motorcycle speedway in Poland, baseball in South Korea and lacrosse in Canada.

And what makes the situation even more dire is that many of the people who are to be seen at county cricket matches are dead. I went once to Lord's and was told that there's a thirty-year waiting list to become a member.

I couldn't understand that because there were many empty seats in the stands and there would have been even more if they'd cleared away some of the corpses.

It was a terrible day. On the pitch a man occasionally threw a ball at another man and then absolutely nothing happened while he got the ball back.

This slowed everything down and I wondered out loud how Wimbledon would get on if the players only had one ball that had to be retrieved after every shot.

Everyone was aghast. 'Speed it up?' they all thundered incredulously. 'No. That's not the point of cricket at all,' they said. Well, it wasn't in 1889, when it was an alternative to a drink problem for an Old Etonian empire-builder. But now, when we are all busy picking the kids up from school? It's absurd to have only one ball. And no ball boys.

And why stop for tea? And how can it be right or fair that I could field a team of deeply unsporting and fat oafs against the West Indies, who in the first innings would get 1m runs for no wickets?

Our team would then go in to bat and score no runs for eight wickets. And then the whole sorry spectacle would be a draw just because it had started to rain.

There is no other sport or game in the world where you can draw against a vastly superior opponent because of the weather. They play football in the rain and do motor racing. So why not cricket?

The trouble is, of course, that cricket is part of the red phone box malaise that came close to ruining Britain. Everyone knew that they smelt of wee and the coin slot didn't work but when a change was mooted, half of Surrey went berserk.

'You can't abandon the red phone box,' they shouted from behind their mangles and from their Morris Minors. 'It's part of the fabric of what makes us British.'

When I googled the phrase 'make cricket more interesting' there were more than 300,000 hits. And in every one I viewed there were people suggesting ways to make the game better and faster and more exciting. And all of them will be ignored because, well, because next thing you know we'll have a bloody president.

My hatred of cricket is not some fad. I went to a school that had fourteen clay tennis courts and what at the time was the largest all-weather games area in Europe. But was I encouraged to use these facilities? No, I was not. Instead, twice a week throughout the summer, I was forced – often physically – to stand in a field so I could endure three hours of solid, uninterrupted hay fever.

As I was so useless, they'd make me stand far from the action in the long grass, where the pollen was at its worst and every so often a ball that weighed more than most commercial hovercraft would come my way at about 6,000 mph. And I couldn't see it because my eyes were streaming so I wouldn't know it had arrived until it smashed into the end of my finger, sending the whole digit deep into my own hand.

Then, after several hours of sneezing and teasing, they'd put me in front of the stumps and make me stand still while a big boy called Phil Lovell threw what was essentially a rock at my testicles.

The only good thing about all this is that I have passed on my cricketing ability, my hay fever genes and my hatred of the club mentality that surrounds cricket to my son. This means that in the coming weeks he will not be tempted by Sky Sports' exciting line-up of matches such as Somerset v Surrey, and Warwickshire v Yorkshire.

Which will dramatically increase the chances of him doing well in his A-levels.

11 May 2014

We'll always have Paris and Polish dumplings – until UKIP wins the day

As the half-term bank holiday Monday dawned, it became clear that I could either spend the day looking out of the window, imagining that the clouds were lifting while the children Instagrammed pictures of their own stools – or we could go to Paris for lunch.

And so, three and a bit hours later, we were sitting in a café in the Place des Vosges, making reservations at the delightful Benoit restaurant off the Rue de Rivoli. A small walk round the Louvre later, we were back on the train and by 9 p.m. we were back in London. It was one of the most wonderful and joyous days I've had in years.

And it was all so easy. Yes, the train station at London St Pancras International has various passport booths and security measures, but unlike the security measures you encounter at airports, you are not made to remove your shoes and your belt, you are not expected to unpack your computer, nobody caresses your testicles and you are allowed to pass through carrying as much toothpaste as you like.

Check-in times? Well, they suggest you should be at the station half an hour before departure but because of the adult way the French treat the terrorism threat, we made it to the Gare du Nord three minutes before the train left. And were still allowed to board.

It's not just the rail link between London and Paris

that's easy either. My son says that on his InterRailing travels last year from Amsterdam to – actually he can't remember where he went after that – he was never asked to show his passport once. And that at no point did stern-looking men with greatcoats and alsatians board the train demanding to see everyone's papers.

It's the same story on the road. You simply don't know any more when you've passed from France into Belgium and the only way you know you've gone from Italy into Austria is because there's no litter, or graffiti, or untidiness of any kind. It's like you've gone from a Roman orgy into a Victorian lady's underwear drawer.

I love Europe and it makes me happy that one day we will have forgotten the difficult birth and made the EU work. I long for a time when I think of myself as a European first and an Englishman second. I crave a United States of Europe with one currency, one army and one type of plug socket. And yes, I know, there will be drawbacks. We're already seeing some of them, which is why more than a quarter of those who went to the polls in the recent European elections voted UKIP.

One of the drawbacks I notice quite often is that in South Kensington, which is a leafy part of south-west London, almost everyone is French. The whole area is awash with lovely patisseries and the pavements are rammed with women so elegant and beautiful I have to bite the back of my hand to stop myself from crying out. This is obviously so much worse than if everyone were lurching around in tracksuits looking for somewhere to vomit.

Just up the road, I know of a Polish restaurant where

you can buy dainty little dumplings. And for sure this is a huge step backwards from the takeaway joint that used to be on the site. Because who wants to be served a dumpling by a charming Polish man when they could have a polystyrene tray full of slime instead?

My local off-licence is staffed entirely by French people who know everything about wine. And that's wrong too. Because what you actually want is a fat school-leaver and a shop full of Carling Black Label.

Outside London there are real problems, of course. In the flatlands of East Anglia farmers are finding that all the traditional home-grown workers are sitting at home playing video games on gigantic televisions, and as a result they are having to employ an army of Romanians and Bulgarians.

The only upside to this is that these recent arrivals are prepared to work twenty-seven hours a day and pay the farmer for permission to come to work, which means fruit and veg prices in the supermarket are low.

Further north we have Rotherham, a south Yorkshire town in which UKIP is now the main opposition party to Labour. Locals are said to be fed up with the number of immigrants and want to go back to the olden days.

Hmmm. I worked for three years on a Rotherham newspaper back in the late 1970s. And, I'm sorry, but back then it was pretty terrible.

There was one sandwich shop and if you discounted the council-run café in the bus station – which I did on a daily basis – there was not one single restaurant.

Going out for dinner meant going to the pub and

buying some salt and vinegar crisps. Prawn cocktail? No, we bloody haven't, you poof.

It was a monoculture. Everyone thought the same and did the same. When one person went on strike, everyone went on strike. They didn't even trust me because I was from Doncaster.

Nowadays when you drive through the town it takes about five seconds to realize that it isn't a monoculture any more. Half the cars sport foreign registration plates. There's an eastern European delicatessen on Wellgate. Many men look like potatoes. The town has become a blend of several things. And is that a bad thing?

Well, I suppose if you think that Rotherham is your town and that all of the jobs in it are rightfully yours, then, yes; it is bad when Mr Zyscyzsky offers his services at the call centre for 32p a year and, as a result, you have to sit at home all day watching *Cash in the Attic*.

But look at it this way. When I worked in Rotherham almost everyone was deeply resentful of the Queen. They argued that entitlement was not a birthright. So by the same token it's quite wrong to say Rotherham is your town just because you were born there.

I know that the EU doesn't work now. I know the currency is a disaster and that it's run by an army of muddle-headed fools. And I know too that they obsess about the correct size for a haddock and the proper shape of a banana. But on the upside you can go to Paris for lunch ever-so easily.

1 June 2014

My mum's final act of love was to throw all her stuff into a skip

Right in the middle of all that brouhaha about sloping bridges and Ecny, Meeny, Miny, Moe, my mum died.

So there I was, in Russia, in the middle of a *Top Gear* tour, trying to organize her funeral and tell the children and sort out all the legal stuff, with the BBC moaning at me in one ear and a reporter twittering on in the other, and I knew that if I wept, which is what I wanted to do, because I was very close to my mother, the *Daily Mirror* would run pictures and claim they were tears of shame. It was a gruesome time.

And I knew that when I came home the BBC would still be bleating and the reporters would still be calling, and I'd have to go to her house and start sorting through her things. And where do you start with a job like that? Where did she keep her pension details, the deeds to her house, her insurance certificates? How do you cancel a Sky subscription? Did she have any shares? Premium Bonds? And how do you find out if you haven't got a sister who's a lawyer?

Luckily, I do have a sister who's a lawyer, but even though she could handle the paperwork, I'd still have to go through my mum's things, and that would be a nightmare because I'm such a sentimental old sausage I even find it difficult to throw away an empty packet of fags. I think of the fun I've had smoking them and the people I've shared them with and I want to hold onto the wrapping as a keepsake, a reminder of happy times.

So what in God's name would it be like in my mum's house, surrounded by everything that made it hers, except her? And there'd be all those childhood memories. At some point it would be inevitable I'd find the eggcup I'd used every morning as a child and the cereal bowl with rabbits on it. That would tear my heart out.

At one stage I received a call from a middle-ranking BBC wallah saying they'd had a letter from some MPs, asking if I was going to be sacked, and I really wasn't paying much attention because I was wondering what on earth I'd do with the mildly fire-damaged Dralon chair that my dad had bought for £4 in 1972.

Even by the standards of the time it was a truly hideous piece of furniture, and the years had not been kind to it. Any normal person would give it to charity or use it as firewood. But it was the chair my dad used to sit in. It had a cigarette burn in the arm from the time when he'd nodded off while smoking. I couldn't possibly give it away, or burn it. And I sure as hell didn't want it in my house. So what would I do?

There is no single thing in the house of anyone's mother that isn't infused with a gut-wrenching air of sentimentality. It's not just her jewellery or her clothes. It's the little things as well. Her kitchen scissors, her bathroom scales, her flannel. Every single thing in each and every drawer is as impossible to discard as a first teddy bear.

I would need a very big lorry to handle all the stuff I'd need to bring home. I'd also need at least two months to go through it all. And I'd need about 4,000 boxes of Kleenex.

However, here's the thing. My mum did not die unexpectedly. She'd known for some time that the cancer was winning and had therefore had time to put her affairs in order. A job she had undertaken with some gusto.

I'd always assumed that 'putting your affairs in order' meant writing a will and remembering to reclaim your lawnmower from the chap at No. 42. But in the weeks since my mum's death I've learnt that actually there's a lot more to it than that.

First of all, she had left many helpful instructions about what sort of funeral she wanted. No friends. No flowers. And no mention of God or the baby Jesus. My sister and I didn't even have to guess what music she would have liked because she'd told us: 'Thank You for the Music', by Abba.

All the financial stuff was in a neat box with everything clearly labelled. And she hadn't stopped there. Before she became too weak, she'd had a massive clear-out. Pretty much everything she owned had been thrown into a skip. 'It'll save you the bother when I'm dead,' she had said.

But by far and away the best thing she did in those last few months was to sort out a lifetime of photographs, putting the ones that mattered into albums and, crucially, writing captions. So now I know that the time-faded sepia image of a stern-looking woman in a nasty hat is my great-aunt and that the blurred picture of what might be a corgi was my grandad's dog.

Ordinarily, I'd have thrown away the endless pictures of what appear to be a building site, but thanks to my mum's diligence, I now know it was the house in which I was born. And how it had looked when she and my dad bought it in 1957.

I don't know how long she had worked on her down-sizing and the clear-out and the organization of her things, but it's something we should all try to do when we know the Grim Reaper is heading our way. Because not only does it spare our loved ones from the hassle of going through every single thing we've ever owned but also it spares them from the grief of deciding that the horse brasses and the Lladró figurines really do have to go to the tip.

The only trouble is that there's one thing my mum did not sort out. Back in 1971 she made my sister and me two Paddington Bears. They were the start of what became a very successful business and they were very precious, but over the years one was lost.

I maintain the sole survivor is mine. My sister insists it's hers. And she's the lawyer . . . so I have the cereal bowl with the rabbits on it, and the Dralon chair.

8 June 2014

Roll up and join the dullards sprinkling frozen peas on the trifle

Since Colorado legalized the sale and consumption of cannabis, property prices have jumped, warehouse rental rates have quadrupled, tourism has boomed and the state government is reporting that it is receiving more than $5m (£3m) a month in tax from sales of the drug. On the downside, however, everyone who lives there is now very boring.

This is something that's rarely debated in the argument for and against the legalization of drugs. Enthusiasts say prohibition never works, that the ban causes more problems than it solves, that it's inhumane to deny someone in pain some organic relief and that it cannot be right for a government to prevent individuals such as snowboarders from setting fire to a plant and then inhaling the smoke, if that's what they choose to do.

Those who seek to ban the bong say that cannabis causes its enthusiasts to become mental, that it's all the devil's work, and that if it were legalized and available over the counter from Boots, children as young as two would soon become addicted. But they never raise the biggest problem of them all: that pot makes people incredibly dull.

Nothing fills me with so much despair as that moment at a dinner party when the architect or the adman produces some hopeless little roll-up and invites everyone to have a toke, or whatever it's called. Mainly this is because if I go within six miles of even a tendril of cannabis smoke I become the colour of parchment. This is followed immediately by some light vomiting. And then I go into a dead faint.

And actually that's good news because at least when I'm unconscious in the nearest lavatory I don't have to sit at the dining table listening to everyone giggling at the salt and pepper pots. Nor do I have to watch them sprinkling frozen peas on a sherry trifle that someone's found in the fridge. And I don't have to join in their conversations about the guitarist Steve Hillage out of Gong or whether the ham is happy. Being at a party where you're drunk and everyone else is stoned is even worse than being at a party where you're not drunk at all.

Cannabis fans say that the drug helps them understand complex things such as the lyrics from Genesis's *Selling England by the Pound*. But I don't believe this because I bet it's not possible to assemble a piece of flat-packed furniture after you've smoked a joint. They also say it enables them to watch and enjoy various daytime television shows such as *Homes under the Hammer*. But they do admit that they can seem distant and forgetful – 'Mmm, sorry, what were you saying?'

I just don't get this at all. Why would you choose to take a drug that causes you to be distant and withdrawn and quietly introspective? Do you think that you are too interesting and too funny when you're sober and that it's better for all the other guests if you smother your exuberance under a fuggy blanket of forgetfulness?

No. In the same way that no one has ever emigrated to Australia because of the success they've made of their lives elsewhere, no one has ever become a regular dope smoker because they are fed up with being the life and soul of the party. No one has ever said, 'I'm bright and witty and everyone loves me so I shall start using cannabis.'

Quite the reverse. It's a boring drug to make boring people less bothered about being boring. But I want to make it absolutely plain here and now that I have no problem with people ingesting whatever takes their fancy. Cocaine out of a prostitute's bottom, heroin through your ankles, Quaaludes for lunch – go right ahead. Just don't expect me to talk to you afterwards.

Because let's be absolutely clear about this. One of the main reasons we were able to win the Battle of Britain is that the pilots of the Spitfires and the Hurricanes were not distant and forgetful. One of the main reasons that America lost in Vietnam is that its troops were.

Nothing great or brilliant has ever happened as a result of weed. Concorde was not designed in a fog of forgetfulness. Nor was the Apollo space programme. 'Where's my slide rule, Hank?' 'Oh sorry, Junior, I was peckish so I ate it.' Obama Barrack said that as a kid he smoked dope and inhaled frequently. 'That was the point,' he joshed. Yes, mate, but I bet you don't smoke it now. 'Sorry, Mr Putin, I wasn't listening. What were you saying?'

It is allegedly the same story with Bill Gates, although he has never admitted it. He is said to have used it when he was young but we can be fairly sure that his empire would be a bit more corner-shoppish if he hadn't stopped.

There's a whole list of extremely successful and talented artists and musicians who have owned up to a marijuana addiction. But I suspect they produced their good work despite their habit, not because of it. Mostly the only tangible thing their drugs produced was the vomit on which they choked to death.

This naturally brings me on to alcohol. And, of course, it's pretty much the same story. Nothing tremendous or brilliant has ever been created by a drunk. It too will make you mental and after you've had some you cannot drive a car or operate heavy machinery or assemble an Ikea dining table. However, unlike cannabis, drink makes people interesting and funny.

Go to a party and note the volume of the chat when you get there. Then note what it's like after a couple of hours. People have become louder and shinier. They beam and they make expansive gestures. They forget their inhibitions, they can't keep secrets and they want to have sex with one another.

The truth of the matter, then, is this: given the choice of spending time with a group of people who've just had a joint and another group who've just had a couple of glasses of wine, I'll take the drinkers every time, which is why I won't be visiting Denver any time soon. Because the Dog and Duck in Dagenham is going to be a whole lot more fun.

15 June 2014

This comedy troupe's lightning wit has ceased to be. This is an ex-Python

I can't remember much these days. Certainly I can't remember whether I've told you this before, but when I was nine my dad came into my bedroom late one Sunday night, woke me up and said I had to come downstairs to watch a television programme that had just started. It was called *Monty Python's Flying Circus* and it was, he said, 'going to be important'.

Well, it didn't look very important to me. There were some sheep in a tree and a man with three buttocks. And every so often a man in army uniform would come along and say, 'Stop that. It's silly.'

Which it was. But that didn't stop my father waking me up every Sunday night for the rest of the show's thirteen-episode run to watch it with him.

Later he took me to watch the Pythons perform their show live in Leeds, and whenever they made a film he was always first in the queue to buy tickets. And you know what? He never laughed once. He never even smiled. He watched everything they did in the way that you or I would watch a burning airliner. With a quiet, fascinated stillness.

And yet while he didn't find Tim the Enchanter funny when he was first seen, on a rock in Scotland, blowing up mountains, he would giggle until he was fit to burst if you mentioned him the next day. Or

Venezuelan beaver cheese or Mitzi Gaynor's pine teeth or sweaty, mindless oafs from Kettering and Boventry.

It's strange. There are some films – *Airplane!* is the best example – at which you laugh in the cinema until you are sick, but Monty Python was not like this. Nothing the team did was funny at the time. But at school or work the next day you would laugh with your friends until your spleen came out of your nose. Python was like cheese. It matured with age . . . and then it went off, but that's another story.

Back then, knowing everything the Pythons had ever done off by heart was a badge of honour. Being able to recite the Spooner poem and every word from the Upper Class Twit of the Year sketch showed that you had the wit. And I would reserve a special type of fury for those who attempted to join in and got the quotes a bit wrong. 'It's not "We were evicted from our lake", you imbecile. It's "hole in the ground". Get it right or get out.'

Thanks to my dad, you simply will not find anyone alive today who loves Monty Python more than I do. You could ring me this morning and give me any quote from any show, book, record or film and I will know where it came from. And what came afterwards. And who said it. I could bore for Britain on Python and have, many times.

So you would imagine that I would have been first in line for a ticket to the Pythons' live show next month. But I wasn't. Partly this is because I'll be in Budapest at the time but mostly it's because I'd rather put out a campfire with my face.

They say you should never meet your heroes, and having met the former test pilot Chuck Yeager I'd certainly go along with that, but even more important is that you should never meet your heroes forty years down the line. And certainly not if they were comedians.

It's often said that comedy is performed exclusively by people whose looks and armpit aroma prevent them from getting laid. It's reckoned that the only way the greasy and the ginger can get into a girl's knickers is via her funny bone.

So, the reasoning goes, once you are old and your gentleman sausage is able to perform only its secondary function, there's no point in being funny any more. That makes sense, of course, but I think there's another reason . . .

Every talent you are given at birth fades with age. A fighter pilot loses his reactions. A footballer loses his knees. And then all his money in a failed pub venture. A model loses her battle with gravity. And comedians lose not just the will but the actual ability to be funny.

I had lunch last week with a columnist on this newspaper who shall be nameless except that his name begins with A and ends with A Gill. In the past these were quite jolly affairs with much laughter. Not any more.

'You remember that man?' I asked.

'What man?' he replied.

'That man you used to eat with at, oh, what's that place called?'

'You mean the man who's married to whatserface?'

'He used to live in Gloucester Road above that pub.'

'The one with the long dog?'

Later we moved on to world affairs. 'What's that country next to the one with all the refugees?'

'Egypt?'

'No, the one where thingy was in prison.'

'Burma?'

'Yes, Burma. Anyway . . . what was I talking about?'

In a whole hour we didn't remember the name of a single thing, person, place or event. And it is hard to be sharp when you are constantly foraging about on the tip of your tongue for the reason you'd embarked on the story in the first place.

I listen to my children chatting sometimes and they're like one of those executive toys. The ones that are see-through balls with purple lightning in them. I can't remember what they're called. Van de Graaff generators? No, wait, they're the ones that make your hair go funny. Anyway, what was I saying?

Yes, I remember. It's a constant stream of nicknames and wit. Machine-gun comedy in which the belt never ends. Kids have the power of instant recall and can leap like water boatmen from an obscure episode of *Family Guy* to someone's new boyfriend who's a professional Frisbee player: 'He can catch it in his teeth and while he's doing a backflip.'

'It's a dog sport,' said my son sullenly. I found that very funny.

I bet your children are the same, and so on 1 July take them out to dinner. Because I bet you any money it'll be funnier than watching five old men reciting the Four Yorkshiremen sketch. And not quite getting it right.

22 June 2014

Being soft, I've robbed my tortoise of any ambition to go hurdling

While I was enjoying a reflective moment on my hotel balcony in South Africa last week, a vervet monkey strolled into the outdoor breakfast area sporting a pair of extremely marvellous pastel-blue testicles. He sat for a while, legs akimbo, allowing the guests to cop a good look at his package, before climbing onto one of the tables and helping himself to the contents of the sugar bowl.

Except – here's the thing – it wasn't the entire contents. He took only the sachets of healthy and nutritious white sugar. All the Fairtrade left-wing brown stuff and the packets of hideous Canderel sweetener were ignored.

And, of course, if you live in a fairy-tale world of princesses and unicorns, this is proof that the vervet monkey is extremely intelligent. I'm not so sure, though, because while it knows to discard sweeteners, and can open plastic sachets, and throw what it doesn't want into the sea to stop its sexual rivals having it, it can't write a symphony or build a steam locomotive or even read the simplest of books.

It might be intelligent compared with a wasp, or an octopus, or a dishwasher, but compared with us? No.

If it really were intelligent it would speak. It has a tongue and teeth, so it could. But all it says is,

'Sceeeeeeeeeeeeee', which, as far as I can tell, means, 'Oh no, a waiter is coming with a broom handle to stop me nicking all the sugar.'

People say that dolphins are intelligent because they can allegedly be trained by the United States navy to deliver and attach explosives to the underside of an enemy aircraft carrier. But if the dolphin were truly bright he would say, 'You want me to do what?' and swim off to play with his mates.

Dobbin enthusiasts are forever telling people, who are usually on the verge of falling asleep, that their horse is intelligent, but it just isn't, or it wouldn't let you ride round on it. If you asked even the most stupid human to give you a piggyback round some fields because you couldn't be bothered to walk, they'd tell you to get lost.

It's much the same story with my dog. I won't tell you his name because I shall probably be accused of racism or homophobia or genocide, but he is capable of displaying what pass for human emotions.

He does guilt when he has misbehaved and elation when I put on a pair of wellington boots. But if he were bright he'd take himself for a walk and run free rather than allowing me to put a string round his neck and pull his head half off every time he so much as looks at a sheep. Or a lady dog.

I'm sure doggists (doggers are something different) would explain at this point that dogs can display love for their owners and that any animal that is capable of such an emotion must be intelligent. Yes, but if you woke up in the morning and you were just an inch tall

I would be amazed, and I would rush about calling for doctors and CNN to come round. Your dog, on the other hand, would eat you without a moment's hesitation.

All of this should be borne in mind during the continuing discussion in various parts of the world about animal equality. Those in favour want all creatures great and small to be treated with exactly the same respect and consideration as humans.

Through 'corporate outreach' they want to see a world in which 'speciesism' is as frowned upon as racism, in which it is wrong to eat a bacon sandwich, or to save a child from a fire rather than a dog just because the child is human. (If you don't understand any of this, the BBC has a web page on the subject, naturally.)

Hmmm. I worry that in fact we are getting too soft on animals and that by doing so we are actually making them even more daft than they already are.

I have many pets, and even the most rabid animal rights activist would say that they are cared for extremely well. The horses, for instance, have burqas to shield them from the things that give them sweet itch, the pigs have a house and a shady spot in which they can recline, the dogs are fed and loved and walked often, and the tortoise is never encouraged to do things that might cause him stress, such as hurdling.

Because of all this they have no ambition at all, which means they are never forced to think for themselves. They just sit about until a human being arrives with something that half the time they didn't even know they wanted.

You see old ladies in pet shops often buying their cats expensive toys, and food made from the most choice cuts of a dolphin. And this is actually cruel because it reduces the need for a cat to do what cats normally do: ignore you and kill songbirds.

Exactly the same sort of thing is going on in the world's game reserves. I'm not suggesting for a moment that elephants should be left at the mercy of the poachers – quite the reverse. I'd love to organize a day when we hunt and attempt to shoot the idiots who buy the ivory, but trying to manage Dumbo's habitat to make life easier for the poor thing is silly.

All he knows now is to eat and mate and stick his ears out when he's frightened. If we provide him with food and ensure he never knows fear, what's left? Very quickly all elephants would become sex maniacs.

There was some evidence in South Africa to suggest this was already happening. Because after the vervet monkey I'd been watching had gorged on all of the refined sugar, which he'd garnished with some fleas from his navel, he sat on a railing for a little while and then, having established there was absolutely nothing else to do, performed what we must call here a sex act on himself in full view of all the hotel's guests.

I found it rather sad.

29 June 2014

No kisses, no bear hugs, please: there's only one harmless way to say hello

Several thousand years before the baby Jesus was born, men decided that the best way of demonstrating that they had no sword-whirling intentions was to hold hands with people they met. And so the handshake greeting was born.

There were a few subtle variations. When someone shook your hand firmly, while smiling, it meant they were strong and trustworthy. If their hand felt like a piece of wet fish, it meant they had social issues and possibly a hygiene problem. And if they did a strange thing with their thumb on your knuckles it meant they played a lot of golf and had risen with suspicious speed through the police service. Or that they were Prince Michael of Kent.

Oh, and if they used their left hand to cradle the shake, while turning their upper body through forty-five degrees, it meant they were a politician and that they were not listening to a single word you were saying. The swivel was performed simply to ensure that nearby photographers got a good shot of them shaking hands with whatever your name is.

We heard, of course, that Eskimos – or Inuits, as we must now call them if we work for the BBC – would greet one another by rubbing noses and we guessed that this was because it would be stupid to take their hands out of their pockets in such cold conditions.

And we heard too about strange rituals in Japan, where visiting American businessmen would attempt to bow but would in fact make themselves look completely stupid. They'd be standing there with their faces pointing backwards through their knees, and their host would be saying to his colleagues: 'I think this idiot thinks he's Olga Korbut.'

Elsewhere, though, everyone apart from Mrs Queen and Johnny Pope shook hands. And that was fine. But recently, and I'm sure you must have noticed this, every single person in the world now has their own way of saying 'hello' and if you get it wrong you are at best socially inept and at worst a racialist.

I have been to South Africa many times over the years and a handshake has always been fine. Not any more. Now, when you are introduced to someone, you must take their hand, hold it steady and perform what in football would be called a marginal shoulder charge. By the time I'd finished moving down a line of dignitaries, I was extensively bruised, and had knocked one poor man over.

Apparently this is a Zulu sign of brotherly love, and should not be done on the 'street'. Here, if you try to shoulder-charge someone, he will treat it as a sign of disrespect and almost certainly cut your head off. What you must do instead is take his hand in the traditional fashion, but then pivot around one another's thumbs. It's a bit complicated and you can end up with a dislocated wrist.

In America the handshake also seems to have gone out of the window. Here, in order to show that they are black, well-to-do young white men now form their hands into a fist and touch knuckles with one another while saying 'Yo'.

But you don't have to travel abroad to be confused because even in Britain the whole system is a complete mess.

God knows why, but when you have known a chap for some time a handshake is considered to be a bit formal. So what you do is take him in your arms and give him an almighty bear hug. The trouble is that you don't know when in your relationship this will happen: you shake hands with someone for maybe a year and then, one day, he bats your greeting away, envelops you and spends a few moments rubbing his gentleman sausage into yours.

I have one friend who goes even further. The bastard takes me in his arms and kisses me. I've told him time and time again that I find this uncomfortable but it makes no difference. So now, if I see him at a party, I always spend the rest of the night in the lavatory.

Which brings me on to the modern-day problem of greeting a woman. In the past this was easy. You shook hands when you were introduced and then planted a peck on either cheek when you parted. Now, though, you sometimes encounter a girl who wants to greet you with a tender kiss on the lips, which causes problems when you meet one who actually doesn't.

So, you home in with your head canted over and she is coming at you with her head at the same angle. It's like two of the Red Arrows heading towards each other when they haven't previously worked out a game plan. So you cock the other way and she follows suit and now you're in real trouble because the gap is narrowing fast and your heads are swaying from side to side as if you are a pair of Thunderbirds puppets and you are thinking: 'There is no way all this can be coincidental. You must want me to kiss you on the lips so here goes . . .' And next thing you know, she's looking at you as though you are basically a rapist.

It was in New Zealand, however, that I really did come a cropper. To welcome me, a group of semi-naked men came barrelling into the airport arrivals lounge shrieking and waving their tongues about. This was the haka, an ancient greeting designed to let a newcomer know he was facing great strength and unshakeable unity. So when they finished, I thought it would be a good idea to respond in kind.

I racked my brains for the traditional British equivalent of the haka, and in the limited time available all I could come up with was: 'You're going home in an ambulance.' This was considered to be a tremendous insult.

So please, can we just go back to the handshake. It's simple, it communicates a great deal, there's no genital contact and no bruising and it's impossible to cause offence by getting it wrong.

6 July 2014

What becomes of the broken-hearted's toasters? I'll show you

A few months ago I came here and said that most of the world's museums are filled almost entirely with stuff that's not very interesting. And that the only reason we pay them a visit is because we think it will make us look more brainy than we really are.

I suggested that each of the world's most well-known museums has only one really exciting exhibit and that all of these should be brought together in Dortmund to create a visitor experience that everyone would want to see. No old coins. No broken pottery. No muddy arrowheads. Just the dinosaur from London's Natural History Museum, the pickled baby from Ho Chi Minh City in Vietnam, the *Mona Lisa* from Paris, the Bell X-1 supersonic aircraft from Washington, the shroud from Turin and so on – all under one roof.

It was a brilliant plan, but it all came a bit unstitched on a recent visit to the Croatian capital, Zagreb. It was a lovely sunny day, and I had nothing to do until the evening so I thought I'd have a little look at the market and maybe people-watch at a pavement café for a while.

But no. As usual, the snob gene kicked in and I realized that I couldn't possibly come back from a trip to the former Yugoslavia and say I'd spent my only day off looking at pretty girls in the sunshine. So with a heavy heart I found myself asking the hotel concierge if there were any museums I ought to visit.

He suggested something called the Museum of Broken Relationships, and that sounded like it mightn't be so bad. I figured it would be full of exhibits from the civil war: some guns and maps and James Blunt's tank, perhaps. So yes. I would go and I would perch some spectacles on the end of my nose and look grown-up and interested and sensible.

It turned out, however, that the Museum of Broken Relationships had nothing to do with the war. But I'm glad I went because it was poignant, bewitching, intelligent, sad and, at times, very, very funny. It was the only museum I've visited where every single thing on display was utterly fabulous.

Most of the exhibits are bits of worthless tat, but each is accompanied by a brief story from a former owner about why it had mattered in a previous relationship. It could be an old boyfriend's hat. An ex-wife's T-shirt. There was even an axe that a cheated-on spouse had used to smash up every stick of her errant husband's furniture.

There was also a battered pocket watch that an elderly chap had bought for his younger lover. 'I thought she liked things that were old and broken,' said the accompanying text. 'But it turned out she didn't.'

All of us have, at some point, been through the breakdown of a relationship. We know how much it hurts, and how it's the smallest mementos that can turn us into sobbing, shoulder-heaving wrecks. We all think that nobody has suffered as we are suffering now. But this museum tells us that they have.

And then it gets even more awful. One person has donated the suicide note left by his mother. I had a very lumpy throat and prickly eyes reading that one. But right next to it was a piece of electric equipment with a short accompanying note that said: 'Wi-fi router: we didn't get on.' I laughed a lot at that. I felt the man's pain.

I also enjoyed the toaster that had been donated by someone along with a note explaining how the relationship with a girlfriend had ended, how she had taken everything and he had been able to save only the toaster, which he said was great 'because now she will never be able to toast anything ever again'.

You can feel the bitterness right there. You know this is a man who even now, even after he has donated the last reminder of his girlfriend to a museum, will still be incapable of having a drink without feeling an overwhelming need to call his former lover to try to win her back and call her a bitch and slam the phone down.

I don't doubt for a minute that anonymously donating an item that symbolized a relationship is extremely cathartic. And, of course, it will provide an element of closure – 'I've given the bloody thing away to a museum.'

But there's more too because I bet that every single one of the people whose stories are on display sits at home every day, praying that the former lover is in the museum reading it.

Especially the woman who could have been Anastasia Thingy from the Fifty Shades of Embarrassment books. She had donated a pair of high-heeled red shoes that had been bought for her by a dominating man who had made her do all sorts of intimate things. She must hope that one day he drops by and dies a thousand deaths as he realizes it's him she's talking about.

Certainly, I must confess, as I moved from exhibit to exhibit, that I felt a tinge of fear that the next would be a teddy bear with a severed head and a short accompanying story about a former local newspaper reporter with an interest in cars and a very small gentleman sausage . . .

Apparently the Museum of Broken Relationships now has such a wide and varied collection of donations that it's currently touring, and if my internet is to be believed, it's now at the Southbank Centre in London. I haven't had time to go but I wouldn't be at all surprised to find that one of the exhibits is a battered red briefcase alongside a note from someone identified only as MG of Surrey.

'I worked in the Cabinet for four years, during which time I used this red briefcase every day. I was good at my job and loyal, and people liked me. But then one day, for no reason at all, my boss called me into his office and demoted me. My new job is to make sure that all the other employees do as they're told. Well, if he thinks I'll put my back into that, he's got another think coming, the snot-nosed little so-and-so.'

20 July 2014

Heathrow's a hole. Our new runway must be at London Hogwarts

As we know, first impressions count. If someone greets you with a weak, drooping handshake, you know immediately you will not like them. They can stand there, telling you that they work for Nasa and Médecins sans Frontières and once saved a party of disabled schoolchildren from a rampaging tiger, but it won't matter because you'll be thinking, 'Yes, but your hand is like a bit of wet cod, which means that deep down there's something wrong with you.'

Halitosis is another problem. And so are dirty fingernails, beige shoes, culottes, Princess Anne hair and that white gooey stuff that some people get at the corners of their mouth. Oh, and for reasons I can't explain, I'm especially troubled by people who have thin lips. They can appear to be amusing and kind, but I'll have already decided that actually they are not.

The writers of American box-set television drama are aware of the importance of first impressions, which is why at the start *Breaking Bad* contained casual sex and nudity. The same with *Dexter*. The same with *Orange Is the New Black*.

Estate agents get it too, which is why even a lopsided and damp wreck will go for more than the asking price if prospective buyers are greeted with the smell of fresh bread as they walk through the door.

Unfortunately, countries don't seem to have cottoned on. If you are greeted at the airport by a cheery and welcoming immigration official, you will think, 'I'm going to enjoy it here.' Whereas in America, with its sullen and rude attitude, you always emerge onto the taxi rank thinking you're not.

Here in Britain, however, the problem is far more fundamental. Because, as journeys go, the drive from Heathrow into London is right up there with the hand-cuffed shuffle prisoners are forced to make on the green mile. West Drayton. Osterley Park. Brentford. A rick-ety bridge that was erected as a temporary measure forty-odd years ago. Then Hammersmith. Nobody is going to emerge from a ride such as that thinking, 'Mmmm. I'm going to love it here.'

And things are even worse if visitors land at Gat-wick, because a management team that couldn't be trusted to run a greengrocer's has ensured there aren't enough baggage handlers, which means nobody's suit-case arrives on the carousel until it's time to fly home.

If you are foreign and you are told you have been waiting for your bag for two days because staff won't work at weekends, you are going to think the whole of Britain is crap. And that's before you learn London Gatwick is nowhere near London.

The situation is even more dire for people arriving in Britain by boat. They may be looking forward to their holiday, visiting the Shambles in York and Warwick Castle and London. But first they must get out of what they've been told is the Garden of England – Kent.

We must assume that if they're in a car, they arrived

in Calais via a super-smooth but expensive-to-use French autoroute. So they will probably be quite pleased to find out that Britain's motorways are free. Until they actually use one.

My God, the M20 is bumpy. Progress would be more smooth if they'd simply left it as a field. But eventually, with double vision and a disintegrating ribcage, they are directed onto the M25 – where things, unbelievably, get even worse. Happily, however, they will not realize this, because traffic here is moving at the same speed as tectonic drift. After an hour they will be geologically closer to their start point in Europe than London.

But then Maman and Papa will turn to the back seat and tell their children – who by this stage have started to shave and have periods – that they are now turning off the M25 and going into London. Trafalgar Square. Big Ben. Tower Bridge. The Queen. Everyone is excited.

It says on the map that the road they've chosen to travel into London goes past golf clubs and woods and commons, and it all sounds very wonderful and Harry Potterish, but mostly it's an ocean of pebbledash interspersed with the occasional parade of shops where you can get a loan or have your nails trimmed. But that's about it.

What if you want to stop for something to eat? Well, unless you fancy a kebab, you can't. It's rubbish. This is Surrey. It's supposed to be pretty and tranquil and expensive. But, honestly, the journey from Leatherhead to Long Ditton, past Surbiton and the Chessington World of Many Traffic Cones, is as featureless and as boring as a journey from Venus to one of Jupiter's outer moons.

I realize, of course, that it's much the same story with most of the world's cities. But they have built motorways that penetrate deep into the centre so visitors don't have to see them. On the way into London from the south, though, there are no motorways. You are forced to pass through the underbelly, and that's like seeing someone's bowel and lower colon before you meet them for real. 'Yes, I appreciate you are witty and wise and well travelled but I can't concentrate on any of that because I have seen your digestive system.'

This is something that should be borne in mind as we continue to hunt for ways of increasing the number of planes that can land at our overcrowded airports. It's all very well looking for sites where there's a limited impact on newts and bats and where residents will suffer the least.

But towering above these requirements should be the first impression visitors get after they've landed. That's why the new airport must be built near Stratford-upon-Avon. Passengers arrive in Anne Hathaway's cottage and are then transported on a Harry Potter steam train down through the Cotswolds, alongside the Thames and into London past Windsor Castle.

Think about it. When visitors arrive at your house, you don't ask them in via the coal chute and the cellar.

3 August 2014

Dear MPs: Weather hot, people being buried alive. Wish you were fixing it

Last week there was a story in one of the tabloids saying that the BBC had offered me a new £12m contract even though I'm a member of the Ku Klux Klan and I spend most evenings erecting burning crosses on Lenny Henry's front lawn.

Obviously, this is laughable because it's August, which means no one at the BBC is drawing up contracts, or doing much of anything at all. Half the senior management is staying at agreeable farmhouses in Tuscany with Polly Toynbee and Alan Rusbridger and the other half is in Edinburgh at some kind of warm wine and canapé festival.

Furthermore, no one read the story because everyone is currently on a beach, trying to clear away half an inch of spurted Piz Buin from the screen on their Kindle ebook reader. And come to think of it, no one with any sort of journalistic qualification could have written it either, because hacks – they're all away as well.

We always used to laugh at the French for upping sticks and moving to Biarritz for the whole month of August and we wondered how Italy could continue to operate as an actual country when for four weeks no one did anything at all. But now we are just as bad.

We learnt recently that more people in Britain have jobs than at any time in history – and what? We are supposed to be surprised by this? I'm not, because every job now needs two people to do it. One for when the other is on holiday.

I was in Italy last week – working, amazingly – and the Amalfi coast was full to overflowing with everyone you need in Britain to take out your teeth, mend your computer, empty your bins and fix your sprained ankle. And then in Tuscany, behind the constant background noise of strimmers and lonely dogs, you could just about make out the sound of various mildly left-wing journalists helping themselves to another plate of arugula before questioning the man from the BBC about why he gives any airtime at all to those brutes from Israel.

Rome? Well, there were several thousand Americans pointing at the Colosseum and wondering how the Roman Empire had put up such an enormous amount of scaffolding but that was about it. You wanted lunch somewhere? Forget it. The restaurant was shut.

I'm in London now and I feel like the Omega Man. And it's all very well saying that traffic is light but there's nowhere to go. Nobody's having a party. Nobody is suggesting we go out for a drink. Nobody's having a meeting. And I can't stay in either, because all there is on the television is news from the only people who do seem to be doing any work at the moment – the Israeli army and those Islamist fanatics in northern Iraq.

I was in that part of the world a couple of years ago and it was beautiful. The cities of Dohuk and Erbil were quiet and graceful and the countryside in between had an aura of peace and serenity. And now? People are having their legs chopped off and their shoulders dislocated before being hanged from lampposts. And women and children are apparently being buried alive.

And thousands have been trapped on a mountain, homeless and starving in the savage heat, simply because several hundred years ago someone in their village chose a different religion from someone in the next village.

And what are we doing about all this in the West? The Americans have dropped some bombs on . . . we're not quite sure what. The French have sent a couple of hand grenades. And we're handing out bottles of water, and offering to send a few guns to the Kurds – if they ask for them. And that's about it.

There seems to be a sense in the West that the days when we could march into the Muslim hinterlands and sort everything out are well and truly over.

I mean, we don't even have the will these days to secure a field in eastern Ukraine, even though this is a friendly state, in Europe, and the field in question was being held by nothing more terrifying than six greengrocers with AK-47s and a plumber whose head was buried in the instruction manual for a rocket launcher that had a best-before date of 1967.

But surely, you're thinking, while the public has no stomach for a scrap, our leaders must be capable of rising above the apathy and doing what's right. So why are we only sending water and making half-hearted offers of weapons? Why not send military advisers to help whip the Kurdish army into some kind of shape?

Ah, well, here's the thing. If we just send water and

blankets, it's a humanitarian project. If we send in the military, to do anything vaguely militaryish, we'd need parliamentary approval and it's August, so guess what: parliament's on holiday.

It was on holiday this time last year when the Syrian rebels were calling for help. And MPs were so annoyed about being told to put down their Jack Reacher books and come back to work, they voted not to do anything at all – wisely, with hindsight.

Who knows? It may be wise on this occasion to sit on our hands and allow time and history to take their course. But I would at least like to think that Westminster was full of people in the know advising our elected leaders on the situation and the implications, so an informed decision could be reached.

Because it's well over 40C on that mountain in Iraq. There's no food. The Islamist fanatics are coming and they have a cruel streak as wide as their tanks. They will show no mercy and as a result all the stranded refugees cannot simply hang on until September when MPs get back to work.

Of course, at this point, the MPs will be jumping up and down , saying that they can't be expected to sacrifice their holiday every time there's a crisis – and I agree. People need a break. But do we need four weeks? If you think so, drop me a line. But don't expect any kind of reply, because I shall be in St Tropez until the middle of September.

17 August 2014

Make a fortune with fake food – no one's got the taste to catch you

Now that Great Scotland Yard is to be converted into a luxury hotel and the few remaining policemanists are either investigating Sir Richard's trip to Sheffield almost thirty years ago or standing round the Israeli embassy dressed up like ninja skateboard enthusiasts, I'm surprised more school leavers aren't considering a career in crime.

There are a few issues, of course. For example, there's no point robbing a bank, because all the money held inside doesn't exist in big piles of crisp tenners that can be carried outside to your waiting Ford Transit van. It's all theoretical.

And if it were easy to steal by using a laptop from the privacy of your own bedsit, then people would be doing just that. And they aren't. Instead it seems the world's brightest and most brilliant computer hackers are only able to steal photographs of Jennifer Lawrence's breasts, which net them the grand total of no money at all.

Perhaps this is why French thieves have been reduced to gassing British caravannists and, as they sleep in a fug of carbon monoxide, breaking in to steal their . . . what, exactly? Their Tupperware? Their Swingball set? Their stash of *H&E* naturist magazines? Certainly it's my bet that no caravan contains a safe full of exotic jewels and cash.

This is the problem. You don't even find cash in most parking meters these days. Which may sound disheartening for anyone who's decided they don't want to be an estate agent or a florist. But happily there is a solution: food fraud.

As we know, the Chinese are extremely adept at making copies of well-known western brands. You can buy fake Chanel handbags, Hermès scarves and Rolex watches. On a recent trip to Burma I found a fake Sony Walkman that was perfect in every way, apart from the fact that Sony was spelt 'Sonk'.

Closer to home, we are regularly asked to buy pirated films and television box sets. The art world is forever being duped by immaculate forgeries and there's a man who comes to my door a lot with a van full of Bukhara rugs that I just know were knocked up in Ealing, west London. So if you can fake a rug, why can't you fake food and wine?

Apparently this has been tried in China but it didn't go well. The fraudsters decided to beef up baby milk with the industrial chemical melamine and six infants died as a result. There was a similar problem in the Czech Republic after a batch of fake vodka and rum, which had been laced with methanol, wound up on the streets. More than forty people died after drinking it.

Don't be disheartened, though, because I'm absolutely sure it is possible to sell fake food that doesn't contain ricin or anthrax or anything that is even remotely fatal.

Take chicken. It requires effort to rear the birds these days. To keep the animal rights people at bay, they have to be housed in four-poster beds and given access to hot-and-cold running satellite television. When their time comes, they must be killed kindly using nothing but lullabies and summer breezes. And the resultant meat must be transported in ebola-style sterile tents to the supermarket, within hours.

But I'll let you into a little secret. Pretty much everything tastes like chicken, so why not set up an operation selling chicken that is actually rat, or crocodile?

Many restaurants already employ this technique. It was discovered back in April that more than half the lamb curries tested in Birmingham contained other, cheaper meats such as beef or turkey. And could the customers tell? Not when the dish was smothered in 1,400 gallons of vindaloo, they couldn't.

Of course you might imagine that if you went round selling chicken that was actually hamster you would be arrested very quickly. But in the whole of Buckinghamshire, where there are about 2,500 farms, and many more businesses associated with selling and retailing food, there are only twenty trading standards officers. In Worcestershire the figures suggest there are only six. The result is simple: you're not going to get caught.

And even if you do, the court is not going to treat you like a drug dealer or a people trafficker.

Which brings me on to an even better idea. Faking household names. Simply make some cola cans, put a silly name on the side such as Greg or Dude, fill them with water and pass them off as Coke. By the time anyone finds out what you've done, you're long gone.

Or better still, go upmarket and target the food snobs. I'm amazed that the world isn't full of fake Fortnum & Mason hampers containing Spam dressed up as pâté, and rubbish wine being passed off as Château Mouton Rothschild. Because who would ever know?

Not me, for sure. During a press junket many years ago BMW played a practical joke on journalists. We were taken to a chateau in France and invited to try the wine . . . which had been laced with vinegar. Like many colleagues, I made lots of heartfelt 'ooh' and 'mmm' noises before buying a case. So could I tell the difference between a bottle of newsagent plonk and a 1945 Pétrus? Nope. And the chances are you couldn't either.

It's easy to tell a fake Rolex from the real thing. Just wait a couple of minutes and the second hand will fall off. Or take it in the rain and watch it dissolve. But with food and drink it isn't easy at all. Could you, for instance, tell the difference, in a blind tasting, between expensive acorn-fed ham and ham from a pig that's eaten nothing but used tea bags and cigarette butts?

Could you tell Norwegian Jarlsberg from cheddar, or caviar from lumpfish roe? Could you tell the difference between a truffle and your next-door neighbour's verruca?

The world of food snobbery is ripe for fraudulent exploitation and the government plainly has recognized this because, as we speak, ministers are studying proposals for a sort of national FBI-style food-crime unit.

I shouldn't worry, though, because it won't happen, and even if it does, the people it employs won't be able to tell the difference between caviar and lumpfish roe either.

7 September 2014

Bombing a spaniel is a step too far, Mr Putin – we're sending in the SAS

When the ebola virus started to run riot in west Africa we were all very sympathetic but nobody rushed to the kitchen with a chemistry set and a handful of Petri dishes to see if they could develop some kind of antidote.

It's much the same story with Ukraine. We keep being told that this is a war that's being fought if not on our doorstep then certainly at the bottom of the garden. And we worry about it in the same way as we worry about our neighbours' marital difficulties. Which is to say, we don't really worry at all.

And then there's this grubby business in the Middle East. It's horrific what these Islamic extremists are doing, we all know that. But we're then not completely sure what exactly it is they are doing. Or where they are. Or what they want. Or what on earth we can do to stop it happening. So we turn over and go back to sleep.

The world is full right now of many serious problems and I think it's fair to say that almost none of us would cross the street to help solve any of them. No, don't argue. You wouldn't go to Sierra Leone to be a nurse. You wouldn't sign up to help the Ukrainian army. And what exactly have you done to help the homeless in Syria? Exactly, and neither have I.

And yet when someone set light to a dogs' home in

Manchester, half the city leapt from their beds and ran into the raging inferno to rescue as many of the inmates as possible. Afterwards, when the flames had been extinguished, so many people rushed in their cars to see if they could adopt a damaged dog, the police had to issue a stay-at-home alert, saying that roads were being overwhelmed.

Twenty-four hours later the charity that runs the home announced that it had received donations totalling more than £1m. That's a million quid to rehouse the 150 survivors. And that works out at at least £6,666 per dog. They will be eating peach and peacock for the rest of their ermine-lined lives, that's for sure. And there's nobody in the whole country, or what's left of it – I'm writing this before the vote in Scotland – who would begrudge them a single penny.

Apart perhaps from a *Coronation Street* actor called Jack P. Shepherd, who went on Twitter to say: 'I have a million "hot dog" jokes.' Straight away there were calls for him to be sacked. You can make jokes about almost anything these days and keep your job. But dead dogs? No. There is a line in the sand, and Rover, trust me on this, is on the other side of it.

It's not just dogs either. It's all God's creatures. I posted a picture on Twitter recently from a shooting party in Gloucestershire and plenty of people stepped forward to say that killing birds is wrong and that, er, we should wait for the partridges to die of old age before we put them in the oven.

Then you have the animal rights extremists who want to kill all scientists. And we're not talking about half a dozen teenage girls here. I'd be willing to bet there are more people in Britain who would lay down their lives for a tortoise than there are who would lay down their lives for Allah.

Which tells us something we have known for a very long time. Britain is a nation of animal fanatics. Here we have believed for centuries that you must feed your horse before you feed yourself. That you can slaughter Johnny Foreigner and win a medal. But that if you cause a dog to be sad, it's time to put your affairs in order and start oiling your service revolver.

Which gives me an idea. An idea that would end the apathy and malaise we currently have about world affairs.

At present, reporters are keen to show us the human suffering in various conflicts. All through the turmoil in Gaza we saw ruined houses, broken businesses and shattered limbs. We heard about dead civilians, and the next morning we went to work as though nothing had happened. But what would happen if we were to be shown pictures of a dead dog?

'I say, Jean. The Israelis have mortared a dog. Well, that's that. I shall organize a bring-and-buy stall in the village hall immediately.'

And Ukraine. At present no one has much of an appetite to poke President Vladimir Putin in the eye. We know he is a megalomaniac with one hand on the nuclear red button and another on the tap that feeds continental Europe with gas. He frightens us.

But one photograph of a dead hamster would change all that. If we thought that soldiers in his employ had hurt an animal, the SAS would be scaling the Kremlin walls by tomorrow lunchtime.

All of which leads me to the sick bastard known as 'Jihadi John'. He stands there, in the desert, spouting sixth-form common-room politics and then cuts a hostage's head off. When I read in the papers about his antics, it makes me seethe with rage and fury. But then, like you, I turn the page and spend a little while reading about some minor celeb's braless trip to the Chiltern Firehouse restaurant in central London.

I cannot believe that I do this. A British man was beheaded on the bloody internet. Somewhere out there, in this green and pleasant land, he has a family who are suffering from a grief that would beggar belief. And what are we doing? Rushing to Manchester to adopt a dog.

We need an event that changes our priorities. Which is why I'm wondering what would happen if an actor dressed up in black robes and stood in a desert somewhere, mimicking Jihadi John. And then, on camera, shot a dog.

Tragically, that would cause the nation to choke on its cornflakes. It'd get us on the streets. It'd cause us to stop worrying about a celeb's side boob.

And who knows? We might even start supporting any action that would bring the real murderer to justice.

21 September 2014

Make no mistake, lives were at risk

It all started to go wrong while we were filming on a mountain in the world's southernmost ski resort, just outside the city of Ushuaia in Tierra del Fuego.

We knew Ushuaia was the port from which the *General Belgrano* had sailed on its doomed voyage at the start of the Falklands War and we knew that anti-British feelings still run hard and deep, here at the bottom of the world.

As a result we were on our best behaviour. We were posing for all photographs, and happily accepting requests for autographs. The sun was out. All was calm. We were even referring to the slopes as 'gradients'. Certainly there was no suggestion that we had walked into the middle of a war we thought had ended thirty-two years ago.

But then came word from the bottom of the mountain. Some protesters had arrived and were keen to let everyone know they were unhappy with our visit. Our producers tried to explain that we were there to film at the ski resort and then to host a game of car football in the city. England v. Argentina. The Bottom of the World Cup we were going to call it.

They were not listening. They were angry. They said that they were not violent but that a group of men from the local truckers' trade union were on their way. And that when they arrived things would definitely turn nasty. Our local fixers advised that we stop filming immediately, leave the cars on the gradients and go to a nearby hotel.

'This is a mafia state,' said one onlooker. 'Best you do as you're told.'

So we did, but going to the hotel did not work. A gang of people were waiting there. They said they were war veterans, which seemed unlikely as most were in their twenties and thirties. Bonnets were banged. Abuse was hurled. The police arrived and immediately breathalysed Andy Wilman, our executive producer – we're not sure why.

Richard Hammond, James May and I bravely hid under the beds in a researcher's room while protesters went through the hotel looking for us. The car park was filling up. More were arriving. This was starting to get ugly.

Back at home, newspapers were saying I had caused the problem by arriving in this political tinderbox in a Porsche bearing the numberplate H982 FKL, which if you turned the H into a 1 and transposed the K and the L, could have been seen as a reference to the 1982 Falklands War.

This, however, was untrue. The car had indeed arrived in Argentina with those plates, but two days into our journey, when we were in Chile, a Twitter user pointed out the problem so we removed them.

When we arrived in Tierra del Fuego the car had no plate at all on the front and a meaningless jumble of letters and numbers on the back. And no, it wasn't

W3WON. Which it would have been if I'd been trying to ruffle feathers.

The numberplate, then, wasn't the issue. But something was causing more and more people to arrive at the hotel. Twitter was rammed with messages from locals saying they wanted blood. One said they were going to barbecue us and eat the meat.

'Burn them. Burn their cars,' said another. Mob rule was in the driving seat.

Government officials then stepped in, saying we were no longer welcome in the city, that our safety could not be guaranteed and that we needed to leave Argentina immediately. Plainly they had given us permission to visit simply so they could make political capital from ejecting us when we arrived.

The problem was: how do you leave when the streets are filled with mobs with pickaxe handles, paving stones and bricks? No one had an answer to that one.

Chile is a spit away across the Beagle Channel but we weren't allowed to cross it because Argentina says it owns the land on the other side, too. We therefore gathered up as many possessions as we could, rounded up the girls from our party and made a dash for the airport.

That night we were in Buenos Aires among sensible Argentinians who couldn't believe what had happened. And the next morning we were back in Britain.

We felt that with us three gone the situation might calm down. It didn't.

We had left behind twenty-nine people; cameramen,

sound recordists, fixers, locals and producers. They had to make their escape overland in a ragtag collection of hired 4x4s, trucks and the three 'star' cars that they had been told to remove from the ski resort.

They faced a long, bumpy and gruelling six-hour trek to the Chilean border and safety. But in the first town the locals were ready. A lorry was blocking the road and as our convoy approached, it reversed at speed towards them, forcing our guys onto the verges, which were filled with people who made it plain they wanted blood. Bricks were hurled, windscreens were smashed and two of the party were cut by flying glass. But they made it through.

And then they had a problem. The next city was Rio Grande. And the word from there was that 300 cars and thousands of locals were setting up an ambush. This turned out to be true.

The British embassies in Chile and Argentina were doing their best to get a police escort. And the nine of us who had escaped were in a hotel room in Buenos Aires working through the night to find a plane and an airfield from which they could get out because, make no mistake, lives were at stake.

Meanwhile, a chase had begun. Our guys were being herded towards the ambush.

So they abandoned the star cars, which were filled with hundreds of thousands of pounds worth of camera equipment – and my new hat – at the side of the road. And took off across the frozen wilderness to a remote border post where there isn't even a road. You get into Chile by fording a river.

We had to get a tractor there to pull them across. And it had to be a fast tractor because we knew our convoy was being chased by the thugs. And you try finding a fast tractor at 2 a.m., in the middle of nowhere. All credit to producer Al Renton that he did it.

With the batteries dying in the convoy's satellite phone, we lost contact and for six hours had no clue whether they had been caught. Whether our friends were alive or dead. That was a long night.

I still haven't had a chance to speak to any of them but I know they were held at the Argentine border from 3 a.m., when they arrived, until 11 a.m. Why? To allow the thugs to catch up? Who knows? All I really care about is that they are now in Chile and safe.

Tierra del Fuego is not listed as a problem for visitors by the Foreign & Commonwealth Office but there is no question in my mind that we walked into a trap.

I know mischievous newspapers in Britain have said it was all my fault because of the numberplate. But that wasn't even mentioned down there because the plate in question had been replaced.

No. We were English (apart from one Aussie camera guy and a Scottish doctor) and that was a good enough reason for the state government to send twenty-nine people into a night filled with rage and flying bricks.

'Look what we've done,' they will say at the next elections. 'Sent the English packing.'

That is true. We got our arses kicked. But there is a glimmer of a silver lining in the whole sorry affair. The game of football would have been a good ending for our Christmas special. But we've been gifted something even better by the region's politicians and their rent-a-mob cohorts.

I'd like to say 'Gotcha' at this point. But I won't.

5 October 2014

You reckon you can talk like us, Hank? Well isn't that just awesome

I spent a couple of weeks recently in South America, where I met a man with the weirdest accent in all human history. He had been born and raised in Argentina but his dad was from Lancashire, which meant that when he spoke English, it was with a mixture of Bolton vowels and Spanish lisping. Think of it as the verbal equivalent of a sausage in a sherry trifle. Both fine individually, but together? Wow.

And what made it even more strange was that because his parents were both English, and English had consequently been spoken at home when he was growing up, his use of the English language was perfect. He described a truck, which he pronounced 'trook', as 'grotty'. Which is the sort of word you can use properly only if you are actually English.

We see this problem a lot with Americans, who use the word 'bloody' when over here, to try to make themselves sound as if they belong. But they invariably put it in the wrong place in a sentence where it simply bloody doesn't belong.

Which brings me on to the footballer David Luiz. Upon arriving at Chelsea, the Brazilian learnt about the word 'geezer'. He liked it a lot. And used it a lot. But not once was it ever appropriate. Only a real Londoner knows how and when to use it correctly.

In the same way as only a Yorkshireman knows how to say 'the'. When people from other parts of the country attempt it – Robert Carlyle in *The Full Monty* springs to mind here – they abbreviate it to 't' ', and that's wrong. It's actually completely silent. You just pause where the word should go and nod slightly to signify you haven't said it. This made buying tickets to see the band The The extremely difficult for people in Leeds.

William Hague knows what I'm on about here. And if you're in Surrey you don't, and if you try you will look idiotic.

I encountered a problem with this sort of thing recently while skiing with a charming Dutch family in the Alps. Keen to let them know that I paid attention to their ways and their culture, I described someone who had queue-barged us as a 'swaffelaar'. It's a word that has no equivalent in English because 'swaffelen' means 'to bash one's penis against the Taj Mahal'.

It turns out, however, that in Holland this is not a word that you trot out in public. It is the worst word in the world. It's a thousand times worse than our c-word. I know, I know. Maybe it's because they smoke a lot of dope, but whatever – by trying to be friendly I ended up offending my new friends and never saw them again.

Languages are a bugger. And there's another example right there. A German may be able to say it perfectly in a perfect Oxbridge accent. But he will never understand quite how to use the word for an unspeakable act in such a way that it's harmless and acceptable.

I can speak French. I know how to ask for directions to the post office and I know how to ask for the pen of my aunt but I once said to an officious Calais dockworker, 'Vous avez des idées au-dessus de votre gare.' And I couldn't understand why he looked so perplexed. This is because knowing the French words for things doesn't actually make me French.

All of which brings me on to a book called *Watching the English*, a new edition of which has recently been published. It's by an anthropologist called Kate Fox, whom I met once. I can't recall what we talked about because I was too busy dribbling. She is very attractive. Anyway, in her book she says that there's one word that sets the English apart: 'typical'.

She may be on to something here. The Americans have 'awesome', which is used to describe the holy grail, the Grand Canyon, the moon landings, a cup of coffee from Starbucks, a new pair of socks and everything in-between. It signifies that they are an upbeat people who are extremely pleased with pretty much everything.

'Typical' signifies that we are downbeat and resigned to the fact that everything will always go wrong.

We use it, Fox says, in the event of all disasters, ranging from burning the toast to the outbreak of the Third World War. But there's more to it than that. Because when we use it – and this comes naturally only to those who were born in Britain – we sound simultaneously peeved, stoically resigned and slightly pleased that our predictions have been fulfilled.

Other expressions Fox identifies as being quintessentially English are 'mustn't grumble', 'oh, come off it' and 'as per usual'. All of which are similarly depressing.

But she seems to have missed the expression that I think best sums up the English. 'It's all right for some.'

If you buy a new car in America, neighbours will come round and whoop and say 'awesome' a lot. Whereas here neighbours will twitch their curtains and say to their husbands, 'It's all right for some.'

Obviously, if you hadn't bought a new car it would have made no difference at all to the onlookers, but they don't see it that way. They think you've done it deliberately to make them feel small and useless. They don't want to live in a world where some people fly business class while they're in the back with the chickens and straw. And they don't want you to eat good food in a restaurant while they sit at home with a bucket of fried chicken.

This would stump anyone trying to learn English. They might be able to say the words but most would wonder why it was necessary. 'I see. So if my neighbour sends his child to a private school, I must not be happy for him. I must adopt a sour face and say, "It's all right for some."'

It's why the citizenship test can never really work. Because while immigrants may know who the Queen is, what the post office is for and how queues work, they will never understand our relentless pessimism, our pettiness and our appalling hatred for those who are better off than ourselves.

12 October 2014

No, it's me, Ermintrude – you're just not my idea of a significant udder

If for some reason you had to up sticks and get out of Britain, where in the world would you live? I'm not talking about retirement here, or running from the long arm of the law. I'm talking about living a normal life, working and raising a family.

We are forever being told by world economic forums that your No. 1 choice should be somewhere such as Canberra in Australia, or Zurich in Switzerland. They argue that nothing bad happens in places such as these, and that's probably correct. But nothing good happens either. I think if I had to live in Zurich I would shoot myself in the head after a week or so.

I've posed the question to many people in the past few weeks, and San Francisco is mentioned often. I can see why. It's very pretty, the people speak an approximation of English and the locals whoop slightly less often than people from other cities in America. But I don't think your calf muscles would enjoy the hills very much, and the fog would surely become wearisome after a while.

New York? Yup, it's very exciting but I bet you'd quickly become fed up with being shot. Rome? Brilliant but it's hard to get a plumber and the television is terrible. Paris? Lovely for a springtime visit with someone you love. But if you lived there you'd be run over within a month.

Many people would choose a tropical island of some sort and I can see the appeal of never having to wear a jumper again. But every day you'd sit on the beach instead of doing any work, which means that pretty soon you'd be a mumbling, penniless alcoholic, stumbling about in the tourist areas trying to steal people's wristwatches.

If I had to leave Britain – and the way things are going with this Argentina business, I might – I'd move to Copenhagen. The climate's the same as ours, so I wouldn't be tempted to sit outside drinking wine all day. The restaurants are delightful, and there's a wonderful sense of fair play.

There is, for example, a voluntary tax on flashy boats. Owners don't have to pay it, but they all do. Because they know that if they can afford a 60 ft Sunseeker they can also afford to help pay for the nation's streetlamps.

If you were to bookend the concept of civilization, you'd have one of those half-ape humans at one end, bashing bison over the head with sharpened bones, and at the other a girl on a bicycle in Copenhagen. I like Denmark a lot. I like its furniture, I like its stereo systems, I like its bacon and its detectives. I also like its Lego, apart from when it's the middle of the night and I'm barefoot and I've trodden on some.

However, even here in this cobbled and cheery paradise, it turns out that there's a problem. The Danish agriculture minister, who looks like he's from a boy-band, announced last week that he is set to fly in the face of Scandi-liberal politics and ban Danes from having sex with animals. Yup. He says no matter how much you love your goat or chicken, you may not express that love physically because it would be non-consensual.

There are so many questions raised by this, I hardly know where to start. How can the courts prove that it's non-consensual? Maybe the goat or the chicken was up for it just as much as the farmer. And more importantly, how widespread does a problem have to be for a government to step in and make it illegal?

Here in Britain our government is busy trying to sort out the mess in Syria and send help to the ebola-ravaged regions of west Africa, but in Denmark they are busy instead debating the rights and wrongs of 'doing the funky chicken'. This would imply that the practice is out of control.

Maybe it is. In the past ten years France, Germany, Belgium and Holland have all outlawed bestiality, so perhaps enthusiasts in these countries – and indeed Britain, where it's been illegal since 1290 – are visiting Denmark so they can be inside a cow and the law at the same time.

We worry – well, I do – when we hear about single fiftysomething men going by themselves on a holiday to Thailand.

So should we be similarly concerned when we hear about someone dousing themselves in a bottle of eau de manure and setting off for a fortnight in Odense?

I'm not sure we should, because if you are attracted to farmyard animals, I can't imagine that you worry too much about what the law says. It's the court of public opinion that would cause you the biggest headache.

I can understand why cannabis users would head to Holland or Colorado to flaunt their hobby in public. But telling people you're going to Copenhagen so you can hang out with a cow? No. I don't see that.

We can tolerate MPs who send photographs of themselves naked over the internet, and we can even sympathize with those who pay ladies to pick imaginary nits from their hair. But sex with a goat? I think we'd draw the line at that, whether it were illegal or not.

Things, however, seem to be different in Denmark, because a recent poll showed that 76 per cent of the population are in favour of a ban. Which means 24 per cent – nearly a quarter – of all Danes are either ambivalent or in favour. Yup, more than a million of them either don't mind if you have sex with a sheep, or would like to have a bash themselves. Which is odd in a country where the former supermodel Helena Christensen would be regarded as 'averagely pretty'.

Certainly it means I shall have to rethink my emigration strategy. Because while I like Copenhagen a lot, I fear that if I lived there I would spend most of my life thinking twice about shaking hands with everyone I met.

19 October 2014

Strewth, down under, feminists don't wear T-shirts, they carry rifles

So I was in a helicopter. The doors were off, I had a rifle and the pilot was hovering 100 ft from the ground so I could shoot a wild pig. Later we butchered it and over a few beers fed it to his pet crocodile. This is the all-male, rough-and-tumble image we have of life in Australia. But it's wrong . . .

The following morning, all I wanted was a cigarette and a cup of coffee in the morning sunshine, but down under, this is no longer really possible.

I made the short 300-yard walk from the restaurant to what was billed as the smoking terrace. But a waiter sprinted over to say that the actual smoking terrace was even further away, in a cave by the bins. And that, yes, he could bring me a coffee, but only in a paper cup.

This is because he'd have to walk past the swimming pool. Never mind that it was completely fenced off, and accessible through a gate so complicated that only a child could possibly work the latch, there was a chance that he would trip over one of the signs advising visitors that it was 0.2 metres deep, that diving was banned, that no lifeguard was on duty and that the water may contain traces of diarrhoea.

I'm not sure there's a country on earth where the global perception is as far removed from the reality as Australia. We see it as a land of spiders and snakes,

where you are born drunk and with an ability to barbecue yourself. But it's not like that at all.

Today the unholy alliance of the nanny state and the
trade union movement has created a culture of health
and safety so all-consuming that no one is allowed to
die, or even fall over. Cigarettes are sold in packets
made from the diseased lungs of dead babies, drinking
outside is not allowed and there are speed limits on
roads where there is literally nothing to hit. You could
have a crash lasting two hours and you'd still be fine.

The last fatality from a spider bite was in 1979, and
every single river in the outback is garnished with floats.
If the daily checks reveal they are riddled with teeth
marks, the rangers know that an inquisitive crocodile
is around and the entire area is then sealed off to the
public, until it has been captured, humanely, and transported in sumptuous comfort to an area where there
are no people.

And it's not just in the area of safety that Australia is
different from the global perception. There's also the
question of feminism. When we think of women in
Australia, nothing springs to mind at all. We think of
their rugby, and their cricket and their pick-up trucks
and their beer and their barbecues and their Crocodile
Dundee. And in all of that, there are no women at all.

I've racked my brains and the only well-known Aussie women I can think of are Germaine Greer, Elle
Macpherson and Kathy Lette. And they all either live,
or have until recently lived, in Britain. Australia then,
we imagine, is a misogynistic nightmare where a woman
can only get a job if she has ginormous breasts.

Nothing, in fact, could be further from the truth. I first noticed this at a remote iron ore mine in the Northern Territory. I was there, in a hard hat and a hi-vis jacket, watching the approach of a tipper truck. It was as big as a block of flats, it was carrying 50 tons of rock and it was about as manly as anything I've ever seen in my whole life. It even said Territory Iron on the cab. There was a danger that if I'd looked at it for any longer, I'd have made myself pregnant. But it was being driven by a woman. And so was the digger that had loaded it.

Later, at a nearby airfield, I was mooching about when an extremely attractive girl emerged from the engine bay of a light aircraft. She was wearing vaguely unbuttoned overalls, carrying a spanner and had oil streaks on her face. And I'm ashamed to say I thought that maybe I'd stumbled into some kind of soft-porn calendar shoot. But no. She was an aircraft engineer.

This went on and on. The pilot who flew missions to a remote farm was a woman. And here one of the sun-hardened cowboys was actually a fourteen-year-old cowgirl. In a Darwin newspaper there was a story on the back page about a seven-a-side football match. The accompanying photograph showed a player tackling another player. It looked normal, but one was a bloke and the other wasn't.

We think we have feminism worked out in Britain. All BBC panel shows must now feature at least one woman, Ed Miliband is to be seen in a T-shirt declaring his love for women's rights and there are many women bosses. But compared with Australia, we are miles off the pace.

If you went to a quarry in Britain and found that the 50-ton trucks were being driven by women, you wouldn't mind. But you'd notice. It'd be the same story if a woman came to mend your lavatory, or fix your roof. And if your light aircraft had been serviced by someone who looked like Katie Price you'd certainly make a few jokes about that at the next lodge meeting.

You could argue that in Australia's Northern Territory they have to use women to drive trucks and make up the numbers in football teams as the population density is 0.4 people per square mile. And that here in the UK where there are more than 650 people per square mile it's a different story.

But is it? We are forever being told that we need migrants to come to Britain to drive our buses and do our plumbing. But how can that be so when half the indigenous population think they've broken through the glass ceiling just because their website selling second-hand children's clothes has fourteen followers?

Australia can keep its ludicrous attitude to health and safety, but we should look long and hard at how it has created an environment where the person in the back of the helicopter on the pig-shooting mission is a teenage girl. And she's got a rifle as well.

9 November 2014

The call of nature means warts and misery. Heed the Call of Duty instead

As the world teeters on the brink of economic collapse, it's not surprising that many people are starting to wonder if we should go back to the old ways: making do, mending and knitting our own jumpers from leaves and peace beads.

Last weekend I dropped in on a Cotswold hedge-laying competition, where I was enveloped in a reassuring blanket of deep calm. All around, countrymen with pink cheeks were to be found hacking away at trees with their home-made hammers, and then bending them over to create a living, natural barrier. There was no talk here of the Footsie or Vladimir Putin, and after an hour or so I was consumed with an urgent need to eat a ploughman.

It was a similar story the next night on the BBC television series *Countryfile*. One blonde girl with a regional accent went to visit a man who sat in an unheated shed all day making rakes from boiled trees. And another with no regional accent built an oven out of mud. There was even a thin veneer of Prince Charles and, ooh, it all looked too lovely for words.

If you were watching, and since there's never anything else on television on Sunday night these days, you probably were, I bet you were thinking, 'Yes. I am fed up with the rat race. I want to grow some rosy cheeks and wear a Viyella shirt and make my own cutlery out of excrement . . .'

But let's just pause for a moment and consider those rakes. I can see that they might have been jolly useful for clearing up the entrails of a drowned witch in about 1347, but today what's the point when you can get a free electric leaf blower with every five gallons of unleaded?

And what of that oven made from mud? It was used to cook bread that we were told was jolly yummy, but was it more yummy than if it had been baked in a kitchen? And what happens when your mud stove gets wet? And who wants to cook everything in the garden? In an oven full of worms and disease?

Not that long ago the television was full to overflowing with a programme presented by a man who would spend some time with a tribe in a jungle. Each week he would finish off by saying, 'We have a lot to learn from these simple people.' Really? What?

They would tell us that to cure a headache they would strip the bark from a worawora tree and then mix the sap with bits of grated parrot before soaking the resulting paste in the heart of a palm nut that had passed through the complicated stomachular system of a ruminant. And the man in short shorts would nod and pull earnest faces and at no point did he ever say, 'Well, where I come from, we just go to Boots and buy some Nurofen.'

In another TV programme about the traditional ways we were shown a fisherman called Sulbin who would leap out of his canoe and then walk about on the sea bed, 65 ft below the surface, holding his breath for what felt like about two hours as he looked for a fish to catch. And?

Is this how we are supposed to catch our supper? By walking about on Dogger Bank until our eyes pop out? Let me put it this way. What do you think Sulbin would say if you offered him an aqualung? Or one of those gigantic Spanish trawlers? 'Oh, thanks, mate. But I prefer to burst my lungs every day because that's traditional.'

All of this was brought into sharp focus on a recent trip to Australia, where a guide took me into a gorge and in hushed, reverential tones showed me some Aboriginal art. Well, I'm sorry but it was no different from the art you see on every fridge door in Wandsworth's Nappy Valley. I'm afraid I may have said that out loud.

The truth is that if you want to see great art you should go to a museum in Europe, not a ravine in the outback. It's the same story with theatre. Cameron Mackintosh will give you a better night out than a bunch of traditional dancers on Easter Island.

And New Zealand's supposedly scary haka routine is nowhere near as effective as a bunch of English football yobs singing, 'You're going home in a f****** ambulance.' I think I may do a television programme on this: I shall call it *Everything Is Better in London*.

It is, though. I look occasionally at silly western tourists nosing around markets in the dustier parts of the world and I think, 'What are you hoping to find here that you could possibly want to buy?' Because here's the thing: if it were desirable in any way it would be in Harrods.

It would. Nobody, no matter how ethically sustainable and traditional they are, would say to the buyer from a London department store, 'No. I do not want to take a hundred pounds for this birdcage that I have made out of moss. I would rather sell it to an idiot in the local market so that foolish Americans can haggle all afternoon and then buy it for £3.75.' The only reason you can't buy it in Harrods is: it's no good.

I know from my day job that the traditional ways never work. When someone says a car is 'handmade', they mean the door will fall off. And it's the same story with everything. A birdcage made in a Tunisian shed will either rot, or give your much-loved parakeet some kind of fatal disease. And a living fence, though lovely to behold, will not keep your horse in the paddock as well as an electric one.

The solution, then, to our economic woes is not to retreat into the woods and live with a face full of warts on a diet of bark and beetles. Instead we should foster the dribble of growth by buying an iPhone 6 and the new Call of Duty game. Which is a lot more fun than hopscotch.

23 November 2014

Is that room service? I'd like flies, diarrhoea and a frog chorus, please

A couple from Mickleover in Derbyshire are suing Thomas Cook, saying their romantic Turkish honeymoon was ruined by disease, insects, small birds and diarrhoea so catastrophic that their ten-year-old daughter ended up in hospital on a drip.

They say that during their stay at the four-star resort and spa (my alarm bells are ringing already) there were birds and flies in the restaurant and that at the buffet (there go the alarm bells again) they witnessed staff putting new food into the trays on top of old food.

Anything strike you as odd yet? Nope. Me neither. And nor am I even slightly surprised to hear that the couple's daughter ended up in hospital with what are described as various 'gastric' events. She's ten. She's in Turkey. And I'm sorry to say this, but in these circumstances it happens.

I'm scratching my head now, trying to remember if I've taken my children abroad without one of them ending up in a surgery or a hospital suffering from some kind of food-, insect- or sun-related incident. And, er, nope. Nothing's coming to mind.

In fact I'm trying hard to think of any hotel I've used that would not make lurid tabloid headlines if I were that way inclined.

Certainly I cannot forget the converted old sheep

station in the uplands of Bolivia where I was woken
one morning by a cleaner who entered my room without knocking, shuffled past my bed with a mumbled
'Buenos días', went into my bathroom and took a noisy
dump before shuffling out of the room with a frankly
insufficient 'gracias'.

The couple from Derbyshire say that at their hotel in
Turkey staff were slow to clear up puddles of vomit left
round the pool by other children. To which I have two
things to say. It's the job of a parent to clear up a child's
sick, not some hapless immigrant waiter who's working
for tips. And if they think that's bad, they should have
tried a place in Uganda I visited last year.

The mattress on my bed was caked in so many
encrusted bodily fluids it was hard to know what sort of
crime scene I was sleeping in. Plainly, though, it had
ended with a murder and the evidence had simply been
covered by what had once been a sheet.

The worst hotel I visited was in Turin. It was on the
hottest, most humid night I've experienced – and I'm
speaking as someone who has been to Cambodia. Outside, there was an overnight lorry park that reverberated
to the sound of a hundred diesel engines ticking over to
keep the air-conditioning in the sleeper cabs working.
At 4 a.m. there was a lot of revving as the lorries finally
left, and then came the banging as the market traders
arrived to erect their stalls. As sleep was impossible, I
spent all night in the pitiable shower, trying to prevent
myself from spontaneously combusting. Through rage,
or heat, or a combination of the two.

And now I am reminded of the hotel in South

America where the room's only plug socket was to be found actually in the shower cubicle. That's the sort of arrangement that can give a man a whole new hairdo.

And what about all those dreadful American motels I've used over the years, all of which came with the same drone from the nearby interstate and the same hourly wake-up call from the rumbling ice machine on the landing outside.

And then in the morning the man who was almost certainly responsible for the crime scene I'd visited in Uganda would offer me some coffee he'd made two months earlier by putting one granule of Nescafé into the tepid bath from which his ageing father had just stepped.

Or then there are those hotels – by which I mean every hotel in the world – where you trudge two miles to your room, only to find your electronic key card doesn't work because it's been within 200 yards of someone's mobile phone. Or the place in Turkey where the barmaid refused to sell me a drink because, 'I don't like the English.'

I travel a lot these days with Richard Hammond, who is from Birmingham and is therefore so badly put together that he gets an upset tummy as soon as he arrives in Calais. If he were to sue every foreign hotel in which he's spent the night not knowing which end to hang over the lavatory bowl he'd be even richer than the *Daily Mail* claims he is.

Which brings me on to our film crews. They're all seasoned travellers. They live out of suitcases for much of the year. Some are so well versed in hotel life that they can even understand how to fill in a laundry form. And on almost every single foreign trip we make, a handful always end with bottoms like broken garden taps.

In Thailand last year the crew of about fifty was reduced in just two days to a functioning outfit of ten.

Obviously, away from work, when I travel for pleasure I stay in hotels that are absolutely lovely in every single way. But even the very best have birds in the restaurant, insects in every room and, as night falls, a symphony of frogs to keep you awake till dawn. At which point you're woken up by a child who's been bitten by a mosquito on the eye, or leant on a poisonous tree, or eaten some dodgy chicken.

Maybe the couple from Derbyshire do have a genuine axe to grind. Maybe they were staying in a godawful hotel – it certainly looks that way in the pictures – and maybe the chef did all his cooking with a urinary disease and unwashed hands.

But my bet is this: they're used to living in Britain, where there are no frogs, or birds, and the water's fresh and the government sends round people in hi-vis jackets to eradicate all risk from every possible place where it may lurk. I said last week that everything is better in London. And, as our couple from Derbyshire have now found out, everything is better in Mickleover as well.

30 November 2014

Well, hello, neighbour. Just call me Erik and spend all my money

You wouldn't believe what it's like these days in Norway. I spent some time last weekend in Oslo and there was no dirt or grime of any kind. The roads gleamed with a shimmering newness, not a single bulb in a single thing wasn't working and every barrier to every private car park rose like a saluting US marine.

At Thief Island, a regenerated district in the centre of the city, everything was sparkling and wondrous. All the buildings were sharp and cool and edged with a blue LED brilliance, and yet the materials used to make them all put you in mind somehow of Whitby's olde worlde centre. It's the best modern architecture I have seen.

And that's before we get to the hotel at which I was staying. The manager was the Duracell bunny. He served the drinks, checked you in, never went to bed and was always smiling the smile of a truly content man.

Outside, there was a kindergarten, and outside that were rows and rows of mini scooters and trikes, all brand new and all paid for by the government. State kindergartens are now so good in Norway that the private alternatives are resorting to madness to compete. One even offers gourmet food and lessons in how to gut fish. For four-year-olds.

Big school is obviously even better. Because every single restaurant is staffed by people who speak forty-three languages and know everything. In one a girl who was so beautiful I kept fainting leant over at one point to explain that my understanding of the Northern Ireland assembly was incorrect. And I checked later. She was right.

There'd be no point screening a Norwegian version of Alexander Armstrong's quiz show, because how would you be able to find a pointless answer in a country where the random selection of 100 people would know everything.

It's not just education and aesthetics, either. The healthcare system is so good that no one has died in Norway since 1982.

The reason all this is possible is tax. I've done some research and it seems that there are many layers of complex structures that mean everyone gives about 102 per cent of what they earn to the government. Unless they earn more than £300,000, in which case they pay about 150 per cent. Then there's VAT, which means everything costs about a million pounds. Apart from cars, which are ten million pounds.

It's odd. Deep-veined socialism doesn't work when it comes in jackboots or fur hats. But dress it up in a sturdy white polo-neck jumper and it seems to be brilliant. Especially when it's mainly fuelled by oil.

In various Middle Eastern countries that sit on reservoirs of the black gold, the money earned goes straight to the royal family, who spend it on yachts and watches. In Russia it goes to John Terry and Gary Cahill, and in

Britain and America it goes to the shareholders of the oil companies. But in Norway the biggest oil company is 67 per cent owned by the state.

So it gets the revenue from that, in addition to every penny everyone earns, as well as £200m every time a tourist buys a beer, and the upshot is simple. If you ignore various weird fiefdoms such as Qatar and Luxembourg, along with Singapore, Norway is the richest country in the world. So. Why can't we do that here?

Well, here's the thing. Would you trust your MP to run a gigantic oil company? No, really. It's a tricky business, with all the refining and shipping and negotiating at complicated international meetings, and I'm not sure you'd entrust that to a man who got his job simply because he has a ready smile and nice hair.

Let's not forget, shall we, that Gordon Brown spent all day as chancellor poring over the books, yet somehow he sold more than half our gold reserves when prices were at rock bottom. And it'd be the same story if we put an MP in charge of our oil.

And then what? How do you find him to express your disappointment? Do you know his name? Do you know where he lives? Do you even know if he's a he?

This is the great thing about small countries such as Norway. The chances are you were at school with the prime minister, and that you live next door to the chap in charge of transport. So if you run over a pothole on your way home, you can pop round and ask him to fix it. This means the politicians are truly accountable. They know that if they have taken all of your money, they had damn well better do a good job when it comes to spending it. Or you're going to poke them in the eye at the supermarket next weekend.

That can't happen in a country with a population the size of ours, because I'm willing to bet you've never met an MP in your local supermarket. Or anywhere else. Which means they've never met you. Which means that they don't really care about your money. Which is why, when everything was nationalized here, nothing worked.

The solution, then, would seem to be obvious: more devolved powers to the regions. Break Britain up into bite-sized chunks, because that way you will have a greater chance of knowing the man who's entrusted to spend your cash.

That all sounds very sensible until you look at, oh, I don't know, let's say Tower Hamlets, or Rotherham. These are local councils run by local people, and do they work well? Are they efficient? Would you trust your local councillor to get the oil from under the North Sea and then achieve the best price at the market? No. And neither would I. Because I don't know his name either.

This is the root of the problem, really. Recent figures suggest that about 70 per cent of people in Britain do not know their neighbours' surnames or what they do for a living.

Which means that the only people we really know and can therefore trust with our earnings are our own families. Which is why the Norwegian system couldn't work here. Because in our hearts we don't want to pay any tax at all.

7 December 2014

Can't cook, won't cook, want everything on a plate: it's Generation Idle

Last week the Tory peer Baroness Jenkin put down her game of Candy Crush, summoned a bank of plebs from beyond her duck house and said that Britain is awash with food banks these days because 'poor people don't know how to cook'.

Naturally this was seen as yet another example of government being completely out of touch with how real 'hard-working families' live, and as a result she was forced to burn herself at the stake for being a witch. Which is a shame, because she had a point.

Of course, if you take the big wide world as a whole, it's extremely foolish to say poor people don't know how to cook, because obviously they do. If you go to the back streets of Calcutta or Tanzania, or anywhere without a benefits system, you'll see lots of extremely poor people making the sort of food that causes you to drool. The absolute nicest thing I've put in my mouth was a pho – a noodle soup – made in Vietnam, on a pavement fire, by a woman with more warts in her mouth than teeth.

In Britain it's a different story. A young couple went on the television news last week to say they were so poor they regularly went to bed hungry and, I'm sorry, but they were in a house, with a roof, and they have access to a doctor and a hospital. What's more, their street has lighting and if one of them has a problem, they can call on a police force to help them out. Poor? They simply don't know the meaning of the word.

If they were really hungry – and I mean properly close-to-death hungry – they'd have been wandering the lanes where they lived, picking berries and scrumping apples.

The fact is – and this is what Jenkin was trying to say – there are many people in this country who are so thick, spoilt and greasily lazy that they think Jamie Oliver is a creature from outer space and that *The Great British Bake Off* is science fiction. Not that they know what science is. Or fiction. Or even an oven.

They sit there on their leatherette button-backed settees in front of their gigantic benefits plasma TV, expecting David Cameron himself to come round with a bucket of KFC and party seven of Worthington E. And when he doesn't, they say they're hungry.

Which immediately prompts a bunch of Liberal Democrats to burst into tears and realize that other people have a greater need for the tinned salmon and Sutherland crab spread that have been languishing in the back of their pantry for forty years. And that it'd be a nice gesture to give it away.

Inevitably this causes the lunatics to rush about in their cassocks and mitres saying that because Britain is one of the richest countries in the world it's absurd that people here can only stay alive thanks to charitable donations and food banks. Which then prompts a bunch of bleeding-heart sandalistas to say that the government should be distributing food to the poor rather than leaving it up to volunteers.

Aaaargh. What's the matter with these people? You could say that of any charity. Why should that poor boy who died of cancer recently have had to rely on Twitter to raise money for research into the illness? Surely the government should be doing that too. And what about the care needed by soldiers who've had their legs blown off while serving their country? Or all those important buildings that need renovating, or all the ducks and bees that are on the verge of extinction?

Would you put someone from the government in charge of the Amazonian tree frog? No, and neither would I.

I would not choose to give anything to a food bank – not in this country at any rate – but if a little old lady wants to give away some Green Giant sweetcorn and a packet of Spangles, who's complaining? Not me, not the person who receives the food and certainly not the little old lady, who can go to bed bathed in the comforting glow of having done something nice for someone.

This is what church leaders and their communist cohorts simply cannot get into their stubborn, stupid heads: that if the state provides everything, it leaves no space for individuals to lend a hand.

And anyway, can you even begin to imagine what a food bank would look like if the government got its hands on it? All the staff would be forced to wear hi-vis jackets and spend all their time filling in forms to ensure the food was picked yesterday, in a sustainable organic way, by a horny-handed son of the soil.

And you wouldn't be able to get into the place because of all the wheelchair ramps, and there'd be nothing on the shelves because it was either out of date, or it had fallen foul of some obscure European law about what shape it should be.

When will people learn that the government cannot be trusted to run anything? And that if we put it in charge of feeding the thick and the lazy, pretty soon there'd be a diarrhoea epidemic and people in the streets saying, 'Bring out your dead'.

Whereas what we have now is a load of unintelligent people who think Oreos grow on trees and that spaghetti is hoop-shaped, milling around in an abandoned branch of Woolworths, passing the time of day with big-hearted neighbours who have a bit of time on their hands. And that to me seems fine.

Sadly, though, none of this could be discussed in the wake of Jenkin's observations because she said poor people don't know how to cook. What she should have said is, 'They can't be arsed to cook'. They want it oven-ready, prepacked, ready salted and handed to them on a plate by people who work for a living so they have the wherewithal at the end of the month to do something kind.

14 December 2014

My dark night of Top Fear

In among all of the televisual holly and the jolly seasonal jumpers, BBC2 will be screening the not-at-all-Christmassy *Top Gear* special in which our thirty-one-strong film crew is attacked by a large mob of stone-throwing Argentine thugs.

By now most people know exactly what happened. Despite claims that it was all just an amazing coincidence (yeah, right) it's obvious I deliberately chose to drive across Argentina in a Porsche sporting the numberplate H982 FKL – a clear and provocative reference to the 1982 Falklands War.

It was all a typical piece of *Top Gear* japery, only this time it went wrong and – you know what – we had it coming. We'd pushed our luck for too long and it simply ran out. Many commentators actually sided with the Argies, thanking them for standing up to our gung-ho blend of racial stereotyping and polar bear-killing nonsense.

Since our return, the Argentine ambassador in London, Alicia Castro, has been stoking the fire. Rightly so. That's her job, and she's good at it. She demanded the BBC apologize and scrap the programme, and when that failed she released a series of statements claiming I'd exaggerated the incident and that when we abandoned the cars we tried to set them on fire for 'dramatic effect'.

The message, then, is clear. We had tried to provoke the Argentinians into some kind of response, and when that didn't work, because they were all at home knitting jumpers and making daisy chains for handicapped children, we had invented some kind of a kerfuffle to boost the show's ratings.

Well, you will get a chance to see for yourself what happened when the two-part Patagonia special is screened on 27 December and 28 December. I'll warn you, though, it's gruesome. I've watched the footage of the attack, grabbed on camera phones as our convoy attempted to get through the Tierra del Fuego town of Tolhuin, and it's like a scene from John Carpenter's *Assault on Precinct 13*.

You get the sense that there's a never-ending supply of – let's call them 'youths' – coming out of the darkness, hurling anything they can lay their hands on. You wouldn't have wanted to be in any of the cars, that's for sure.

But I'm not going to start another war of words here. Ms Castro has presented her arguments and soon we shall show you what we saw. Then, as I say, you can make up your own mind.

Of course I don't doubt that after the programme is aired many people will say that I should be ashamed of myself for putting all those innocent people in danger and that it really is time for the show to be turned into something more benign – *Countryfile* with windscreen wipers perhaps. But here's the inconvenient truth. On this occasion, for once, we did nothing wrong.

I've given up telling people that the H982 FKL

numberplate was a coincidence because absolutely nobody believes me. I have the email chains that show exactly why that particular car was chosen – only two were available at the right time for the right price and the other was black, a colour that doesn't work on television.

Everyone on the show knows the car was not chosen for its numberplate and no one believes them either. Because *Top Gear* has a reputation: we're troublemakers. Driving across Argentina with a Falklands War message hidden in the numberplate? That's exactly the sort of thing we would do.

You're right. It is. I mean, we once turned up in Germany in three Spitfires, and when our Australian colleagues came to the UK to take us on in a selection of motor sport events we had them collected from the airport in a prison van – so they could come 'home' the same way they had left.

It all sounds very terrible but when you actually analyse our 'crimes' we really aren't any worse than those three other fools who earned a living from falling over on *Last of the Summer Wine.*

Things we've been accused of in the past include 'driving into a tree'. Er. Everyone's done that at some point. Or saying that an Albanian we'd apparently murdered was 'fat'. But he was. We were also criticized for driving over Botswana's salt flats even though we actually screened a scene with the then vice-president of the country wishing us well. And then there was the time I drank a gin and tonic while driving to the magnetic North Pole. I can't even be bothered to justify that one.

Oh, and then we were accused of faking after the incident in Alabama when a small army of burly locals decided that because we'd driven through their state in cars bearing messages such as 'Nascar sucks' and 'I'm bi', it'd be best if we were murdered.

It definitely wasn't faked, I can assure you of that. From a personal point of view, I would say it was even more scary than what happened in Argentina, because in the Southern states the missiles tend to come from the end of a Remington pump-action shotgun.

Top Gear is always in the newspapers for something or other. It's almost a sport, finding two people on Twitter who've been offended and then running a story saying we've sparked fury.

As a result you may have the impression that the *Top Gear* production office looks as if it is one of Jordan Belfort's Quaalude trips – birds, Rizlas and a handful of discarded dwarfs behind the filing cabinets. But right now there are more women than guys and it's a proper healthy mix of backgrounds, sexual orientation and colour. We even employ one man from Birmingham.

It's quiet too, for the most part, and studious because to put a show such as *Top Gear* together takes a lot of effort. You sign up for *Top Gear*, you wave goodbye to a social life, that's for sure.

Of course there have been some actual proper mistakes in the past but that's inevitable when you've spent the past twelve years sailing as close to the wind as you dare. We once had two Ofcom rulings against us for a single show: a record, I think. But I don't mind saying sorry when I've messed up.

I particularly enjoyed apologizing to the Mexican ambassador after I'd accused him on TV of being asleep a lot, because he took me into the back of his embassy and forced me to drink my own body weight in tequila. I still socialize today with his cultural attaché.

There are those who after the untransmitted n-word incident and the regrettable 'slope' palaver say we are basically a bunch of little Englanders but if that's the case, why is *Top Gear* the world's most watched factual programme? If we really were a bunch of modern-day pound-shop Enoch Powells, to coin a phrase, why would 350m people in 170 countries around the world regularly watch us?

'Mon Dieu. *Top Gear* is on the television again ce soir. Let us sit down and watch ze, 'ow you say, UKIP enthusiasts making fun of our onions and our surrendering.' It wouldn't happen. Well, it does in Poland – they quite like it when we are rude about Germans but that's an exception.

Some say this global success is the only reason *Top Gear* hasn't been put in the recycling bin by the BBC. But that's unfair. Yes, *Top Gear* makes a lot of money, which is then ploughed back into the pot, but there's more to it than that. The BBC takes a licence fee from a wide range of people and is therefore duty-bound to provide a wide range of programmes: hymns, strange sea creatures, Gary Lineker, Alan Yentob, wannabe singers, Wimbledon, *Cash in the Attic*, and three clowns falling over and catching fire. There's space across four channels for all that.

Well, I hope there is because we're just putting the finishing touches to what will be our twenty-second series. It starts in late January and will see us endlessly thanking the Chileans for their help after the incident in Argentina, then thanking them again. Then, after we've showered praise on Chile and talked about the magnificence of its hotels, its food and, yes, even its weather, we shall be cattle herding in Australia's Northern Territory, racing a hovercraft through St Petersburg, making fun of the French car company Peugeot, designing our own ambulances and trying, but not very hard, to rescue Richard Hammond who was marooned on a frozen bear-infested mountain in Canada.

To film that episode, the crews chose to travel in a selection of GMC off-roaders. And I couldn't believe it. 'What's the matter with you idiots?' I said. 'Have you learnt nothing after what happened in Argentina?' GMC is plainly a veiled reference to General Montcalm who was defeated by General Wolfe at Quebec.

Strangely the Canadians either didn't notice, or did and didn't mind. Certainly nobody threw any stones. So we can learn a lot from these simple people. Except the way they pronounce roundabout . . . And there you are. I'm at it again. I've learnt nothing either.

And on that bombshell . . .

21 December 2014

Guns down, survivalists – it's the cheesemakers who'll inherit the earth

For several million dollars you are now able to buy a second home deep in the dreary flatlands of Kansas, buried deep underground in a former nuclear missile silo. There's no fresh air, no view and not much to do, and all your neighbours will be gun enthusiasts. Tempted? No. Neither am I.

The apartments are the brainchild of a chap with a tucked-in polo shirt who believes that soon the world will collapse and that in the ensuing anarchy vast marauding hordes will roam the land, killing and eating anyone who isn't living up to 174 ft underground, behind 9 ft of concrete, in a silo full of automatic weapons.

Defence seems to be quite important in his sales pitch. 'If someone tries to climb the fence, we can stun them. If they try to break into the system, we can put an end to that.' I think he means 'shoot them'.

It's all slightly bonkers, of course. Or is it? Our friend in the tucked-in polo shirt – I haven't actually seen him wear one but I bet he does – talks about ebola, another global financial crash, terrorism and all sorts of geological issues that may bring about the end of society as we know it. And argues that he's simply being prepared.

Apparently this is becoming a big deal in America.

There are many people called 'preppers' who really do believe that the end is nigh and that they should prepare by buying some gas masks and soup now, along with a few automatic weapons. And maybe the odd pump-action 12-bore shotgun. And a few pistols.

It's easy to dismiss all this as Americans using paranoia as an excuse to do what they want to do anyway: go camping and shoot stuff. It's in their genes because they are all descended from people who travelled from somewhere else very recently and could only survive by camping and shooting stuff.

Obviously, over here, on the civilized side of the pond, we do not fancy the idea of 'prepping' for post-apocalyptic survival because if it comes to a choice between tenting and being dead, most of us would tick the box marked 'Kill me'. Camping is the preserve of the very young and the terminally idiotic. And we will shoot something only if we are wearing tweed shorts.

There's another difference as well. Americans have a fundamental mistrust of their government. They look at what happened after Hurricane Katrina hit New Orleans – people waited five days for federal agencies to deliver water, and that was just a bit of wind in one city – and say that in the event of a global emergency it'd be every man for himself.

We're different. We moan all the time about our government, but when all is said and done we're happy to sit about playing Monopoly and nibbling on that old tin of corned beef that's been at the back of the pantry for years until someone in authority sorts everything out.

You may recall the film *Shaun of the Dead*. In the

middle of the zombie attack, the hero, played by Simon Pegg, comes up with a plan: 'Go to the Winchester, have a nice cold pint and wait for all this to blow over.' In Hollywood they head for the hills with their guns.

However, I wonder. What would we actually do if the problem didn't blow over, if there was no government and no one in authority? What if there was no military, and no police or emergency services of any kind? What if there was no food at the shops, no electricity and no phone service? What if you woke up tomorrow in the Stone Age? What would you do?

You can't head for the hills with a gun because you haven't got one. And even if you have, and you are able to shoot a deer, then what? Could you peel it? Would you be able to gut it without being sick? Thought not.

So what could you do? Could you, for instance, make a candle? It sounds simple. You soak some string in some paraffin and then wrap it in a tube of wax. But where do you get the string, or the paraffin, or the wax? I don't know.

So what about a pencil? Nope. Sorry. I've seen lead in its natural state and I'm not sure I'd be able to roll it into a cylinder and then insert that into a hollowed-out twig. And even if by some miracle I managed to succeed, what would I write on? Because I have absolutely no clue how to turn a tree into a sheet of paper.

Over the years I have acquired a special set of skills, but in a world where civilization has fallen to pieces I'm not sure there'd be much call for someone who can drive round a corner too quickly while shouting. I'd be useless and dead in a week.

I have only one survival skill. It's this. If you hollow out a palm nut that's been through an elephant's digestive system, you can use it as a whistle to attract a bird, which will then lead you to a bees' nest that will be full of honey. I'm not sure, however, that this would be of much use in Chipping Norton, where there are no palm nuts. Or elephants.

Which brings me back to that silo in Kansas. I'm sure they think they've thought of everything. It has a pool, a cinema and a shooting range, but could they make cheese? Could they manage a colony of bees? Could they grow an onion or make string? Because if the world is hit by events that cause society to break down, these are the skills we shall need, not the ability to waste people who are climbing over the fence.

That's why our friend in the tucked-in polo shirt is doomed. Because the sort of preparations you actually need to make to survive aren't interesting or manly and don't involve anything made by Glock. He'll die. But, weirdly, a little old lady in a cottage in Devon who has spent her life making do and mending – she'll be fine.

Have a very happy new year. See you on the flip side.

28 December 2014

Ah, you're a tonsorial architecture consultant . . . I wanted a barber

For years we've been told that in polite society you should never open a bout of small talk by saying: 'What do you do?' But what are the alternatives? 'What's your favourite jungle?' 'What do you think of the situation in South Sudan?' 'How long is your gentleman sausage?'

I was once trapped in an upside-down armoured personnel carrier in Sweden – don't ask – and as we had some time to kill before we could be rescued, the officer sat the crew and me down and said: 'Right. So how much do you all earn?' That didn't work at all.

Back in the 1980s I spent most of my life at dinner parties in Fulham, south-west London, eating awful spaghetti bolognese to the musical accompaniment of Brothers in Arms, and it was jolly useful to discover that the man to my right worked at Goodyear, Stickleback and Bunsen Burner because then I could explain my flatmate was at Nose, Kosygin and Ovary and immediately we'd have a conversation cornerstone on which we could build something useful.

Back then, small talk was easy because everyone did one of three things. They worked in the City, in which case you'd turn to the person on the other side and talk to them instead. Or they worked in advertising, in which case you could relax, knowing the evening would be sparkling. Or they were estate agents, in which case you'd empty the fondue pan on their heads. Everything was clearly defined. Everything was easy.

Only once was I ever stumped.

'What do you do?' I asked the man to my left. 'I sex the Queen's ducks,' he replied.

Sadly, in my early twenties, I didn't have the gumption to look amazed and say, 'What? You make love to them? Or you go down to St James's Park and explain to Her Majesty that the ones with green heads are men ducks and the ones with brown heads are lady ducks?' So instead I just said: 'Oh,' and turned to the girl on my right who, mercifully, worked at Knight Frank.

But then along came *Blind Date* and everything started to change. Because every Saturday evening the nation would sit down and watch a girl with preposterous hair and a large forehead explain to Her Cilla-ness that she was a retail marketing consultant. 'You're a shop assistant,' I'd scream. But it was no good because Her Cilla-ness was on to the next contestant, a girl from Leeds who was a beverage and comestible manager. 'Why can't you say waitress?' I'd bellow.

This had a profound effect on the nation's small talk. Because suddenly no one was prepared to say what they did. Hairdressers became business managers, strippers became business managers, tyre fitters became business managers. Everyone else was a consultant and everyone had marketing in their job title, apart from plumbers who suddenly became technicians, ambulance drivers who became paramedics and firemen and women firemen who all became firefighters. All of this meant you had to keep digging to find an answer that you weren't very bothered about in the first place.

'Really?' you'd say with glazed eyes, a heavy heart and sagging shoulders. 'You're a business marketing consultant manager. And what does that involve?'

I knew one girl in the late 1980s who would tell strangers she was a business consultant manager. Then, under further inquiry, she would say she worked in advertising, for the creative team. If you could be bothered to question her for longer she'd explain what accounts they handled, and which office she worked at, and then only after you had ripped the plug from the nearest electric appliance and threatened to shove the bare wires into her eyes would she say that she was a secretary.

Today things are even worse because even after you have waterboarded the person to your left at a dinner party and held a knife to his wife's throat as you scream: 'No, but what do you do for a living?' you will still have absolutely no idea what they're on about.

I met a man the other day who explained that he uses money he doesn't have, and which doesn't exist, to buy companies that have gone bankrupt. And somehow this provides him with enough income to run a house in the Caribbean and a snipe shoot.

Another man at the same party said he rents shares from people and sells them. Which sounded to me like a fancy way of saying he was a thief.

I know one girl who takes pictures of bits of lace and puts them on Instagram. I started out pretending to be interested in how this qualifies as a job but then I became genuinely fascinated. So much so, she thought I was being sarcastic and clammed up.

My daughter was described by the Mail Online last week as a marketing consultant. How does it know? I have lunch with her twice a week and I've tried – really, I've tried – to get to the bottom of what her business does but it baffles me. It's something to do with the internet.

Normally the conversation ends with her rolling her eyes and saying: 'Daddy. A lot of businesses are run by old people who don't understand social media so they have to employ young people who do.' Wow. This means she is taking money from people who don't know what she does with it. Go girl. And can I come and stay when you have a Pershing superyacht in Portofino?

Last weekend I had a look through the appointments section of this newspaper and discovered that someone is offering £67,000 a year for a 'road user director' and someone else wants a 'chair'. What's the successful applicant going to say when he's quizzed at a dinner party? 'I'm a chair.' That's ridiculous.

And then of course we have the *Guardian*'s jobs pages, which are full of opportunities for people to do health and safety stuff that simply isn't work at all. Seriously, how can you earn a living by trying to stop people falling over?

Then again, how can I earn a living from driving round corners a bit too quickly while shouting? God knows. But I do.

18 January 2015

Ladies and gentlemen, I begin my speech with a request . . . shoot me

I think I'm right in saying that in all of human history no one has ever woken up and thought: 'Ooh, good. I'm making a best man's speech today.' Even the most cocksure and confident young man knows that the words 'Ladies and gentlemen', when spoken loudly in a room full of expectant faces, move your saliva glands into overdrive and cause your testes to disappear back whence they came, turning your velvety baritone into a spittle-flecked, prepubescent squeak.

And that's before we get to the touchy subject of what you're going to say. Everyone knows that if you tell raunchy and amusing stories about the groom's chlamydia-ridden past, you will get an industrial-strength glower from the bride's po-faced aunt that will cause you to develop a hot neck and a stammer. And that if you are sweet and kind, you will annoy the groom's mates, who will throw bread rolls at your head.

A best man's speech is impossible to get right. It's either dull or toe-curlingly embarrassing. And there's no way out of it, because when you are asked, it's impossible to decline. Which causes me to wonder: what possesses someone to agree to make a speech when it's not compulsory?

Even top politicians who enjoy talking and are schooled in technique get it wrong. David Cameron does a shifty thing, glancing down at his notes every few seconds, the other man does nothing memorable at all and Ed Miliband has developed a habit of staring down the barrel of the camera, which a) means he's ignoring the audience and b) makes him look mad.

Then you have professionals such as Rob Brydon. He's a properly funny man with a properly funny routine. But at a recent awards ceremony in America he addressed his pitch-perfect impression of Dustin Hoffman to the actor himself, who was in the audience – and who was visibly and ostentatiously not amused. This created an atmosphere in the room and in circumstances such as these it's impossible to soldier on with any kind of dignity. It's like trying to be funny while they're tying a noose round your neck.

Which brings me on to those 'I'm not saying my mother-in-law is fat' after-dinner speeches that are given during trade-and-industry-type dos at swanky London hotels. First point. At an event such as this, where people have come to the capital from places such as Wednesbury and Stockport, everyone is trying to get their secretary into bed and doesn't want to break off and shut up while Clive Anderson rambles on for half an hour about caravan holidays and how he once spilt some milk over the vicar. Especially as all the wine on the table has a habit of running out at the precise moment he begins. Only Bob Monkhouse was any good on the after-dinner circuit and he's dead.

And point two. Nobody wants to give an after-dinner speech either. Everyone knows that. Which means everyone knows the clown on the stage is only there for the money.

I vowed early on in my television career that I'd never take the corporate shilling. But then one day someone offered such an enormous sum I couldn't say no. So there I was on the stage at the Grosvenor Hotel in London, addressing a bunch of – I can't remember who they were; double-glazing salesmen probably – and much to my surprise and delight it was going well. There was much laughter and I felt good.

As a result I decided I'd do another, and so a couple of months later I was back at the Grosvenor delivering exactly the same routine to another group of portly men in dinner jackets . . . and it was a total disaster. Every punchline was greeted with the sort of silence normally experienced by astronauts in the vast emptiness of space. I died hard and have never done an after-dinner speech since.

The same cannot be said of one of my colleagues. To spare his blushes I shan't name him here. I'll only say he has a reputation for driving slowly, that he lives in Hammersmith, west London and that his name begins with J. And ends with ames May.

Friends asked if he wouldn't mind awfully going to pick their son up from his school one night. 'It'd be such a surprise,' they said, 'and all his friends would love it.' So my colleague, being a kind and gentle soul, arrived at the school and, as he entered the hall, heard the words from the headmaster at the lectern: 'Ah, good, he's here now. So would you please welcome our guest speaker for the evening . . .'

Words you'd rather hear include: 'Take aim. Fire.'

The only solution really is to bound onto the stage and do something outrageous. Seriously. Goose the school secretary. Say you're late because you've been snogging Norman Lamont. Wet yourself. The only best man's speech I can actually remember featured a man so drunk that halfway through he vomited onto the cake.

All of which brings me on to the televised election debate that seems to be causing all sorts of fuss and palaver. Mr Cameron argues that if Nigel Farage is allowed to take part, wooing traditional Tory voters with the sort of right-wing rhetoric he'd like to use but can't, Mr Miliband should have to share the stage with the loony-left Green candidate who wants to abolish shampoo and make her armpit hair the foreign secretary.

I don't blame him. Because he knows that one bead of sweat, one forgetful moment or one stray hair will cost him the keys to No. 10 and that this time next year he'll be at the Grosvenor, in a frilly dinner shirt, telling an audience that isn't listening how he used to be so fat as a child you needed a bus pass to go round him.

There's only one solution, really. Don't bother making a speech at all. Nobody will be listening anyway. Just wait until one of the other candidates is being really annoying and then punch him in the mouth.

25 January 2015

Call the mansion tax what it is, Ed: a kicking for the wealth makers

When I'm in London I stay in a modest flat on the top of a tower block just a few yards from the extremely unglamorous and very noisy Shepherd's Bush Green. By no stretch of the imagination is it a mansion, but if we get Ed Miliband as prime minister he'll say that it is and charge me £30,000 every year for the privilege of owning it.

That isn't completely the end of the world while I have a job, but one day, when my bladder has become leaky and I've been sacked, Miliband will still be on the doorstep every April demanding that I hand over 1 per cent of what my flat is worth.

Apparently, if I really can't afford his stupid new tax, he'll let me pay after I've died and the flat has been sold. So that's good news. To meet his demands I shall have to commit suicide.

Now I'm not going to get bogged down here in a verbal assault on the Labour leader. Because what worries me is that we are living in a country where he stands a very real chance of winning the election.

The mansion tax is popular. People have been told – by the *Daily Mail*, oddly enough – that the rich spend their time quaffing champagne, gorging on swan and jetting in and out of Los Angeles international airport with a dead leopard on their heads. And they think that it's only fair these people should do their fair share to help those who live in Scotland.

Oh, for crying out loud, they already do – apart from Lewis Hamilton, obviously, but don't worry about him, because to avoid paying his whack he has to live in Monaco, which on the Clarksometer is the second-worst place in the entire world.

No. Most rich people do contribute, and contribute massively. In fact it has been said that Britain's wealthiest 1 per cent pay almost a third of all the income tax received by the Treasury. But still Miliband wants them to cough up more. And the electorate may well decide he should get it. Which will cause the rich to move elsewhere, which will cause tax receipts to go down, not up (see France for details).

The mansion tax makes absolutely no sense, but it's popular because in this country there's a sense that the sun will shine every day and Scarlett Johansson will tuck you in every night if the pigs at the top have less on their table. This, however, is a theory that only really works in a weed-infested sixth-form common room.

Let's take Warren Buffett as an example. He's worth £48bn, which means he's richer than Cambodia and Ghana put together, and there are those who say no single person should have this much money. Fine. So what if we took his fortune away and spread it out evenly among everyone else? You wouldn't even get a tenner.

Let's bring it closer to home. Let's say we confiscated the assets of the Duke of Westminster and gave them all to the NHS. An excellent idea, a firebrand leftie would say. But his £8.5bn would be gone in less than a month.

I spoke the other day with a man who was cruising around the Caribbean on his extremely beautiful yacht. He told me that he would be there for a month more, after which he would switch to his slightly smaller yacht and sail to the Galapagos Islands for a few weeks.

Then he would fly in his private jet to Nice, where he'd rejoin his bigger boat for a summer in the Mediterranean, after which he'd go to his game reserve in South Africa.

Today this sort of thing is seen as revolting, and I cannot see why. Yes, he was born into a wealthy family and that makes him very lucky. But what difference does it make to you that he is spending the next six months on holiday?

It doesn't matter whether he's swimming with the turtles in the Pacific or working as a filing clerk in Watford: you will still live in the same house with the same stains on the carpet and the same wonky car.

Let me put it this way. If you hit a supermodel in the face with a tyre iron, would that somehow make the rest of the nation's women more beautiful? Would your horse be faster if you cut one of Frankel's legs off?

A couple of weeks ago a buffoon called Chris Bryant said it was iniquitous that the arts in Britain were dominated by people who'd been educated privately. There's James Blunt, and Chris Martin out of Coldplay, and, er, Florence Welch out of the Machine, and, um . . .

The fact is this. Of the UK artists who had a top forty album between 2010 and last year 72 per cent went to a state school and 62 per cent did not go to university.

So the shadow culture minister is talking out of his privately educated back bottom. Pop music is dominated by public-school kids in the same way as parliament is dominated by Liberal Democrats.

And anyway, who gives a damn? When I hear a tune I like, I don't think, 'Well, I'm not buying that because it was recorded by a load of smelly, poor people from a council estate', any more than I think when I hear 'The Lady in Red', 'Ah, this chap went to private school so it must be marvellous.'

Normal souls don't think like the bitter and the twisted. I look at the people with whom I socialize now and I don't have a clue where half of them went to school. I don't care. Nor does anyone I know.

We employ the best candidates, choose friends based on their kindness and sense of wit and go to work to earn as much as we can. It's not complicated.

But if Miliband wins the election it'll get extremely complicated because everyone whose home is worth more than £2m will have to become a rent boy – or dead. Happily I've come up with a plan. I shall start a business and tour the country, valuing everyone's house, no matter how big it is, at £1.9m.

1 February 2015

Step aside, RoboPlayer, sport will simply die without Johnny Hapless

Like half the population of Britain, I spent last Sunday morning watching Novak Djokovic and Andy Murray have a game of upside down tennis in Australia. And halfway through the third set I realized something: I was watching the beginning of the end for sport.

Both players had plainly spent every waking moment of their lives playing tennis and every sleeping moment dreaming about it. Both had been force-fed with the right sort of lumpy nutritional sludge and tweaked, mentally and physically, until they had become human G-strings. No avenue had been left unexplored. No crease had remained unironed.

And as a result they were evenly matched. Both could play any stroke faultlessly. Both had the best rackets that current technology could provide, both had comfy shoes and both were fit enough to play for a year, should the scoreline necessitate that.

But then something began to trouble Murray. It could have been a fly buzzing around one of the lights, or a bit of self-doubt. And because of this tiny detail, his game went to pieces, he lost the fourth set 6-0 and that was the end of that.

Well, I'm no particular fan of Murray, but I don't think that a tennis Grand Slam final should be decided by a fly buzzing around a light. Or by some teenage issues about self-worth.

Things are even worse in the athletical world of running about and throwing things for a great distance. Your success in a high-jump competition now can be affected by a light breeze and in a cycle race by a microscopic drop in barometric pressure. And then it gets worse.

In 1954 Roger Bannister covered a mile in less than four minutes and everyone wondered if the human being would ever be able to go more quickly. But just twenty-five years later Sebastian Coe shaved ten seconds off the time.

So what does this mean? That man will one day be able to cover a mile in three minutes? Two? A thousandth of a second? Plainly the answer is no, so at some point no more records will ever be broken. High jump. Long jump. All of it is doomed.

Football too. Last year the Premier League was won by Manchester City simply because one of the Liverpool players fell over at a crucial moment. All that training, all those Aston Martins and all that television time, and it all comes down to a dodgy shoelace. This year's Champions League could easily be decided by a header that's knocked off course by a player's idiotic hairstyle.

I went last week to watch Chelsea play Manchester City, and both teams were so good and so well disciplined that nothing interesting was going to happen. As indeed it didn't.

Even Scrabble has been ruined these days because

you get two people who have spent their lives learning the dictionary and think it is acceptable to use words such as jo, qi and fiz, and I sit there in a puddle of incandescent rage, shouting: 'It's a game of imagination. Not to see which of you is the best at being a parrot.'

We've reached the point in all professional sport where the rewards are so bountiful that it's worth pushing your body and your mind to a point where the only way you can shine is by growing an extra lung or two brains. Which means you can't shine at all.

Technology is the only answer. I'm talking about tennis rackets that can read the position of an opponent and then adjust the head to ensure the ball goes to a point on the court where he can't reach it. Or snooker cues that work out the correct angle. And cricket bats that emit a loud and piercing whistle to keep the crowd awake.

But do we want to live in a world where I could become the world golfing champion simply because my bat, or whatever it's called, can direct the ball to the hole thing in one go, in all weathers, and on all courses? Not really. Because that's not sport.

For evidence of this we need to turn our attention to Formula One motor racing, in which the driver simply drives around in a computer algorithm and can win only if his agent has secured him a place in whichever team happens to employ the best aerodynamicist.

Yes, he could throw caution to the wind and try to drive outside the box, but if he does that, the stewards, a Honda dealer from Jersey and a man with an earwig on his face will make him sit on the naughty step until he has no chance of winning at all.

The time is fast approaching when all governing bodies need to start appointing judges who are not especially bothered by how well a person has boxed or how efficiently a team has defended, but are very bothered about who has shown the most grit and determination and spirit.

It would be a sort of Eddie the Eagle-type deal in which the person who flies for the longest time after leaving the ski jump gets a pat on the back, a £2 postal order and a medal of some kind. But the chap or chapess who comes down in a tangle of limbs yet with a suicidal grimace of determination parked on their face gets £1m.

If someone wins a motor race having done nothing interesting at all, then his place on the podium is taken by someone who has. Even if he's in a pine box as a result.

And football? Yes, the number of goals will still count, but the number of tackles and shots on target will be considered as well, to stop managers parking the bus, or settling for a draw.

It is often said these days that sport is business, and that's true. But the business in question is entertainment. And in a world where all the competitors are trained, fed, massaged and psyched to perfection, it's like watching robots. And that's not entertaining at all.

8 February 2015

The sewers are full and I'm about to raise the Second Great Stink

Back in 1848 London's politicians decided that the smell of sewage was becoming intolerable and that all of the city's cesspits must be closed forthwith. And as a result 14,137 Londoners immediately died of cholera.

Scientists refused to believe that the epidemic had anything to do with the sewage that was now flowing freely through the city, and so in 1853 the cholera came back, killing 10,738 more souls.

The scientists, displaying the same sort of stubbornness that we see today with their global warming argument, still wouldn't back down, blaming something called the 'miasma'. Anyone who dared to disagree was labelled a miasma denier.

But by 1858 the stench was so bad that the politicians decided to solve the problem using engineers. They therefore contacted a chap called Joseph Bazalgette and asked him to construct a network of tunnels that would carry the city's sewage into the Thames estuary and then out to sea.

The project he developed was vast: 450 miles of main sewers, 13,000 miles of smaller ones and a network of exquisite pumping stations. He would use 318m bricks and excavate 3.5m tons of earth.

And then he thought, 'Hang on a minute. What I'm proposing would serve London now, but the population is expanding at an alarming rate. One day it might be home to more than 8m souls, so it'd be best if I doubled the size of all my tunnels just in case.'

It worked, of course. The stench went. The cholera went. And since we are still using Bazalgette's sewerage system today, you have to credit the man with extraordinary vision. But sadly it wasn't quite clear enough. Because he never foresaw the arrival of Alan Titchmarsh.

Alan spent almost ten years telling us all to put decking into our back gardens, which meant that the rainwater could no longer seep into the earth. It was all channelled into the sewers. And here's the horrible irony. Alan's show *Ground Force* was conceived and produced by Peter Bazalgette, the great-great-grandson of the man whose sewers were now being overwhelmed.

This wouldn't have been so bad, but then along came something else that old man Bazalgette didn't predict: Kevin McCloud's *Grand Designs*. This gave the nation an appetite for home improvement, which in London meant creating a home cinema room by digging out a new basement . . . below the level of the sewerage network.

So on a wet Sunday afternoon you sit down to watch *Battle of Britain* and before Leigh-Mallory's 'big wing' strategy is airborne you find yourself sitting in a puddle of your next-door neighbour's distressingly aromatic number twos.

From my point of view the upshot is a bit annoying, because I've had a letter from Thames Water telling me that it wishes to solve the problem by digging an extremely large hole outside my London flat. The project will take two years to complete; there will be twelve-hour working days for the first twelve months and round-the-clock activity thereafter. Vehicular access will be impossible, noise will be inevitable and the smell will be bad.

I was then informed that representatives from the company would be on hand at a local school should I wish to drop by and discuss the implications.

Sadly, however, the representatives chosen by Thames Water to attend this meeting were mostly engineers. Now, I like engineers and I must confess their enthusiasm for the project was admirable. They had diagrams and flow charts and spoke with flailing arms and mad eyes about how much concrete they'd need and how big the hole outside my front door would be – chuffing massive, is a rough translation of what they said.

Eventually, though, I had to interrupt and ask about what the company intended to do to make life even vaguely tolerable while it was making merry with the TNT. 'Um,' seemed to be the answer.

The engineers were talking about building a new sewer junction in a hole 70 ft deep, along with a weir. It would have to be gigantic because it would be handling the waste from every single property in a giant arc from Brent in the north all the way east to Camden. So while the work was under way I'd have Ed Miliband's turds bobbing past my window every morning.

We don't need a crystal ball to see what will happen

next, because it always happens when a large engineering project is mooted these days. A residents' action
committee will be formed and Thames Water's proposals will be fought every step of the way. I'll be in a
T-shirt with a slogan on it, up a tree, with Swampy, and
the water company will have to employ lawyers at great
expense to get me out again. And as the years crawl by,
the cost of the project will spiral, and meanwhile we
residents will not be able to sell our properties for more
than about £2.75.

And while all this is happening, everyone with a
basement conversion in London – which is everyone
these days – will be sitting up to their armpits in
an unholy cocktail of sanitary towels and wee and
engine oil.

This annoys me. I know that London cannot use Victorian sewers for ever. I appreciate that work must be
done. And I like a big engineering project. But it was a
shame Thames Water sent engineers to win the hearts
and minds of those whose lives are about to be ruined.
That was foolish. When you've been sentenced to death
by firing squad you want a priest, or a prostitute, not
someone to explain with great enthusiasm how the gun
works.

If the board of directors had rocked up, saying that
of course they'd temporarily rehouse people who were
being asked to take one for the team, they could have
started tomorrow morning. That would have been the
decent thing to do. And ultimately it would have been
the cheapest thing to do as well.

But they didn't, which is why I'm now doing two

things: spoiling for a fight and setting up a competition to find Britain's noisiest motorbike. Which will be staged every night on the road outside the house of Sir Peter Mason, chairman of Thames Water.

15 February 2015

Phrasebook, tick. Local currency, tick. Tracksuit, tick. I'm off to the north

Over the years my trips to Liverpool have always been extremely memorable. On one occasion I found that the door to my hotel room was blocked by a girl who was lying in the corridor, having apparently died. On another the constant burglar alarms meant that I checked out of my hotel at 2 a.m. and drove back to London for a bit of peace and quiet. Oh, and I nearly forgot: there was the time a blood-soaked chap sprinted into the restaurant in which I was dining and ran amok with a knife.

However, I went to Liverpool last weekend and it was all very agreeable. There was a lot of postmodern urban-chic architecture and many museums, hotels and waterfront cafés. It looked really good. I liked it.

Yet behind the veneer of modern loft living were one or two incidents that warrant a mention. I stayed, for example, in an extremely stylish hotel with mood lighting and a lot of exposed brickwork, and for breakfast I asked the waitress if I could have a kipper.

'What's a kipper?' she asked.

'It's a sort of smoked fish,' I said.

'Fish?' she responded. 'For breakfast? No. We don't do that.'

It turned out, however, that they did do that, and a kipper was duly brought to my table. Sadly, though, it had to go away again shortly afterwards because it hadn't been what you'd call cooked.

For lunch I had a Caesar salad that the menu said was done 'our way'. Their way was interesting. There were some prawns, lettuce and a handful of croutons that were bits of bread that appeared to have been dipped into a bowl full of lukewarm washing-up water. It was like eating a docker's wet vest.

That night we did one of our Top Gear Live arena shows and went out afterwards to a private room with catering from the restaurant below. There were oysters. Yummy.

'Could I have some Tabasco?' I asked the waitress.

'Some what?' she said.

'It's a hot sauce,' I explained, and off she scurried.

She was gone a very long time, and as she returned I worked out why. She'd obviously decided that serving anything in a bottle wouldn't be 'posh', so she'd emptied it, one drip at a time, into a saucer.

And if I'm honest, I wish she hadn't bothered, because Tabasco doesn't really work as a dipping sauce. You end up with too much on your oyster, so every mouthful feels as though you're snorting Harpic. It sounds risible, yes? And it was, thanks entirely to me. Seriously. When I visited Israel a few years ago I didn't barge into the restaurants at night demanding the chef cook me a pork chop with added grasshopper. And neither, when I was in a Burmese temple last summer, did I say to the monk: 'Oi, fatso, fancy a kickabout? Altars for goalposts.' I know I have a dreadful reputation for putting my foot in it, but when I'm abroad I do my best to fit in.

These days I even check my registration number to make sure it's not offensive in any way.

So what the bloody hell was I thinking of in Liverpool, splashing nasal C-4 all over what the waitress plainly thought were lumps of raw snot? And then washing it down with a bottle of la-di-bloody-da rosé wine?

Ordering Whispering Angel in Liverpool is like a Liverpudlian strolling into the Savoy at teatime, in a shell suit, and demanding seven pints of vodka. He's going to be shown the door. And I should have been shown the door too.

This is the root cause of all the problems surrounding the north–south divide. And not just in Britain either. In Europe we have states in the north imposing their rules on states in the south: 'Look here, Stavros. Just go to work and pay your taxes and everything will be fine.' But Stavros doesn't want to pay his taxes. It's not the Greek way.

Closer to home we have soft-living, champagne-soaked southerners imagining that they know what's best for northern cities such as Liverpool. 'My dear fellow, why don't you simply give up heroin and start a book club? Because if you don't, we'll cut your benefits.'

We go up there and say, 'Look what we've given you, Gary: a Tracey Emin hotel and slavery museum, all full of Ed Miliband bumper-sticker slogans. Aren't you grateful?' But Gary isn't grateful because he doesn't like Primrose Hill sensibilities and bloody mood lighting.

Or does he? I don't know because I'm not a Liverpudlian. But I am a northerner, and what I therefore know is this: the north of England has never been more different from the south of England.

People up there earn less, die more quickly, have fewer jobs and live in houses that are worth the square root of sod all.

I know of no country in the world in which the biggest city is so dramatically different from the second-, third-, fourth-, fifth- and sixth-biggest cities.

For those who live in the south the north has become 'abroad'. Going up there and sitting about sipping pinkie-up Earl Grey tea while inquiring of the good man on reception where one might avail oneself of some E. M. Forster reading material is therefore as offensive as driving through Alabama with 'Man-love rules OK' on the side of your pick-up. Oh, hang on a minute. I've just remembered. I did that. We go to Rome to eat pasta under some wisteria. We go to France to sit in a café, people-watching. We go to Morocco to haggle with market traders. We expect and hope that these places will be different from home. So why should we expect the north to be the same as Esher?

This weekend I'm in Newcastle, and I shall therefore make sure I have toast and dripping for breakfast, some kind of buttie for lunch and several pints of brown ale for tea. Then I'll go clubbing in a vest.

22 February 2015

When a fat man gets suspended there's only one thing to do – get cooking

We read often about active and busy people who die the day after they retire because they simply can't cope with the concept of relaxation. So as I seem to have a bit of time on my hands at the moment, I thought it would be a good idea to take up some kind of hobby.

I began by watching daytime television, and soon I felt myself starting to slip away. So I turned over to the news and it was all about a not very interesting fat man who had been suspended from his not very important job. But watching the fat man made me hungry and that's when the penny dropped: I'd take up cooking.

I've never really bothered with cooking in the past because it would have meant using a recipe book. And as a man I can't do that, for the same reason I can't use instruction manuals or listen when someone is giving me directions; because it means admitting that someone out there knows something I don't.

And besides, recipe books are full of beautifully shot photographs showing you what your food should look like when it's finished. No, it won't, because you haven't painted everything with varnish and employed a stylist to make sure the sultanas are all in the right place. Recipe books are just cruel.

There's another problem as well. Anyone who can cook is able to control ingredients using their minds.

This means it's witchcraft. Don't argue with this because it is. You put butter and flour into an oven and somehow it comes out after a while as a delicious fluffy cake. How? Why didn't it come out as a Yorkshire pudding? Or a profiterole?

And what is the origin of cooking? I think it's almost certainly sinister because, let's face it, nobody accidentally stumbled on the recipe for bread. You take the bullet-hard and completely tasteless seed from a sheaf of wheat and grind it into a powder. Right. I see. And how many other seeds did they try before they arrived at that? 'Morning darling, I'm trying laburnum today and . . .'

But anyway, they ended up with a powder that is still tasteless and inedible but they kept right on going, adding water until they had a paste. Which is still a long way from yummy. Undaunted, however, our early-days Marco Pierre White then thought, 'Hmm. I'm on to something here. I think if I just add the stuff that gathers in my navel if I haven't washed for a while, this will be delicious.'

The whole idea is as preposterous as the idea when someone one day decided that tobacco wasn't very suitable as a sandwich filler but that it was lovely when rolled up in a piece of paper and smoked.

Anyway, I decided not to cook bread. Oh no. I decided to get ambitious and cook the most delicious thing I've eaten in my whole life: a pho.

A pho is a Vietnamese noodle soup that contains about 128 different ingredients, and, unlike bread or smoking, it's very easy to see how it was invented.

Someone who was very poor heated some water and thought, 'I wonder if this would taste nicer if I put some weeds in it? And maybe a bit of that cow that has died.'

Today of course the weeds have pretty names such as star anise and coriander and cost more than cocaine. Mostly they are also harder to find than cocaine. But luckily I'm holed up in a part of London where you stand in line behind Alan Rickman, who's buying half a pound of myrrh, and Jimmy Page, who wants a bag of lemon-infused pistachio nuts.

My greengrocer was full of Damon Albarn, who was buying all the things he needed for an exotic chicken korma, and naturally the place had everything I needed for my even more exotic pho. It was the same story at the butcher, which stocked beef knuckle and bone marrow. And so within minutes my son and I had all we needed to start my hobby.

Except a pan. I do of course have pans, all of which are easily big enough to handle some beans or a bit of Heinz tomato soup. But to make a pho you need a dustbin, really. We had to resort to a wastepaper basket.

We also didn't have a rolling pin, which we needed, apparently, to 'lightly bruise' the ginger. But I did have a hammer, so we used that instead. It didn't go particularly well because ginger, it turns out, can't really be bruised. You tap it and it just sits there undamaged. So you use a bit more force and it falls to pieces.

The instruction manual said that during the four-hour cooking process we should also spoon off the scum that formed as the broth boiled. But there wasn't any that I could see. This might have been down to the fact that I couldn't see much of anything at all, or talk properly.

The problem is, when you are cooking, you are near a fridge and fridges have wine in them. Well, mine does, because I haven't been drinking much for the past few weeks. And with time to kill until the broth was ready, I came over a bit Keith Floydish.

This may explain why I didn't roast the bone marrow or the knuckle before boiling them to bits and it certainly explains what happened later. I hadn't really been listening properly when the man in the greengrocer's asked what sort of chillies I'd like. And I must have selected some that sat on the Scoville scale just above lava.

I only used one or maybe two but it was enough to ruin four hours of work. The only good news was that my spoilt broth was already in the wastebin.

I went to bed that night hungry, drunk and with an ulcerated, gangrenous mouth from a tasting sip that I'd taken to make sure I hadn't used too many chillies.

I think, therefore, some people are not born to be cooks. They lack the special powers needed to influence the outcome of what is basically sorcery.

So my new hobby is called 'going out to restaurants and letting people who know what they're doing cook my food'.

15 March 2015